AMERICAN DIPLOMACY AND THE SPANISH CIVIL WAR

INDIANA UNIVERSITY INTERNATIONAL STUDIES

AMERICAN DIPLOMACY

AND THE SPANISH CIVIL WAR

RICHARD P. TRAINA

BLOOMINGTON · LONDON

INDIANA UNIVERSITY PRESS

TO MY PARENTS

CONTENTS

PREFACE

THE MOST COMMON historical judgment of American policy toward the Spanish civil war begins with the notion that the Spanish conflict was the prelude to World War II. This has led to the proposition that the United States should have assisted the Spanish government in its struggle against the Rebels and their Fascist allies. Had Hitler and Mussolini been defeated in Spain, they could not have pursued their subsequent designs: mankind would have been spared the horrors that followed.

The simplicity of that thesis has made it at once suspicious and attractive. Since its outlines took shape during the course of the Spanish conflict, those men in Washington who made policy became quite familiar with the idea. Conscious as they were of the spectre of world war, they could ill afford to ignore alternatives which might offer brighter prospects. When they pondered the probable consequences of active involvement in Spain, however, they did not arrive at favorable conclusions. Even though they sometimes found their decision difficult, the policy-makers continually rejected arguments for military assistance to the Loyalists and instead pursued a policy of non-involvement. The reasons for this grew increasingly complex as the conflict progressed, but almost from the beginning of the

ix

civil war interventionist arguments were believed to be fraught
with unreasonable hopes and perilous contingencies. The purpose of this study is to follow the development of that noninvolvement policy, to investigate the reasons for its adoption
and continuation, and to explore those domestic and international issues which were so closely bound up with it.

During the research and writing of this work, I became indebted to many people for their generous assistance and encouragement. Of that kind of gratitude which can only be due one's
mentors, I could not have more for both Armin Rappaport and
Raymond J. Sontag. Their help cannot be measured. I appreciate this opportunity to acknowledge my many debts to Robert
H. Ferrell, as well. The manuscript, in various stages, was read
by all three men and additionally by Jules Davids, Gabriel
Jackson, and Paul Seabury. Each offered valuable criticisms
and suggestions for which I am more than grateful. It cannot
go unmentioned that any errors or faults in this book are my
responsibility alone.

It is difficult to single out individuals from a long list of
librarians and archivists who rendered so much assistance during the course of my research. But special mention must be
made of Dr. E. Taylor Parks of the Historical Office at the
Department of State, and of Miss Elizabeth Drewry of the
Franklin D. Roosevelt Library at Hyde Park, New York. By
no means do I wish to minimize the courteous help and thoughtful counsel of many others at the Roosevelt Library and at the
Historical Office, or of those whose responsibility is the care of
Department of State records at the National Archives. I re-
ceived the same gracious assistance at a number of other ar-
chives and libraries as well: the Manuscript Division, Library
of Congress; Houghton Library, Harvard University; the Yale
University Library; the archives of the American National Red
Cross; Tamiment Institute; Butler Library, Columbia University; College of the Holy Cross Library; the Department of
Archives and Manuscripts, Catholic University of America;
University Library, University of Delaware; Lilly Library,
Wabash College; and the University Library and Bancroft
Library, University of California, Berkeley. To the directors
of most of these archives and libraries, I also owe special thanks
for permission to use, and to quote from, manuscript collec-
tions. The note on sources, at the conclusion of this study, in-

dicates the specific manuscript collections used at each institution. I am obligated as well to Mrs. Albert Lévitt for permisson to quote from the papers of Jay Pierrepont Moffat, and to the United Church Board for World Ministries for permission to use the papers of the American Board of Commissioners for Foreign Missions.

This study could not have been accomplished without financial assistance, and I am very grateful to the Woodrow Wilson Foundation and to the University of California for grants-in-aid to cover travel expenses during the first year of my research as a graduate student. I am likewise pleased to express my thanks to Wabash College for two grants which have covered a substantial portion of my research and secretarial expenses over the past four years.

To Mrs. Wilma Louise Barton I owe special thanks for her patient and careful typing of the manuscript. And Mrs. Barbara DeKruyter deserves much gratitude for helping me handle the seemingly endless correspondence required by the book.

There are many relatives, friends, and colleagues, not already mentioned, to whom I owe a great deal—not least for their encouragement and forbearance. The list is long and their contributions various; it would be unfair to mention any individuals but one. I thank my wife, Margaret Warner Traina. Never did she fail to give aid and comfort to this study, which might for several years have been considered a demanding intruder in our household.

R. P. T.

AMERICAN DIPLOMACY AND THE SPANISH CIVIL WAR

1

SPANISH AND
AMERICAN BACKGROUND

W̱ HEN THE SPANISH CIVIL WAR erupted with a right-wing
military revolt on July 17, 1936, the uprising was not unexpected by the Department of State in Washington. Since
the February elections, won by the Popular Front, there had
been increasingly grave reports of turmoil in Spain. While the
confused political developments during these five months defied
analysis, the Spanish government was quite clearly meeting
only limited success in its efforts to maintain public order.
American officials specifically predicted a right-wing military
rebellion as a strong possibility.

Upon the outbreak of the war, Claude Bowers, the American
ambassador, was away from Madrid in San Sebastián. He consequently found it difficult to obtain accurate information concerning the seriousness of the revolt, and conflicting reports
from the opposing sides further confused the situation. But on
July 19, at three o'clock in the morning, the Government resigned, and President Manuel Azaña appointed a new cabinet.
It was clear the revolt had reached critical proportions.

I

The civil war was long in the making and, had Europe not been so torn by Fascist and Communist ideologies during these years, the Spanish strife of the thirties might well have been like that nation's internal struggles of the nineteenth century. The war had Spanish origins and a Spanish conclusion, but for thirty-three months—from July 1936 to April 1939—the country was an international battleground.

The origins of the civil war can be detected well back in the nineteenth century. In that age of national unification in the West, Spain was increasingly unable to control its own divisive forces. In that age of imperialism, its empire was disintegrating. One can overemphasize the role of the United States in these developments at the end of the century, but the fact remains that the war of 1898 contributed to Spain's decline. While the Spanish-American war marked the debut of one nation as a world power, it took from the other almost all the last remnants of its once vast empire.

For Spain, this American venture into imperialism did more than take away symbols of a glorious past. Men in their twenties during that war were fifty and sixty during the years of the Republic. Some of them had been brought home from army duty in the lost colonies, home to unemployment, to discredit for their military humiliation, and with thoughts of an older Spain in which the army held at least the balance of political power. The war affected yet another body of young Spanish men—the "generation of '98"—determined upon a new Spain of arts and intellect (but not always practicably modern and not, as was later proved, of a liberalism competent to deal with the rebellious working class and peasants). Further, the economic setback attending the loss of the colonies had effects throughout the already unstable economic structure and reached far down to the lower classes. Spanish anarchism as a result became more institutionalized. Marxism and syndicalism attracted more followers. Neglected when they were not exploited, the lower classes were to become one of Spain's most unruly forces.

Nor could the Crown and the bureaucracy of the central government escape the effects of the humiliating war. The monarchy had been crumbling for more than a century; it never really recovered after the Napoleonic wars. But the bureaucracy managed to hold Spain together during the nineteenth century with a corrupt parliamentary system. Now the additional loss of power and prestige in the central government increasingly encouraged separatist movements. The desire for regional autonomy was a historical phenomenon in Spain, and some Spaniards began to turn to it as a hope for achieving their goals of reform. Contrarily, the more conservative elements, such as the large landholders, more and more attached themselves to Madrid.

Finally, there was the Spanish Church. Any ill effects upon the military, the court, and the bureaucracy could not but add to the burdens of an increasingly unpopular Church. Whatever might be said for the village priest as a respected counselor of the people, he was provided with few means with which to relieve them of their material discontents. Meanwhile the hierarchy still nursed its wounds inflicted by the fits of liberalism which marked nineteenth-century Spain; shorn of much of its landholdings, the Spanish Church took its wealth into the world of finance. And wealth unseen created a suspicion more dangerous than the earlier contempt for the Church's vast landholdings. The great error of the Church, as it is so often remarked, was that it stepped backward rather than forward at this time, that it made no effort to court the young men who envisioned a new Spain. But a marriage of the Spanish Church and what wealth it possessed to the liberalism of a new middle class was impossible, whether or not it was ever given consideration. The vitality of the generation of '98, for example, was due very largely to its rebelliousness, shaking off the shackles of old Spain to which the Church was so closely bound.

Then, too, the devotees of the new anarchism were peasants who by their rigorous asceticism robbed the Spanish Church of one of its oldest and most memorable spiritual contributions. Opposition to drunkenness, and even to excessive use of tobacco, was fanatical among many of the landless. The new anarchism was more "religious" than the Church, and it was barefoot as well. For the Spanish Church to have joined with the progressive elements at this time would have required the erasure of more than a century of Spanish history. The Church did not appeal to the youthful Spanish intellectuals, nor could it compete with the anarchist teachings of Michael Bakunin and the syndicalism of Georges Sorel among peasants and city laborers. In 1930, a few leading figures in the Spanish Church reflected, as Hugh Thomas has pointed out, Pope Pius XI's "Wilsonian mood," and they appeared to favor democratic reforms. But there was virtually no chance for alliance with liberals. Spanish liberals were traditionally anticlerical. And for many men in the Church, liberalism had come to signify simply a preface to Bolshevism.

The first two decades of the twentieth century brought troubles to the army, monarchy, bureaucracy, and Church. The generation of '98 and some of the anarchist and syndicalist political movements, while still for the most part ineffective, showed growing vitality. The two major forces of division during these years came from the continual wars in Morocco and from the Catalan separatist movement (an attempt by the more progressive Barcelona to free itself from the central government). Spain was at least spared the horrors of World War I, and beginning in 1923, under the dictatorship of General Primo de Rivera, it shared some of that deceptive prosperity of the next half-dozen years. The Moroccan wars were ended and a grand program of public works was instituted. As a result of Primo de Rivera's passion for roadbuilding, Spaniards were heard to murmur that "they had asked of him bread, and he gave them paving stones."

The dictator's fall in January 1930 came not as a result of popular uprisings but of pressures from the monarchy, nobility, Church, and army. The very forces which brought him into power now lacked confidence in his ability to deal with the problems wrought by the world-wide depression and by the dissatisfaction of liberal elements with the dictatorial restrictions on their freedom. While it was true that the dictator fell but the dictatorship remained, the dormant forces of liberalism and radicalism came more into the open during the new regime of General Dámaso Berenguer. In choosing him, it was reported, King Alfonso XIII had passed by a number of trained statesmen and selected a cavalryman. It was a makeshift arrangement; the best for which the monarchy could hope was a return of the public apathy of the mid-twenties. But by the autumn of 1930, Ortega y Gasset dared to declare before a group of liberals in San Sebastián: "Spaniards! Your state is no more." In April 1931 the King took leave of Spain after failing to gain a vote of confidence in a plebiscite. The Spanish revolution of 1931 was nonviolent, swift, and bewildering.

The "revolution" was undefined. The new men in power were largely republicans, and while few had political or administrative experience, many had several years of self-preparation in theory. Their various "republicanisms" ranged widely over the political and economic spectrum. Nothing should be taken away from several of these men as theorists and dedicated reformers, or from the agony which many experienced in the subsequent necessity to compromise and even sacrifice their most cherished ideals. But the necessity of ruling by unstable coalitions sapped much of their energy. Even the most dynamic leaders were not trained for political life, they were compelled to it—posthaste. They were particularly baffled by the adjustment of long-range goals to immediate needs. Each man thus encountered conflicts within himself as well as with others. As a consequence, they characteristically adopted a posture of certitude and resolve which poorly shielded their bafflement and vacillation.

If some, like Azaña, were attracted to middle-class liberalism (as exemplified in England), others were, like Francisco Largo Caballero, devoted to the cause of the working class and strong doses of socialism. But not only the bourgeoisie and the lower classes placed their hopes in the new Republic. Influential elements in the Church also gave their sanction. The first president of the Republic was Niceto Alcalá Zamora, a devout Catholic; and a number of the members of the Cortes, or parliament, were priests. Even further, men from Catalonia and Galicia, desiring substantial regional autonomy, suspended their plans and backed the new central government with the hope of obtaining their ends through parliamentary procedures. The optimistic hopes which representatives of these groups placed in the parliamentary system was threatened, however, by forces of disruption and subversion. Although they were at first weak, extremists of both left and right made increasing use of the freedoms of the Republic for the purpose of its destruction.

The Spanish Republic faced three primary and interlocking problems: land reform, regionalism, and the strength of the Church. The many landless wanted their land, various regions wanted some measure of autonomy, and anticlericals and antireligionists wanted to strike down the power of the Church.

Sometimes, as in Extremadura, peasants simply seized the land. Church-burnings and crimes of violence against priests and nuns were not uncommon. As a consequence of the demands of its most militant citizens, the new Republic was, after a surprisingly smooth first year, pushed considerably to the left. The forces of old Spain which might have been compelled to an honorable compromise with a moderate regime were soon in ardent opposition to the Republic in liberal hands. Too many antagonistic groups expected sympathy from the new government, and compromise proved incredibly difficult.

The problem of regional autonomy was never solved. Land reform was both slow and ineffective. The Spanish Church and those sympathetic to it were antagonized by the harshness of the measures enacted against it, even though these were not always enforced. The Church faced the loss of its financial resources, its buildings, and its right to teach. According to law, only the right to worship remained. Regionalists were antagonized, the landless were impatient, and the Church's feelings toward the Republic passed from warm to cool, then to outright opposition against the ruling liberal coalition. Important factions within the army also felt outraged. Military pride, as well as the army's size, was dealt severe blows during "these days of the liberals."

The first attempted revolt against the Republic came from the right, an unsuccessful *pronunciamiento* led by General José Sanjurjo Sacanell in August 1932. Then in January 1933, "an almost mortal thrust" came from the left, an anarchist uprising in Casas Viejas in the province of Cádiz. The government, still under the premiership of Azaña, was widely attacked for brutality in suppressing this rebellion. As the moderates of the right found their cause seriously discredited by the revolt of Sanjurjo, the more moderate wing of the left never really recovered from the effects of its treatment of the anarchists at Casas Viejas. By the end of 1933, the liberal coalition was falling apart, and there came a surge of conservative strength with the active support of the Church. For the next two years the Spanish right tried to manage the faltering Republic. Between June 1933 and December 1935, there were twelve governmental crises. The most serious ordeal of this period was the October Revolution of 1934.

Following a tactical political victory by the Catholic party, which placed three of its members in key ministerial posts, a general strike was called by the more radical leaders among those who had brought the Republic into existence. The October Revolution was born in the violence which followed; and though it was soon quelled in Madrid and Barcelona, continued armed resistance came from thousands of miners in Asturias. Generals Francisco Franco and Manuel Goded, subsequently leaders of the insurgents during the civil war, were called in to suppress the rebellious miners. When the fighting and the continued repression were over, there were more than 30,000 political prisoners throughout Spain and an estimated 1,300 miners had been killed. The terrorist methods of the Spanish Legion and the Moorish *Regulares* did nothing to endear the conservative government to the Spanish people. Neither did the strength and organization shown by the Asturian miners comfort the upper and middle classes. From that point on, Spain was in periodic anarchy. As Bowers reported to the State Department a year later, the "lack of parliamentary spirit" is both "disconcerting and disabling." "Disunion," he wrote, "exists everywhere."[1]

The return of Azaña to the premiership in February 1936, and his appeal for calm, did not prevent further degeneration into arson and bloodshed. Extremists of the right and left benefited from the very crimes they perpetrated, as the center was pulled apart. More than three months before the civil war, Ambassador Bowers informed Washington that should Azaña fail "to maintain the upper hand, the danger exists that civil war or communism may ensue." Two months later he reported: "Recurring rumors to the effect that Fascists and other reactionary elements are plotting a military coup d'etat are in some measure borne out by recent developments. . . ."[2] It was true that Communists and Fascists came to have an influence out of proportion to their numbers in Spain. With the decline of the moderates both the proponents of radical socialism and the advocates of a militarist state secured greater followings. One suspects, too, that the physical realities of the Soviet Union and Germany and Italy provided means of identification which were otherwise missing. But too much can be made of this. Few Spaniards were ever devoted members of parties under foreign direction. Involvement with Fascism, Nazism, and Communism was really a wartime phenomenon. The violence perpetrated by extremists on both left and right before the outbreak of the civil war was of Spanish origin.

While a right-wing military revolt had been forecast for some time, both in Spain and in the foreign offices of other nations, the dimensions, the full meaning, of the rebellion of July 17 could hardly have been discerned beforehand. The revolt, beginning in Morocco, quickly spread to the mainland, and within a very few days the Spanish strife had international repercussions of major consequence. Developments in Spain, in their own tragic way, were to influence European affairs to a degree which Spain had not matched since the Napoleonic wars.

II

Despite efforts made during the years of the Republic, Spain had not yet assumed an integral role in continental affairs. Thus it was not until after the outbreak of the civil war that the United States government was compelled to consider its relations with Spain in the framework of general European developments. American policies toward the Spanish conflict were quickly dominated by a set of policies and attitudes which had developed apart from previous considerations of Spanish-American affairs. But if there was one factor in previous relations with Spain which influenced the response of the State Department to the developments following the outbreak of the civil war, it was the obvious instability of the Spanish Republic.

The Republic's relations with the United States had not been particularly friendly, nor even important. During the Hoover administration they were decidedly poor. There was an uneasiness on both sides, primarily attributable to the Spanish government's anticapitalist legislation and to Ambassador Irwin B. Laughlin's ill-concealed antagonism toward Spanish liberals. From 1931 to 1933, these poor relations were reflected in threats of confiscation, the raising of prohibitive tariffs which practically excluded United States merchandise, and the enactment of measures which were prejudicial to American banks operating in Spain. These problems continued in less drastic form during the first years of the New Deal. Additional friction existed because previous American diplomatic officers were considered by some Spanish liberals, justifiably or not, as having been on too friendly terms with Primo de Rivera and King Alfonso. Three weeks before the monarchy fell, Alfonso's government received a $60 million credit from an American banking group. Spanish Republicans later intimated that the American embassy in Madrid had approved the loan as being sound.[3] In January 1933, not long before he was to be replaced by Claude Bowers, Laughlin added to the ill feeling by declining an invitation to a state dinner. He reportedly objected to the order of precedence, the speaker of the Cortes being seated ahead of the ambassadors.[4]

As expected, Spanish officials were subsequently pleased when Laughlin was replaced by Bowers, who was reported to be a true democrat of the Jeffersonian school. During the three years between Bowers' arrival and the coming of the civil war, Spanish-American relations steadily improved. The sorest point in dispute between the two governments involved the threatened confiscation of the International Telephone and Telegraph Company. The problem was solved after the coming of the Roosevelt administration, although negotiations were reaching toward a solution even before then. All difficulties, however, were not eliminated. Uneasiness continued despite Bowers' very patient and amicable manner. Shortly before the war broke out, he was unsuccessfully attempting to improve the situation by negotiating a trade agreement. Relations between the two nations in the summer of 1936 were still really of little consequence and provided no clear guide for what was to come.

In the summer of 1936 American statesmen were deeply concerned over the growing aggressiveness of Germany and Italy and the timidity of Britain and France. These considerations largely determined American policy toward the Spanish civil war. In the days immediately before the eruption in Spain, a number of events highlighted these developments and sharpened Washington's awareness of them. July was an anxious month. It began with Emperor Haile Selassie's anticlimactic address before the League of Nations. "What answer," he asked, "shall I take back to my people?" An embarrassing silence marked the final collapse of the League's weak resistance to Italian aggression in Ethiopia and the failure of Great Britain and France to renew some life in the dying hope of collective security. Days later came the Austro-German accord, purportedly one of mutual noninterference. It immediately strengthened both Hitler and Mussolini, in large part because it made Italo-German cooperation more feasible. The Ethiopian and Austrian problems were only the most important events of this brief period; there were others causing additional worry in Washington. The United States and Germany were rapidly approaching a trade war. France was shaken by civil disorders, and French resolve continued to deteriorate. There was also the tell-tale vacillation of Great Britain at the Montreux conference. Twice the British reversed position on the vital question of belligerent passage through the Dardanelles during war; and these dizzying changes suggested to the assembled diplomats that the "pro-French" and "pro-German" schools on Downing Street were exchanging authority. From the Far East came news no more encouraging to American policy-makers. Internal conflicts in China reached a critical stage—with the involvement there of Japan. And the Japanese meanwhile announced plans for stepped-up naval construction, following their refusal to become a party to the London Naval Treaty of 1936. Even in Latin America, where Washington's anxiety was generally diminishing, there was still the explosive boundary dispute between Ecuador and Peru (which President Roosevelt that month agreed to arbitrate).

This series of events, taking place in little more than two weeks' time, raised every important consideration of American foreign policy since World War I: the issues of economic nationalism, limitation of armaments, and neutrality legislation; the question of coordinating policies with those of the League and with those of Great Britain and France; the advocacy of the Open Door in China; the Good Neighbor policy; the Hoover-Stimson doctrine of nonrecognition of territorial gains made by force; and, most fundamentally, the character of American pacifism and isolationism. Whether or not it could later be excused, it was then to be expected that the President and his Department of State would be respectful of habits of thought, continuing forces of circumstance, and past policies —of which they were currently being reminded—when they first viewed the Spanish crisis. While there were of necessity more proximate determinants of American policy toward the Spanish conflict, it was ultimately an acknowledgment of the weight of the past which early led the United States to pursue a policy of strict noninvolvement in Spain's civil war. That 1936 was an election year could only strengthen the idea that controversial departures were to be avoided. The surest comment which can be made about American policy early in the Spanish strife was that it was normal, obvious, and unimaginative. In short, the position quickly adopted toward the civil war was consistent with the major attitudes and policies which preceded it.

It was as commonplace in internationalist circles in 1936 as it is today to observe that the major development behind American diplomacy in the 1930's was the refusal of the United States to acknowledge the fullness of its involvement in European affairs in the years following Versailles. In relation to the later Spanish crisis, this early and almost continuous retreat from Europe's most perplexing postwar problems led to the question of whether or not the United States could be expected, or trusted, to sustain its commitments should it again be inclined to take some initiative. The idea that American policy toward the Spanish conflict would be, and ought to be, in keeping with its general, ostrich-like, European policy was especially prevalent in the British Foreign Office. This was partly because the British had a good understanding of the influence of public opinion upon the European policy of the United States. The British, while they sought American cooperation, did not expect or want American initiative in Europe.

The aims of American policy toward the whole of Europe had long been ill defined. However quickly the United States attempted to disengage itself from the European scene after World War I, it was unable, even unwilling, to disengage itself altogether. Having changed from a debtor to a creditor nation, the United States could not lose interest in the economic fortunes, or misfortunes, of Europe. What attracted the hopes of most Americans was the prospect of disarmament—from the Washington conference of 1921 to the Geneva conference ending in 1934. With every failure to resolve the dilemma of each nation's demand for security, and the failure of some (like the United States) to make military and political commitments which would provide it, there was a more desperate plea in the United States for protection against war. During the 1930's the internationally oriented peace groups in America began to lose their fervor and strength. Those which had rejected international cooperation, out of a disgust with European "corruption" and "deceit," began to attract more followers among Americans with pacifist inclinations. Security against war was soon sought in the halls of Congress rather than at international conferences—which is to say that security against war was redefined in terms of security against American participation in war.

Contacts between the United States and Europe broke down in the other major area of mutual interest. The devastating depression of the 1930's brought an irresistible wave of economic nationalism. The extremely high Hawley-Smoot tariff during the Hoover administration was, from a European point of view, a prelude to the economic nationalism which dominated the early New Deal of Franklin Roosevelt. The one major attempt to deal with the problems of the depression internationally occurred in 1933. Whatever success the London economic conference of that year might have achieved in the face of grave difficulties, no one was more responsible for its complete failure than the President of the United States. To the great dismay of Secretary of State Cordell Hull, who believed that economic nationalism was the primary cause of international war, President Roosevelt issued the well-known "bombshell message" which virtually withdrew the United States from vital and effective participation in the conference. The President's action made a lasting impression upon foreign statesmen, especially the British.

One other aspect of American foreign policy previous to the Roosevelt administration was particularly relevant to future relations with the European states. Much has been written of the inclination of American statesmen to pursue the course of moral suasion. The most recent example had been the Hoover administration's handling of the Manchurian crisis beginning in 1931. In an attempt to deal with Japanese aggression in Manchuria, the American government invoked a doctrine of non-recognition of territorial changes brought about by force. This was no effective deterrent to Japanese ambitions. The other major nations were similarly unwilling to take strong action in the matter, being first of all occupied with the depression.

The entire incident caused almost as much misunderstanding between the United States and Great Britain as it did between the United States and Japan. Secretary of State Henry L. Stimson felt the British damaged Anglo-American relations by refusing to cooperate with the United States in pursuing a stronger policy against Japan. And the American public lost further respect for the League of Nations, which had accomplished little more than driving the Japanese out of the organization—still another blow to international cooperation. The British, had they been inclined to act against Japan, recognized that the Hoover administration was unwilling to risk a war to halt the Japanese. Without the threat of force, there was no hope of curbing Japan's policy toward China. And it would appear that influential British leaders saw a strong Japan as a deterrent to Soviet penetration in the Far East.

The unwillingness of the United States to use any device much stronger than moral condemnation, even in those areas where it professed to have substantial interest, was not forgotten in Europe—including Italy and Germany. Neither the British nor the French felt they could place much confidence in American power as a preventive to future aggressions by European states. The French were additionally upset by the American failure to treat them as equals to the British during the postwar period, and now that their strength was ebbing they were faced with the even greater likelihood that any American influence on European affairs would be thrown behind Great Britain rather than France.

Under these conditions, the United States could not play more than a minor role in continental affairs, even should it wish to do so. The European democracies would be highly unlikely to permit American initiative in Europe for fear that the Americans would back out and leave them alone to face any resulting crisis. During the Spanish civil war the British made their feelings on this point quite clear.

British and French opposition to American initiative only deepened after the enactment of neutrality legislation in the United States in 1935 and 1936. Troubled by these developments for even better reasons were the majority of officials in the State Department. Preoccupied as President Roosevelt was by domestic troubles, he appeared uncertain about, and almost uninterested in, this problem of neutrality legislation, which so basically affected his administration's conduct of foreign policy. Then, too, he feared any action which might cost him vital votes in Congress for his domestic program. Lacking the President's support, the State Department was incapable of thwarting the demands of congressmen who sought to insure peace for America by limiting the freedom of action of the State Department. The first neutrality act, passed in August 1935 and effective for six months, compelled the government to place an embargo on shipments of arms, ammunition, and other implements of war to all nations involved in war. Thus the State Department was more than ever compelled to "tip its hand" in advance of international crises. The opponents of this legislation argued that, since it would not permit the government to discriminate between aggressor nations and their victims, such legislation might encourage potential aggressors to pursue their designs on weaker states.

While the President signed the Neutrality Act of 1935 with some misgivings, he had his reasons for accepting it. He apparently felt that such problems as the nondiscriminatory provisions of the act could be dealt with at the next session of Congress. Second, the nondiscriminatory aspect of this neutrality act did not particularly bother him as regards the Italo-Ethiopian problem—for in this particular case, an arms embargo applied to both sides operated to the greater distress of the aggressor, Italy. Finally, the President saw some advantage in neutrality legislation that would provide him with powers to deal quickly and effectively with such problems as the shipment of arms and the travel of Americans on the ships of belligerent nations. He was therefore in sympathy with the idea of neutrality legislation but not with the mandatory provisions of the Neutrality Act of 1935.

In February 1936, a second neutrality act was passed. Rather than providing for presidential discrimination, it further limited his freedom—requiring him to ban loans to belligerents and to extend the embargo to any nations entering the war after it had begun. It further prevented him from banning the sale and shipment of raw materials. It was found, however, as in the case of oil shipped to Italy, that raw materials could be of greater importance to a belligerent than implements of war. An omission, later so important in Spain, was the failure to make any provisions for civil wars. The neutrality law applied only to international conflicts. By this legislation, every nation in the world received advance notice of American policy in the event of international war.

As they witnessed developments in Europe during the last half of the decade, American policy-makers encountered a problem of critical proportions: how is it possible to affect the course of events so as to avoid war without making political and military commitments, and having already informed the world what American policy would be in the event of war? With all these limitations upon his actions, Secretary Hull chose two related policies. First, there was "exemplary diplomacy," as specifically embodied in the Good Neighbor policy. Hull, proud of his accomplishments in the Western hemisphere, continually referred to the Good Neighbor policy as worthy of emulation abroad. Second, there were trade agreements, sought for the purpose of arresting the tide of economic nationalism. Both of these approaches antedated the neutrality acts, and both were subsequently continued. The first alternative was terribly ill suited as a guide to European statesmen to solve continental problems. In the Western hemisphere, the policy of the "good neighbor" was workable to the extent that the United States, negotiating from a position of supreme power, had much to gain by helping to increase the strength of its southern neighbors. No European nation was in anything approaching a similar position. The second course, that of reciprocal trade agreements, was just about as hopeless. In Germany, economic nationalism was already intimately bound up with militarism and racism. And Great Britain would have been compelled to make drastic readjustments if it were to depart from its policy of establishing a Commonwealth economy. Even if Hull's policy had been widely adopted, it would have been tardy in bringing about the desired results.

As Hull became frustrated at the European failure to adopt policies which he believed calculated to insure peace, he resorted to moral exhortations—in keeping with the postures assumed by his predecessors as well as his own inclinations. The Secretary pursued still another course. Hull, as an advocate of international cooperation, lent what support he dared give to the League of Nations. As the League's influence was all but disappearing, the Secretary felt compelled to shift the focus of this limited support. By 1936, the European policy of the

United States could be defined, however inadequately, as one of acting in concert with France and Great Britain, and particularly with the latter. It is doubtful that the Secretary grasped at this policy enthusiastically. He was strongly opposed to the formation of blocs. He preferred the collective action which an effective League of Nations might provide. Later, when the European Non-Intervention Committee was proposed by the French, primarily to localize the Spanish crisis, it could be expected that Hull would be sympathetic to the effort.

When "Judge Hull, from Tennessee," became Secretary of State in the spring of 1933, he was, in the jargon of his day, a confirmed Wilsonian. He possessed an obvious concern for the moral contribution which he felt the United States could make to diplomatic conduct around the globe. His preference for "exemplary" and legalistic diplomacy, his dislike for balance of power and spheres of influence, and his suspicion of economic power—these attitudes were characteristically Wilsonian. During the course of his twelve terms in the House of Representatives and two years in the Senate, Hull developed a concern for tariff reform which occasionally bordered on an obsession. There were times when knocking down international trade barriers became a moral crusade to which he tended to sacrifice other causes and which left him slightly lopsided as a statesman. His fellow congressmen were inclined to admire the meticulous quality of his speeches for the cause of low tariffs. But they sometimes wondered at a man who preferred to ruminate in his office, gathering and studying statistics, than to fraternize with his colleagues. As a far more gregarious politician, Tom Connally, later observed, Hull "wanted to avoid rough-and-tumble debates."[5] He even had his speeches entered into the *Record* without delivering them—perhaps because he had a slight speech impediment. The single-minded dedication and personal aloofness which characterized his behavior in the 1920's carried over into the New Deal years.

Because of his experience on Capitol Hill, Hull brought to the State Department an intimate knowledge of the workings of Congress as well as congressional contacts. Yet neither this knowledge nor these acquaintanceships helped the Department appreciably in its major conflicts with congressional leaders. The Secretary's previous experience seems to have encouraged him to back away from congressional battles more than it helped him to win them. From the point of view of some influential men on the Hill, he did not help matters. Just as he had earlier avoided debates on the floor of Congress, he now sought to remain aloof from the Senate Foreign Relations Committee. He had his reasons. Men like William Borah and Hiram Johnson could be anything but friendly. Even those who were sympathetic toward him, however, were sometimes irked by his reluctance to appear before them. Further, Hull still held Washington society at a distance, preferring a quiet evening at home with his wife in the fashionable Carlton Hotel. For most government officials, the Carlton was a cocktail center of special importance; for Hull it was an extension of his office—a convenient retreat located on Sixteenth Street at the base of Embassy Row, and only four blocks from the old State Building. The Hulls did not live there for the purpose of entering into the social life of the capital. As a consequence, the hard-working, withdrawn Secretary did little to increase his limited circle of friends, and in Congress he still lacked those intimate acquaintances whose personal loyalty toward him might have proved valuable.

The only apparent means of winning Congress to the views of the State Department was to use the power and influence of the President. But this path was closed to Hull. In addition to Roosevelt's reluctance to endanger his domestic policy by challenging Congress on questions of foreign affairs, there were also personal obstacles. The Secretary's relations with the President, while amicable, were anything but close. The lack of intimate conversations between the two men during the Spanish civil war was not an aberration. Sometimes stung by Roosevelt's tactless repudiations of his ideas—as at London in 1933—Hull became unwilling to push his views on the Chief Executive. Wilbur Carr, with four decades of experience in the State Department, once recorded that the Secretary "seems amazingly diffident, lacking in courage or lacking in close relationship to the President. Other cabinet members demand things of the President. Why not he?"[6] The Secretary of State was not only affected by his personal distaste for conflict, he was also wary of Roosevelt's sometimes cavalier manner. The fact is that Hull did not altogether trust Roosevelt. From Hull's point of view, the President's actions were too often determined by small-time politics. When Hull told his friends that he aspired to be an American equivalent of a Japanese elder statesman, he was not entirely joking; he very much wanted to be above politics (especially the politics of the New Deal). Hull was increasingly alienated by Roosevelt's domestic programs; they violated his border-state conservatism.

The Secretary continued at his post out of a dedication to principles. The President appreciated Hull's presence for equally purposeful reasons. In the first place, the Secretary could be trusted. He was not devious. Second, he served as an excellent foil. Always the cautious student, Hull could be highly attentive to details and capable of finding objections and obstacles to virtually any policy proposed. If this led to inaction, it enabled the President to counter the arguments of others who demanded this course or that. The President, too, was sympathetic with Hull's internationalist views and was still, however erratically in practice, a Wilsonian himself. Further, the Secretary, as a Southern Democrat, was politically valuable in a cabinet dominated by Northern liberals. If the President required an additional reason, there was always Hull's popularity. He was never subjected to the right-wing hate campaigns which were directed at so many members of Roosevelt's controversial administration. Even when during the last year of the Spanish war the State Department was accused by the left-wing press of Fascist inclinations, Hull was excepted from the charge. The Secretary's forthright expressions of moral indignation and his distinguished appearance made him attractive to the American public. Although the Secretary was widely respected, he possessed neither the dynamism nor the imagination to secure a dedicated popular following. In fact he can be numbered among those men who have been appreciated in their own times for what they were—in Hull's instance, diligent, principled, and gentlemanly. "Almost everybody is fond of Hull," wrote the unenthralled John Franklin Carter. His "upright character embellishes American public life much as an upright piano embellishes a farmhouse parlor."[7]

The Secretary was not a creative thinker. As Donald Drummond has pointed out, he "too often thought in clichés," and "generally was much better at holding the line than at formulating new departures."[8] At the time he became Secretary of State, he was in his sixties, and his patterns of thought were well set. When Herbert Feis, from the Department's Division of Economic Affairs, first came to know the new Secretary, he discovered that Hull was well versed in international economics; but he also observed that Hull's mind was "not flexible in this sphere and vague outside it."[9] These were problems with which Hull's advisors had often to contend, although it is also clear that many of them were gratified by his persistent fact-gathering consultations, his cautious, studied manner, and his habit of treating them as associates rather than subordinates.

The Secretary's penchant for collecting data and opinions resulted in making almost any problem readily susceptible to conflicting interpretations. As a consequence, he was sometimes immobilized. Hull possessed no self-confident will, and no sense of daring, which might lead him out of the morass of conflicting details and toward decisive action. While it is true that he did not possess a particularly incisive intellect, it is also true that much of his "vagueness" proceeded from his appreciation of the complexities he faced. When it came to issues involving economic nationalism and internationalism, he behaved much more decisively; here his ideological commitment enabled him to subordinate conflicting evidence.

Related to his indecisiveness was Hull's basic humility. He is probably better remembered for his statements of righteous indignation, which sometimes slopped over into self-righteousness. But such public, and even private, remarks came largely out of feelings of frustration, not from arrogance. Sometimes uncertain of his grasp of the relevant data, and extremely sensitive to the complexities of a problem when he did feel he had the facts, Hull appeared to humble himself into inaction. His respect for those advisors who could provide the information he desired, combined with his measured self-estimate, fed his need for constant consultation. It also encouraged his habit of considering his advisors as associates.

The chiefs of divisions, within the Department, tended to value such treatment, but Hull's behavior did not always help his relations with the two most prominent advisors. Under Secretary William Phillips, at 58, and Assistant Secretary Sumner Welles, at 44, had between them more than fifty years' service in a variety of diplomatic and State Department posts. Whatever Hull's stature and talents, they were likely to consider him a novice. His prudence sometimes appeared to be

plain weakness, and his attempt at a kind of "fraternal administration" occasionally led to permissiveness. Gentleman that he
was himself, the Secretary did not expect his advisors to abuse
or exploit his style of administration, or to misinterpret it as a
sign of personal inadequacy. Different from Hull in background and in temperament, both Welles and Phillips were
annoyed by his administrative manner. They possessed the
self-assurance, and Welles the ambition and determination,
which Hull so seldom displayed. Welles, in particular, did little
to bolster the Secretary where he was really weak but instead
tried to provide through independent effort what the Secretary
lacked. The Assistant Secretary might, for example, have used
his ability to communicate with the President to Hull's advantage, but Welles plainly wanted to be Secretary of State himself.

Phillips and Welles were, like Roosevelt, Harvard men; and
both were used to the comfort and security of wealth and high
social position. The broad common ground they held with the
President goes far to explain the easy relationships they had
developed with him over many years. This gave them an advantage with Roosevelt which Hull always lacked, and it quickly
became a source of difficulties in the State Department.

Of these two top-level officers, Welles was more ambitious and
imaginative, and less congenial. He was almost invariably described by contemporaries as occasionally brilliant and regularly aloof. Marquis Childs wrote that Welles "had what could
be called, with a wide margin of understatement, a disciplined
exterior."[10] According to Phillips, he "suffered somewhat from
an unbending personality."[11] By comparison with Phillips,
Welles was intense and dissatisfied. The men were two of a class,
but not of a kind.

The major source of difficulties between Hull and Welles lay
in the Assistant Secretary's close relationship with the President—and his exploitation of it. Carr's indictment of Welles'
behavior, while it exaggerates the problem, gives a fair indication of the impression Welles could leave upon his colleagues.
According to Carr, he went over the heads of Hull and Phillips.
When he disagreed with the Department's Personnel Board, he
would threaten the other members with his White House influence. He was guided by "personal motives" and "partisan politics." And "he found it impossible to stay with his prescribed

area of activity."[12] Hull did not openly admit it, but he had much reason to blame himself. He never forced the issue with Welles or with Roosevelt and, as a consequence, became involved in a running feud with his subordinate which lasted into the war years. It was remarkable that they cooperated as well as they did in the formulation and execution of the Good Neighbor policy.

Phillips, in recounting the differences between his relations with Roosevelt (and Hull) and those of Welles, maintained that he never made an appointment with the President without first consulting the Secretary. Certainly Phillips was more respectful of the chain of command. Despite this, he and Hull did not work together very easily. The handsome, "azure-blooded New Englander" respected the Secretary, not least for his integrity and diligence. But Phillips thought Hull not only lacking in firmness but provincial. The Under Secretary was the kind of diplomat who seems to feel capable of averting disaster through the international brotherhood of diplomacy. It was not surprising, for example, when he later became ambassador to Italy, that he counseled the State Department in the fashion of Chamberlain. Nor was it unexpected when he felt frustrated by Roosevelt's and Hull's refusal to recognize Italy's Ethiopian claims. If Hull lacked decisiveness, he was not Phillips' kind of appeaser.

Another of Hull's most important advisors was R. Walton Moore. This "bald and charming bachelor," already in his seventies when he came to the Department, was closer to Hull than was any other officer. (And he was no friend of Welles.) Formerly a legal counselor for railway and steamship companies, and a six-term congressman from Virginia, he was an old acquaintance of the Secretary. The choice of Moore as an Assistant Secretary was otherwise a curious one. In many respects a talented man, he lacked experience in foreign affairs, and he viewed diplomatic problems from an excessively political and legalistic standpoint. Because of his background, it was probably believed that Moore could assist the overburdened Secretary in developing good relations with congressional leaders. Whatever the case, the State Department paid a high price, because Moore held views similar to those of the more ardent isolationists. Soon after entering the Department, he concurred with Senator Johnson of California that it was dan-

gerous to give the President discretionary powers in the application of an arms embargo; Moore felt it was too difficult to
discriminate between aggressor and victim.[13] His isolationist
tendencies did not abate, and this was to have no little effect
upon American policy during the Spanish civil war, when
Moore once again showed his inclination to sacrifice presidential discretion.

Considering the attitudes of these men, and the uneasy relationships among them, it becomes doubly important that they
did agree on the basic policy toward the Spanish conflict.
Welles was influenced in large part by the connections between
the Latin American and Spanish policies: United States support of the Loyalist government would have compounded the
difficulties he faced in developing the Good Neighbor policy.
Phillips, fearful that a Loyalist victory would strengthen Communism throughout Europe, and especially anxious about the
danger of starting a larger conflict, believed noninvolvement in
Spain an appropriate policy. And Moore, finding Congress
opposed to the shipment of American arms to Spain, and believing that American interests were not really involved anyway,
hardly considered the adoption of an alternative course of
action. Agreement among men who were often at odds with one
another made the noninvolvement policy appear additionally
correct—particularly as the reasons for agreement were not
uniform.

Each of these men—Phillips, Welles, and Moore—helped to
formulate American policy toward the Spanish civil war. Of
additional importance were the roles played by William C.
Bullitt and Claude Bowers. Bullitt, a consistently controversial
figure, was ambassador to Moscow. In October 1936, he was
transferred to the embassy in Paris. To officials in Washington,
Bullitt was both an asset and a liability. He was appreciated
and trusted by many foreign statesmen. They consequently
talked freely with Bullitt when they might have been reticent
toward another man. On the other hand, Bullitt was independent. What he did was not always made clear to the State
Department. He also had the habit of deluging the Department
with lengthy telegraphic reports not easily digestible. Additionally troubling was Bullitt's vision of diplomacy as a perpetual
drama in which the cabal and the conspiracy played command-
ing roles, and in which (because of this) all kinds of fantastic

possibilities might await an unsuspecting world. Still there is no doubt that the ambassador often received valuable information, and his analyses of European affairs had considerable standing with many officials in Washington, including the President. Bullitt constantly sought some basis for a rapprochement between France and Germany, for he believed this the only way a general war could be avoided. The reasons he presented for this hope of a Franco-German settlement were too feeble for Roosevelt and Hull to accept, but it is important that Bullitt's attitude, here, had much to do with his failure to counsel American intervention in Spain. Such a policy would only complicate Franco-German difficulties.

With respect to having influence on the policy-makers in Washington, the opposite was true of Bowers, U.S. ambassador to Spain, who became increasingly frustrated by the failure of the Department to pay proper respect to his opinions. For Hull's part, while he was certainly free to reject the ambassador's views, he never once called Bowers home from his duties for a thorough briefing on the Department's view of the Spanish situation and its relationship to general European and Latin American conditions. The ambassador was professionally and personally neglected. Bowers was in a way a wise choice for the Madrid post, for he had many qualities attractive to Spaniards. Open and friendly, sympathetic to the Spanish experiment while wary of its excesses, romantic, and capable of intense feeling and affection, he apparently enjoyed good relations with leaders from antagonistic political factions.

Bowers had long been a journalist in Indiana, eventually becoming a political columnist for the *New York Journal*. At the same time he was increasingly active in national Democratic politics. He is now probably best remembered for his popular, dramatic, and partisan historical writings on Jefferson and Hamilton, the Jacksonian era, and the reconstruction period. These writings furnish one of the best clues to Bowers' diplomatic reports from Spain, for they indicate his flair for the dramatic and sensational. So colored were many of his reports by highly connotative language that they may sometimes have failed even to express accurately his own views concerning the Spanish situation. But, more important, as Bowers later became increasingly convinced of the necessity of a government victory over the Rebels, he apparently forgot what he had earlier reported. Before the civil war, he had warned of the possibility of a Communist take-over. Later, during the war, when such a take-over seemed much more feasible, he came to feel that the State Department was overly concerned about Communist elements.

No doubt Bowers was handicapped by being outside Spain for all but the earliest days of the war. He and many other diplomats went from San Sebastián to St. Jean de Luz, France, for their safety. And while he was in constant personal contact with Loyalist and Rebel representatives there, the ambassador did not actually observe political or military developments in Spain.

Upon the outbreak of the civil war, the view from Washington was obscured. The strength, resolve, and popular following of each party were in doubt. Even though Bowers had warned the State Department of the possibility of a military revolt, matters were far too confused to develop a policy in anticipation of events. Moreover, Spain was immediately catapulted into the center of European affairs. To American policy-makers what happened in Spain was actually of secondary importance (except for the protection of American lives and property). What mattered more to them was what the British and French believed was happening and might happen. Those attitudes and policies toward Europe which had been developing for almost two decades now came into play in the formulation of Washington's Spanish policy.

Shortly after the war began, Secretary Hull chose a course which very rapidly became a policy of inaction—in concert with the foreign offices in Paris and London. Such a policy suited the Secretary's disposition to pursue the path of least resistance and his desire for international cooperation—a desire which had already become restricted to back-seat cooperation with the British and the French. Anglo-French policy toward the Spanish civil war dominated the policy of the United States.

2

PARIS AND LONDON

BY THE SUMMER OF 1936, officials in the State Department could not avoid the fact that their freedom to make policy was severely restricted. If the United States was to make any contribution to the cause of peace abroad, it would have to coordinate its efforts with those of other powers. It was everywhere unthinkable that the United States should attempt to lead the forces of peace, for the American people did not have the will, American diplomatists did not have the experience, and Europeans would not have accepted the risk.[1] Only slightly less unthinkable was the idea that the United States should coordinate its policies with those of any governments to the exclusion of Great Britain and France, the two nations with which the United States had the greatest affinity, and in which the State Department's dilemma was best understood and its hopes best appreciated. American policy, guided by the highest intentions, became wedded to the policies emanating from the British and French foreign offices.

London and Paris were the only European capitals in which it might even be thought that Americans struck bargains and were made intimates. And, yet, even at Downing Street and the Quai d'Orsay American representatives did not really "strike bargains," they simply sought to cooperate; they were not really "intimates," but rather were confidants—for they largely reflected the views given them by the French and the

British, and they did little more than impress those foreign offices with the idealistic hopes of and the isolationist pressures on American policy-makers. Washington's picture of the civil war in Spain was very like a double exposure which combined the angles of vision from Paris and London.

I

The nation most intimately concerned by the fortunes of Spain was France. The French, themselves badly divided internally, were not well prepared to deal with the effects of the rapidly developing ideological war across the Pyrenees. The Spanish strife only deepened existing cleavages among the French people, and the involvement of the Catholic Church further complicated the issue. In France the war was to cause almost as much trouble in domestic politics as in foreign relations.

French foreign policy since the end of the world war had been a signal failure, the most recent humiliation being the German reoccupation of the Rhineland. This in large part brought about the victory, albeit a marginal one, of the Popular Front under the premiership of Léon Blum, in May 1936. The Popular Front, a flimsy coalition of middle-class Radical Socialists, Socialists, and Communists, immediately faced a labor crisis in which the Communists were heartily involved. Not only was there a resultant Red scare which fortified the center and right opposition, but the whole foundation of the coalition was threatened. The confidence of Popular Front leaders was shaken.

French foreign policy, even before this time, reflected a mood of indecision stemming to a large extent from those same deeply etched internal divisions. Externally, the rise of Hitler and the growing intractability of Mussolini contributed to the anxieties of the French people. The same lack of resolve which plagued earlier governments now threatened the Popular Front. After the Blum Government assumed power, an uneasy consensus determined the larger aims of French foreign policy, leftists and moderates concurring to various degrees on the necessity for ties with Britain and the Soviet Union. For each group, close association with one of these powers was considered an

unfortunate necessity. The left felt no special attraction to the
British Conservative Government of Stanley Baldwin; the
moderates plainly felt uncomfortable in association with Stalin.
Among those French leaders who placed particular importance
on securing stronger ties with the Soviet Union were Blum,
Edouard Herriot (whom Soviet officials were shortly to favor
above Blum), and Robert Coulondre, ambassador to Moscow.[2]
Leaning more toward Great Britain as the key ally of France
was Alexis Saint Léger Léger, the experienced and respected
Secretary General at the Quai d'Orsay. Léger's motives for
courting Great Britain proceeded from his conviction that the
British were not natural allies of France and must continually
be impressed by the good will of French leaders—which because
of the Popular Front the British currently might well doubt.
Léger exerted sufficient influence upon Blum to swing the Premier away from the views of Herriot and Coulondre. He was
aided in this by the ambassador to London, Charles Corbin, and
by the Ministers of Foreign Relations and War, Yvon Delbos
and Edouard Daladier. All three men distrusted the Soviet
Union and were angered by Communist interference in France.
Among the higher officials, it was from Blum, Delbos, Daladier,
and to some extent Léger that American diplomats received
most of their "official" information on French interpretations
of European affairs. This was particularly true after William
C. Bullitt was made ambassador to France in the fall of 1936.
And, it was primarily the views of Delbos and Daladier which
Bullitt reflected.[3] During more than two and a half years as
ambassador to Moscow, he too had developed a deep distrust of
the Soviet Union.

At the same time, the views of the French right were not lost
upon American officials—again primarily Bullitt, convinced as
he was that ultimately only a rapprochement between France
and Germany could secure European peace. Those on the
French right began with a demand only somewhat less unrealiz-
able. They wanted something like the "Stresa Front" of sixteen
months before, in which the French joined with the Italians and
the British against the Austrian aspirations of Germany. How
far some of these men would then have gone toward an accom-
modation with Hitler is difficult to estimate. Among these men
were Pierre-Etienne Flandin and Pierre Laval, who helped to
form the Stresa Front. Along with them was a close friend of

Laval, André François-Poncet, ambassador to Berlin. Having been at the French embassy on the Pariserplatz since 1931, François-Poncet was officially and socially intimate with Nazi leaders as well as with the old guard at the German Foreign Office. On the extreme right were some who, to simplify the issue, preferred Hitler to Stalin. Among the latter group, which wielded not a little economic power, were a few influential industrialists. Having considerable investments at stake in Spain, this group feared the anticapitalist character of the Spanish Popular Front and preferred a Rebel victory.[4]

But, whoever determined French policy toward the Spanish conflict, there would be two consistent considerations, one strategic and the other commercial. A Spain in unfriendly hands would be a threat to communications between France and its African colonies, and to the whole of the Mediterranean defense system as well. Furthermore, the French held 60 per cent of the foreign capital investment in Spanish industry, the loss of which would not only be a financial problem but an internal political problem for any French regime.[5]

Two problems were necessarily clear to Blum during the early summer of 1936. First there was the possibility of a Fascist encirclement of France. Second, the popular basis of his support was very like that of the Spanish Popular Front. One source was a spirit of supranational working-class radicalism. If that spirit were shattered in one country, the other nation could not escape its effects. The other source was the uncertain support of the middle class; widespread defection would destroy the Popular Front. The issues brought about by the Spanish war threatened to cause just that. The precarious situation of the French Popular Front could not but affect the attitudes of American policy-makers. Already disposed to lean toward British attitudes on European affairs, those in the State Department now had further reason to look more toward London.

Britain, like France, was interested in the fate of Spain for strategic and commercial reasons. Western access to the Mediterranean was vital to British trade interests and possibly to the protection of its Mediterranean holdings. A stable, friendly, and independent Spain was almost as important to Britain as to France, but while the French Popular Front had a stake in the success of its Spanish counterpart, the British Government would have looked favorably upon a moderately right-wing Spain.

The British Conservative Government was not torn, as the French Popular Front was, over the problem of seeking ties with this or that nation. What the British wished most of all, in fact, was to avoid the division of Europe into two hostile blocs. To this extent, Léger had probably been correct to be concerned for the course of Anglo-French relations. To Cordell Hull, British opposition to bloc-building in Europe was probably not the least attractive aspect of British policy. London wanted a viable situation, one which would permit the solution of international problems through negotiation. For this, a large measure of "impartiality" was thought to be necessary. Prime Minister Stanley Baldwin had nothing directly to do with the formulation of this policy—for Baldwin was notoriously uninformed about, and really uninterested in, international affairs. Duff Cooper, one of the most ardent opponents of the policies of appeasement and restrained rearmament, afterward wrote that "the topic of foreign affairs was so uncongenial" to Baldwin's mind "that he preferred to ignore it."[6] As a consequence, Baldwin gave his foreign secretaries a good deal of freedom. Sir Samuel Hoare had abused that freedom with the attempted Hoare-Laval pact in 1935, which would have given the Italians the larger part of Ethiopia, gratis. So great was the shocked uproar from the British public, and all over the world from adherents of international cooperation and the League of Nations, that Hoare was compelled to step down from the Foreign Office to the Admiralty. Anthony Eden, who replaced him, turned out to be a little more circumspect with the latitude Baldwin again conferred upon the Foreign Office.

If the Prime Minister did not directly influence foreign policy, his appreciation of internal political realities and his reputation as an uncanny interpreter of British opinion influenced a good many Conservatives and not a few Laborites as well. What appeared most obvious was that the British people did not want a "risk policy," nor did they want to spend money on a large-scale rearmament program. Costly social reforms were too badly needed. Should the Government fall into Labor's hands because the Conservatives alienated the voters with a sizable rearmament budget, the British would only be more unprepared for war. A good deal of the strength of the Labor party rested upon its pacifist and antirearmament platform. Such was the dilemma in which the Prime Minister found himself. Whether or not Baldwin was personally uninterested or incapable in the area of foreign affairs, the policy adopted by the Foreign Office was in keeping with the internal political situation as he interpreted it.

It became the Foreign Office's aim to secure peace through accommodations which would satisfy the "legitimate grievances" of Germany and Italy. Even when it was felt necessary to secure the peace further by strengthening themselves militarily, the British placed their greatest hopes for peace in expressions and measures of good will toward the Fascist states. Such was the point of view of most Conservatives, including Neville Chamberlain, who would become Prime Minister in a matter of months, Sir Samuel Hoare, now First Lord of the Admiralty, Geoffrey Dawson, influential editor of the London *Times*, and Anthony Eden, the Foreign Secretary, who gradually became disenchanted with the policy of appeasement as it failed to bring its expected rewards. An even more sternly "antirisk" and certainly antirearmament policy was advocated by the leader of the Laborites, Clement Attlee. The most persistent opposition came from Duff Cooper and Winston Churchill, whose concern for the military strength of Germany and the radical nature of National Socialism were a long time in being appreciated by their Conservative brethren. The Labor party was even slower to heed their warnings to rearm with greater haste.

Concerning the Soviet Union, the British Government was not to any degree attracted by the idea of closer ties such as many French leaders had determined were necessary. The position of the reigning Conservatives on this matter was very like that of the French right and never further left than Delbos and Daladier. Again and again the fear was expressed that the Soviet Union wished to incite all Europe to war, a war from which the Russians would remain aloof so as to reap the spoils from the wreck of Western civilization.

As for the Fascist states, the British knew one necessity— that Germany and Italy must not be permitted to pursue too close an association. Upon the collapse of the Stresa Front, the lame attempt to curb Mussolini's ambitions in Africa, and the failure to encourage French resistance to Hitler's reoccupation of the Rhineland, British policy progressively revealed to the Germans and Italians their common position in relation to the British Empire and the disposition of the British people to avoid the threat or use of force. With good reason, the British grew disappointed over the increasingly close relations between the Fascist states, and this problem assumed critical proportions very early in the Spanish civil war.

II

The revolt in Spain did not long remain a purely Spanish affair. General Emilio Mola, with his Rebel forces in the north, and General Franco, at first isolated after his victories in Spanish Morocco, had anticipated spontaneous and widespread public support which would bring about a victory within a matter of days. The failure of this support to materialize caused the Rebels to turn, with hardly a moment's hesitation, to Germany and Italy for the military aid necessary to carry out a prolonged campaign. It is likely that without the aid of German transports ferrying insurgent troops from Spanish Morocco to the mainland the revolt would have been quickly suppressed. Even before this, however, the Madrid government felt compelled to seek from foreign nations the implements of war necessary to quell the revolt. The rebellion was, after all, primarily led by the army. Making its situation even worse, the government only commanded the loyalty of about half the air force; and while it kept a larger portion of the navy, a good many officers defected to the Rebels.[7] The Spanish government therefore turned to France. But little more than a week after the rebellion began, the Azaña regime found itself deserted by the very foreign government from which it felt it could expect the most sympathy and aid.

This was brought to the attention of Washington on July 27, when the State Department was informed that the French government—largely under the influence of the British—favored a policy of "strict neutrality." The French wished to prevent the export of arms to either party to the civil strife. Ambassador Straus reported the sequence of events which led to this decision as given to him by "an informant." On July 21, four days after the Spanish strife began, the French Minister of Aviation,

Pierre Cot, along with others in the Blum cabinet, decided to comply with a request from the Spanish government to send the arms and ammunition which were urgently needed. "To this decision," Straus reported, "it is understood that Blum gave his tacit approval." The following day, the French ambassador at London telephoned Blum, indicating that the "British Government was extremely worried about this contingency." On July 23, at the French ambassador's urging, Blum went to London—officially to take part in a previously scheduled Three Power Conference of Britain, France, and Belgium. When Blum returned to Paris on July 25, he called a cabinet council during which he, Daladier, and Delbos argued for "strict neutrality" and "won out." Blum succumbed to the viewpoint in London, where Anthony Eden called attention to the positions taken by Germany and Italy toward the Spanish situation. Also reminding him about German troop movements currently near the French border, Eden mentioned the fear in Britain that French aid to the Madrid government could bring about "grave international consequences."[8] As with the Rhineland crisis during the spring, the French were compelled to choose between going on alone and holding back.

Impressed by the "hands off Spain" attitude of the British, reports of German and Italian complicity with the Spanish Rebels, and divisions within his own cabinet, Blum sought a policy at once calculated to prevent the Spanish strife from becoming a European war and to pacify those supporters of the Popular Front who demanded that he aid Madrid. Straus shortly learned that the Blum Government would propose to the British and Italians that "they join in a formal commitment not to furnish arms to either side nor to interfere in any way in events in Spain." The impression left by Straus's informant was that if Italy should evade a definite commitment "it could hardly be expected that the French Government would continue its present strictly hands off attitude." It is difficult to estimate whether the French were attempting to bluff the Italians into such an agreement, or whether they would really have resumed the exportation of war matériel had the Italians finally refused to join.[9] Here again Blum would have been compelled to decide between the French left on one side and the French right and the British Foreign Office on the other.

The Baldwin Government, believed by many to have initiated

the French-sponsored plan of a European nonintervention agreement, responded favorably to the Blum proposal. Even the Labor Party, although pro-Loyalist, supported the nonintervention plan.[10] With the British response in their hands, but still lacking that of the Italians, the French forwarded notes to Germany, Portugal, Belgium, Poland, and the Soviet Union requesting their views toward a declaration of nonintervention. The French were by this time extremely concerned over reports of Rebel concessions to the Fascist states for aiding them in the revolt. Among other things, these rumors concerned the granting of naval and air bases to the Germans and Italians in the Balearics and in Spanish Morocco.[11] The French were consistently more concerned about this possibility than were the British, who, apparently from an early date, thought it very unlikely.[12]

The French went further in an effort to bring about a European accord by announcing independently a prohibition on the sale of war matériel to both Spanish factions. The British, by doing the same some days later, also gave a "practical demonstration of their earnest desire" to bring about such prohibitions in other countries. Anthony Eden has since reminisced that he "had not yet learnt that it is dangerous to offer such gestures to dictators, who are more likely to misinterpret than to follow them. For the moment, these moves appeared to produce the effects we desired."[13] But apparently it was not these gestures which brought about "favorable" responses from Germany and Italy. Johannes von Welczeck, the German ambassador in Paris, and earlier ambassador to Spain, informed the German Foreign Ministry: "I am convinced that postponement of final assent to the arms embargo must work to the disadvantage of the rebels, since, from considerations of geography alone, deliveries from countries which sympathize with them could not compete with French support." Welczeck concluded that if an international arms embargo did not materialize within a few days, "Blum and Delbos fear that they can no longer resist the growing domestic political pressure and they will have to give unlimited support to the Spanish Government." Welczeck cannily added that adherence to a nonintervention agreement "would preclude official participation of governments."[14] The Germans thereupon "officially" placed an immediate embargo upon shipment of arms to Spain. But Hitler the same day decreed an increase in the term of military service in Germany. The French, thus pleased on the one hand, were troubled on the other.[15] In an exchange of views during the last week of August, the Italians agreed with the Germans that further delay in setting up the nonintervention agreement would work to the advantage of the Madrid government.[16] Apparently, both were at least momentarily convinced that Blum might indeed be forced to rescind his embargo policy unless they made a show of cooperation.

The Germans and Italians became involved in the Spanish war only after receiving appeals from the Rebel generals.[17] Hitler's motives, often obscure even to the German Foreign Office, cannot be explained with any certainty. In addition to the economic advantages, particularly with respect to strategic metals, likely to be gained from a friendly and indebted Spanish regime, and in addition to the opportunity to experiment with new weapons and such military techniques as the Blitzkrieg, the audacious policy pursued in Spain was probably calculated to keep France troubled by the prospect of a Fascist encirclement. The policy was continued for the further purpose of storing up a reserve of good will with Mussolini and keeping him at odds with France and Britain. Whether or not it was Hitler's additional aim at the time to enroll the Vatican in his anti-Bolshevist campaign, by siding with the Church-oriented Franco, is not known. German attempts to accomplish this in September failed, but by January they were beginning to succeed.[18] Mussolini's reasons for involvement in Spain were less complex. Anxious to spread Italian influence in the Mediterranean, and thus deal another blow to Britain and France, he seized upon this opportunity. Furthermore, as they persistently pointed out, the Italians were determined to prevent Communist domination in Spain. It is likely, because of Mussolini's distrust of the Germans, that he also did not want to allow Hitler to get an upper hand in Rebel circles. If so, this was probably a later development, coming at a time when the Italians felt they were competing with the Germans for prestige in the Spanish venture.

For the Soviet Union the Spanish war presented an unusual problem. It appeared that Soviet Russia could benefit regardless of which party won. Should the left be victorious, Soviet prestige would be enhanced at a time when the Russians were having their difficulties in the nations sandwiched between Germany and Russia. Spain need not even have a Communist-led government, so long as it was anti-Fascist. A left-wing victory would also prevent Fascist control of Gibraltar. Still, should the right win, France, and perhaps Britain too, might be forced into closer association with the Soviet Union in order to counter the spread of Fascist influence. But Soviet leaders could not be so sanguine when it came to the necessity of choosing a policy. If Russia acted vigorously, thus aiding the international Communist movement, it was likely to injure its relations with France and Great Britain, and also the United States. At the same time, should the Soviet Union act timidly, the Communist International would suffer.

As a result, there arose a heated debate among Soviet leaders very early in the war. Those favoring some kind of sympathetic action prevailed, and it was decided that funds would be collected from Soviet workers for their Spanish brethren. Following this there were shipments of nonmilitary goods to Loyalist Spain. The prevailing opinion was that in the interest of maintaining hegemony over the international revolutionary movement, the Soviet Union must assume leadership and not hesitate in periods of crisis.[19] It was several weeks after the war began before the Soviet Union decided to send military aid, and for this aid the Spanish government was to pay dearly—slightly over 70 per cent of the Spanish monetary gold (amounting to $578 million) left Cartagena for Odessa on October 25, 1936.[20] And there were political as well as financial costs.

So as to protect its ultimate hope of establishing an anti-Fascist bloc, the Soviet government, on August 23, exchanged notes with France and agreed to prohibit the export of arms to Spain if the governments of Germany, Italy, Portugal, France, and Great Britain would join such an agreement. The French chargé d'affaires in Moscow informed American officials that the Soviet Union had been less than willing to make the agreement, for the Kremlin feared it might be criticized by "the more militant world revolutionary forces." Soviet leaders were also concerned that they would be placed in the position of assuming responsibility for the actions of Communists outside Russia over whom they had many times professed to have no control.[21]

By the end of August, the French government secured the replies of all the great powers in Europe, in addition to twenty-three other European states. The most stubborn of the nations was Portugal, whom the British were having difficulty bringing into line. When the Portuguese did join the pact, Lisbon made little effort to conceal its partiality for the Rebel cause. In receipt of these replies, the French proceeded to invite all states concerned to form an international committee which would not only supervise the application of the nonintervention agreement but also discuss other forms of nonintervention. Both Italy and Germany were said to be concerned about the actions of private individuals who might ship arms, volunteer for service with the Spanish government, or act as propagandists in Spain. There was also some concern over the possibility of intervention by non-European states.[22] Of prime importance in this last respect was the United States.

Despite reservations from all quarters, each of the major European powers had good reason to join the nonintervention pact. France and Great Britain feared that the war would otherwise spread across Spanish boundaries and become uncontrollable. The Soviet Union, under the influence of Foreign Minister Maxim Litvinov, believed it necessary to stay in the official good graces of the Western democracies. And Germany and Italy thought it possible that the French government might otherwise feel compelled to aid Madrid. Meanwhile, the discredited League of Nations gave up its initiative and blessed the formation of the Non-Intervention Committee. Finally, considering the prevalent disposition in the Department of State to follow Anglo-French leads, to encourage peaceful negotiation, and to steer clear of explosive European problems, it was not likely that Washington would do anything to disrupt this apparent convergence of self-interested policies on the continent.

The British having offered to act as its host, the Non-Intervention Committee (NIC) held its first meeting in the Locarno Room of the British Foreign Office on September 9. Conspicuously absent from the first session was Portugal, which could not be persuaded to attend until almost three weeks later. During the first month, informal subcommittees and technical subcommittees were formed to deal with aspects of supervision. Discussions ranged over a number of topics, from aspects of nonintervention to methods of reporting violations, from interference by non-European states to tentative methods of control. The daily business of the committee was regularly made farcical by all manner of irrelevant disputes between the German and Italian delegates and the Russians. Debates were as likely to concern national philosophies as the Spanish strife, and the purpose was far more often that of obtaining propagandistic advantages than of reaching a settlement of the pending issues.[23]

While the European powers debated, among other things, the fate of Spain, the Spanish government predictably opposed the formation of the NIC—on the ground that it effectively denied a legitimate government the right to purchase arms for its protection, and also because it implicitly placed the Rebels on a level with the government.[24] Most of all, the Non-Intervention Committee had failed to prevent foreign intervention in Spain on behalf of the Rebels. The Spanish government, a half dozen times during the war, brought these matters and related ones before the League of Nations. This was done to little effect except to use the League Assembly as a world forum before which to air Spanish grievances. On December 12, 1936, the League Council unanimously adopted a six-point resolution which, in addition to other matters, asserted the League members' duty to respect the territorial integrity and independence of other states, urged more effective action by the NIC, and declared the desirability of humanitarian efforts to relieve the suffering of civilians. The general view at Geneva was that the Spanish government, by that resolution, gained all it had expected.[25]

The Non-Intervention Agreement came at a critical moment for the Spanish government. Unable to purchase arms in France, the government forces suffered a severe loss at Irun in northern Spain (a loss largely attributable to Italian planes). On August 28, while agreements were purportedly being reached, Italian aviators and airplanes and two German vessels carrying "pineapples and grapes" arrived at the Rebel-held port of Vigo.[26] All the time there were reports, disheartening to the French, that the Rebels had promised economic, territorial, and strategic concessions to the Fascist states. Soviet Russia meanwhile became increasingly critical of the position assumed by the Blum Government. (Litvinov reportedly said that Blum had the compromising qualities and "the defeatist character of a menshevik.") Soviet representatives demanded, unsuccessfully, that the NIC take action against Portugal and the Fascist states on charges of violating the agreement. Then in October, the Russians began to suggest the possibility of withdrawing from the committee. Feeling themselves no more bound by the agreement than other states, they began during October to provide military goods to the Spanish government, which then faced a critical attack against Madrid.[27]

As the Rebels reached the suburbs of the capital, the NIC was existing on a day-to-day basis, "held together by British determination and a general reluctance to risk openly the alternative of its collapse."[28] Russian aid and a new resolve on the part of the Spanish Loyalists prevented the loss of Madrid.[29] The organization of the International Brigades under the aegis of the Comintern also brought renewed spirit (and fresh shock troops) to the Loyalists. Then came the formation of a new Spanish Government, with broader support and greater discipline, and largely influenced by the Communists because of the aid received from Soviet Russia and the Comintern. From all this there were two important results. It was rather assured from the moment the Rebels failed to take Madrid that the war would be a long one.[30] It was also evident that the two sides, as they received more and more aid from the totalitarian states, were becoming increasingly identified with the regimes and ideologies in Moscow and in Berlin and Rome.[31]

Actually the increasing military involvement of the totalitarian states during October and November was only one of the problems encountered by British and French diplomatists.[32] On November 18, both Italy and Germany accorded full recognition to the Rebel, or Nationalist, government located at Burgos, an act which caused an immediate crisis for the NIC; it confused the already muddled issues of the right to blockade ports, seize cargoes of neutral shippers, and other matters of international law.[33] Coming on the heels of the formation of the Rome-Berlin Axis, it was a further blow to those who felt it necessary to keep Hitler and Mussolini apart and to curb their commitments to Franco. The democratic states had already considered the possibility of recognizing a state of belligerency. While this would have helped to clarify legal technicalities, it would have brought forth new problems. Having been harassed by Nationalist warships in the Mediterranean, the British would have seemed to be kowtowing before Franco. The Blum Government rejected the idea of recognizing belligerency as it would have further alienated the French left by according additional status to the Rebels. Of some importance to Eden, because of his desire for solidarity on this matter, was the disinclination of the United States to recognize a state of belligerency.[34]

In view of the extended foreign intervention and the apparent increase in the commitments of intervening nations to the success of one party or the other, the British and French were more than ever determined to keep the Non-Intervention Committee functioning. During this critical period, both London and Paris never ceased to press upon American officials the absolute seriousness of the situation and their own resolve that nothing more should be done to endanger European peace. Only slightly less obvious during these days was the further disintegration of the spirit and substance of the French Popular Front. Internally it had lost much of its authority, largely because of its compromising stand on the civil war. Externally, its Russian ally was weakened by Stalin's great purges, and the fear was again common that Soviet leaders wished to provoke a general war from which they would stand aside. Then too, the more critical the Communists became of Blum, the more distrustful he became of them.[35] The French increasingly committed themselves to the policies emanating from "London City," for otherwise they feared the dreadful possibility of isolation. They must do nothing to endanger good relations with Britain.[36]

Returning to London from the League Assembly at Geneva, on October 9, Anthony Eden had stopped at Paris and lunched with Premier Blum. Eden later reported that during this meeting "the French Prime Minister said categorically that he continued to think nonintervention was the correct policy. We must do all in our power to make it effective."[37] But it is doubtful that either the British or the French had any real hopes of making the agreement effective. During the last three months of 1936 it was made clear to everyone concerned, including the United States, that even a faulty nonintervention agreement was felt to be better than any other alternative. As Ambassador Bingham learned from the French embassy in London, "the French and British were extremely anxious to continue the Non-Intervention Committee on almost any basis and at almost any price. They both realize it was largely a face-saving device but it had reduced the amount of arms shipped to the belligerents and did help to localize the conflict." Bingham was further informed that they did not think that the "belligerent members of the Committee were particularly anxious to withdraw."[38] On October 29, before the House of Commons, Eden called the NIC "an improvised safety curtain." Almost two months later, he again addressed the House of Commons, saying that the NIC had "on the whole reduced the risk of a European War." Twenty-five years later, his view was unchanged: "Tattered and full of holes no doubt, but better than total war in Spain, and a European war out of that."[39]

The fear of a general war was much more prevalent in Paris than across the Channel. On November 24, Bullitt wrote personally to President Roosevelt that Blum and Herriot, plus some of the representatives of the smaller countries and even the British ambassador, were convinced that war was about to break out. Some believed that it would come during the spring or summer of 1937, others not until the following year.[40] The next day Bullitt telegraphed the State Department to say that the French government believed the Soviet Union wished to push the conflict in Spain to its "bitter end," bringing about a *Nationalist* victory. From that would come an Italian attempt to take possession of the Balearics and a German attempt to acquire a new status in Spanish Morocco, bringing the Fascist states into conflict with France and Great Britain.[41] So suspicious of Soviet intentions that he continually saw goblins where there were none, Bullitt probably placed some credence in this view. Even while it could not be said to be entirely beyond possibility, this interpretation put more confidence in the Russians' ability to foretell and determine events than they deserved. Still, it was not so much a difference in interpretations of Soviet policy which caused the British to be less concerned than the French about such a possibility. It was rather the British conviction that Franco would never grant such concessions to any foreign power, even those which helped to bring him victory. Ronald Lindsay, British ambassador to the United States, spoke of this at the State Department early in November.[42] Before the year was out, there was enough evidence to indicate that the British were not terribly concerned about the greater prospect of a Nationalist triumph.[43]

The main problems, as British and French diplomatists saw

them, were to devise some means by which to keep the NIC in operation—primarily by gestures that would hold Soviet Russia on the committee—and to keep their own relations with both Spanish factions fluid. By these means they hoped to contain the Spanish conflict and to secure good relations with whichever party won the war. To meet the first requirement, they began to consider proposals for the control of shipments of men and materials to Spain.[44] Having begun that, and since it would be some time before a scheme acceptable to all parties could be drafted and put into action, the French and British quickly turned to their second aim. Avoiding the NIC, with all its delays and its reputation for hypocrisy, they issued a joint demarche directed only to those nations most immediately involved—Germany, Italy, Portugal, and Soviet Russia. The Anglo-French demarche proposed to stop all assistance to both parties, and, offering to mediate the conflict, asked for a plebiscite throughout Spain in order to form a new government. It was an act aimed not at mediation, for the chances of its acceptance were nil, but at demonstrating the disinterestedness and good will of France and, particularly, of Great Britain. As expected, the demarche was not greeted with enthusiasm by anyone; but the offer of mediation was a device to which the British would often turn during the next two years.[45]

The success of the Anglo-French policy during 1936 might first be judged by how well it succeeded in achieving its limited aims. It had, thus far, successfully avoided the spread of the war beyond Spain. On the other hand, thousands of Germans and Italians, along with Fascist arms, ammunition, planes, and tanks, were brought to the support of the Nationalists; and thousands of volunteers, formed in the International Brigades, were joining the Loyalists. The latter had also received many shiploads of war materials, hundreds of trucks and tanks, and upwards of a hundred aircraft. Most of this came from Russia (although few Russians went to Spain), but some also came from Mexico and other sources. Both volunteers and weapons reached the Loyalists through France, where the will to enforce nonintervention was not always present. But the Loyalists never did receive men or materials anywhere near the number or amount furnished the Burgos government. In the context of the aims of Anglo-French policy, however, all this foreign intervention was only highly disturbing, not absolutely destructive. No

European war had arisen out of the Spanish conflict. There was still reason to believe that Spain would not ultimately be under foreign domination. In these terms, the policy had yet to fail.

In the context of the larger aims of French and British foreign policies, the situation was somewhat darker. The French were less sure of both the strength and the intentions of the Soviet Union. The civil war also menaced any hopes for French national unity, which was so necessary to provide a common front against Germany. Further the French had during the first few months of the war turned over their initiative to the British, and their influence on European events could now only be exerted in support of British policy. As for London, its larger aims were in danger, but the future was still open. There was, despite the value to Germany of keeping Italy involved in Spain, some reason to doubt the firmness of Hitler's commitment to Franco; for Hitler's real interests were known to be directed toward those states neighboring the Third Reich. It must also be remembered that these were the days when rumors of a military revolt against Hitler were not uncommon; and there was speculation that the German economy could little afford the continued pressure of full-speed military preparation.[46] Second, British determination to keep Mussolini and Hitler apart had seemed to fail; but the British persisted in the belief, and not without some reason at this time, that the two dictators were not irrevocably tied to one another. Despite the formation of the Axis and joint recognition of the Franco government, the Germans and Italians were known to be distrustful of each other. There was, lastly, the question of how long the Italians could afford the continued exertion required to push the Spanish Rebels to victory. As the British viewed the problems within and between the Axis states, they still had hopes that Mussolini would find it to his own best interests to avoid making camp with Hitler.

As early as November 1, in a speech at Milan, Mussolini appeared to open the door to some kind of agreement with Great Britain. The following day the British ambassador to Washington conveyed to the State Department the idea that all was "lovely and bright" between Britain and Italy.[47] But the rest of November brought nothing but adverse news, including a report from Paris that Italy would continue to intervene even if the Soviet Union should stop. During December, the tide seemed to turn once again. The British appeared to be achieving some success in demanding the withdrawal of Italian "volunteers." There were also reports of a food shortage in Germany, of which the French hoped to take advantage by offering economic cooperation in exchange for German abandonment of some of their "more alarming policies."[48] And, as the captured German documents indicate, the Germans were at this time concerned about the posture being taken by Mussolini. On December 18, the German embassy in Rome reported that a stronger solidarity among the Western powers, including the United States, could be of some importance in connection with Italy's physical power and morale. It was added that the Western powers, with Soviet Russia, held a balance of power which neither Germany nor Italy wished to see established. What bothered the German embassy in Rome was Mussolini's current attempt "to bury the hatchet with England" and "his unmistakeable desire for a *rapprochement* with the United States." In fact, what the Western bloc might have in mind was "to draw Italy over to itself in accordance with the motto, 'divide and rule.' " The embassy advised the Foreign Ministry of the necessity of keeping Italy involved in the Spanish affair—a point which Hitler himself repeated in November 1937, according to the famous Hossbach memorandum. Of further importance was the advice that Germany ought to be pessimistic about the future of German Fascism in Spain and the future of German-Spanish relations.[49]

By Christmas 1936, with Mussolini appearing less truculent, with distrust evident between the Axis powers, and with internal problems sapping the vitality of each of the totalitarian nations, Anglo-French policy toward the Spanish strife seemed to be taking a better turn. Despite the fact that Mussolini still held the best bargaining position, it was possible to believe that the policy of postponement, of avoiding provocations and awaiting a favorable turn of events, might succeed after all. An important factor in the entire development of Anglo-French policy was the cooperation of the United States, which London and Paris had sought since the second week of the civil war. As will be seen, without that cooperation the Non-Intervention Committee might never have gone beyond the proposal stage.

3

MORAL EMBARGO

INTERNATIONAL COOPERATION and nonintervention in the affairs of other nations were principles of international conduct to which Secretary Hull attached great moral and political value. The Secretary felt that these principles were cornerstones of the Good Neighbor policy, and he consistently advocated them as part of a general policy of "moral influence" which both he and the President wished to pursue. It was natural that he should call upon these principles in the first instance of American involvement in the Spanish strife. Out of this disposition grew a policy which coincided with, and quickly came under the influence of, the policies of Paris and London. The significance of this development, particularly the resulting inflexibility, was not wholly revealed during 1936.

From Hull's point of view it was not difficult to pursue a policy in concert with France and Great Britain when such a policy was thought to have a reasonable chance of resolving the major difficulties arising out of the Spanish trouble, when a refusal to act in concert was strongly believed to risk further and more serious complications for the whole of Europe, and when (with few exceptions) American citizens were willing to comply with an embargo policy which was not even legally binding.

During the first five months of the conflict, President Roosevelt assumed a passive role in the formulation and execution of the policy toward Spain. He is not known to have suggested what the policy should be or even what modifications might be desirable. It is possible that he saw no reasonable alternative to the course advocated by his Secretary of State. Only later did the President bring that attention to international affairs that he had earlier brought to the domestic crisis.

Congressional leaders and the American public also failed to give much attention to the development of American policy toward Spain during 1936. The American press provided almost continuous headline treatment of the Spanish strife, but, until 1937, Washington's policy did not receive much comment. Among the prominent newspapers and magazines of the day, only *The Nation* early opposed that policy.[1] During the course of the war there developed a series of public controversies over the Spanish issue serious enough to constitute a kind of "holy war." But this "holy war" materialized only after the foundations of the policy toward Spain were laid. The angry battles between pro-Loyalist and pro-Franco organizations really began early in 1937—and only after that time did public disputes over the Spanish war affect American policy. In at least one respect, the course chosen by the State Department early in the Spanish war helped to forestall serious domestic arguments. In 1936, public wrangles over foreign policy concerned internationalism versus isolationism, and partisans on both sides of that familiar issue were early satisfied by the American policy toward Spain. To that extent then, the course chosen by the State Department could be interpreted as politically conciliatory—whether or not it was so intended. While the union of internationalist and isolationist sentiment barely survived the year, it lasted until the policy became firmly established.

Up to the end of 1936, there were two major developments in the State Department's Spanish policy. The first was that of "nonintervention." The second was the normal diplomatic function of protecting American citizens and property. Both of these were complicated by the postures of the other major powers, the intensely ideological character of the Spanish struggle, and the personalities of American policy-makers.

I

The situation in Spain was still obscure when the Secretary was compelled to make his first decision affecting American policy. In coordination with the military movement on the Spanish mainland, the Rebels won control of Spanish Morocco only two days after the uprising began. Almost immediately the Committee of Control governing the nearby international port of Tangier faced serious complications. On July 21 the American consul general, Maxwell Blake, reported that the question of fueling warships of the Spanish government was "causing a menacing situation," for General Franco threatened to bombard any vessels attempting to supply Spanish warships in Tangier harbor. It was in fact possible that the *re*fueling of war vessels would constitute a violation of a neutrality article of the Statute of Tangier. The Vacuum Oil Company, an American concern, was advised by Blake not to make deliveries until the situation was clarified. While the Committee of Control, dominated by France, Great Britain, and Italy, was delaying action on the question, Blake sought instructions from the State Department.[2]

Actually the United States government had never accepted the Statute of Tangier, and any decision reached by the international administration there would not be applicable to American nationals. It was against this background that Hull drew upon those principles which he felt were so relevant to the cause of peace. He instructed the consul general that the State Department, "in the interest of international cooperation for the avoidance of complications, would not be disposed to support American nationals in Tangier in any efforts to furnish supplies to either side to the present conflict, [should such efforts be] contrary to the policy adopted by the constituted authorities of the Tangier Zone."[3]

That same day, July 22, the State Department was informed that airplanes had circled an American steamer in the Straits of Gibraltar. The captain of this ship, the *Exmouth*, reported that three bombs had been dropped but that neither casualties nor damage resulted. An American protest was then delivered to General Franco by the British consul at Tetuán, who also made protests in behalf of British merchantmen. Blake reported that "Franco promised to give strict orders to prevent recurrence of such regrettable incidents although his explanations . . . were obviously unsatisfactory." Franco claimed the bombs were released unintentionally because of defective apparatus on the planes.[4]

Hull's responses to these two incidents foreshadowed the direction in which American policy moved for the duration of the Spanish strife. The United States was not a party to any international arrangement; Hull's decision to cooperate at Tangier was freely made. Further, there was his desire to avoid complications. It was not unexpected, considering his views toward the past four decades of American diplomacy, that the Secretary should seek to avoid interference in Spanish affairs by attempting to remove the possibility of incidents which might involve the United States. Untoward events, such as the near-bombing of the *Exmouth*, could only demonstrate to the Secretary the practical wisdom of avoiding involvement in the Spanish strife.[5] Hull's conduct was clearly in keeping with the self-denying spirit of existing neutrality legislation.

It was during the week following these incidents that the State Department learned of the Eden-Blum conversation concerning nonintervention and of the French desire for an international agreement. The French proposal to England and Italy, made on August 1, was discussed by the French chargé d'affaires in Washington when he called upon Secretary Hull three days later. He informed Hull that his government "desired the American Government to be made acquainted with its actions in the premises." And Hull responded to this discreet inquiry of American intentions with an assurance: "I remarked casually in closing that of course the Chargé was aware of the general attitude of this Government towards the doctrine of non-intervention." The Secretary was aware at the time that should agreement be reached among England, France, and Italy, the French proposal would doubtless be forwarded to other European nations including Germany. And on the same day that Hull saw the French chargé, the Blum Government— not yet in receipt of the Italian acceptance—forwarded notes to Germany, Belgium, Portugal, Poland, and the Soviet Union, seeking their views concerning a declaration of nonintervention. Hull later wrote that before the war was three weeks old it was evident that the French and the British believed that "the best means to prevent the spread of the conflict" lay in a European nonintervention agreement. He similarly concluded that "the initiative in dealing with the Spanish problem lay with the European nations."[6]

Up to this point the State Department had not issued a public statement of American policy. On August 5, for the purpose of discussing this possibility, the Secretary called together several of his advisors. The most prominent of these were Under Secretary Phillips, Assistant Secretaries Moore and Welles, the Legal Advisor, Green H. Hackworth, and the Chief of the Far Eastern Division, Stanley K. Hornbeck. The proposed statement considered at this meeting referred to the "clearly defined" policy and attitude of the United States government respecting nonintervention "in the internal or external affairs" of another nation. The statement mentioned, as an example of this policy and attitude, Article III of the Montevideo Treaty with the Latin American states (ratified in 1934). The statement passed on to "the other and different policy" of the government as defined by Congress in the existing neutrality legislation. The latter applied only to a war between two or more sovereign nations, but not to civil conflicts. Thus making clear that the State Department was applying neither a concept of neutrality nor a law of neutrality, the statement enunciated the adoption of a policy of nonintervention toward the Spanish affair—a policy applicable to a nation whether "at peace internally or engaged in civil strife."[7]

There may well have been several reasons for the particular choice of terms in this proposed declaration, but the most inclusive and apparent reason was the desire to be vague regarding the legal status of both the conflict itself and the rebellious faction. The use of the term "civil strife" avoided the usual progressive categories of insurrection, revolution, and civil war—terms which international jurists had already found difficult to define, but on which there was some measure of agreement. Also, the scrupulous care taken to dispel any idea that the United States was assuming a *policy of neutrality* indicated that the State Department had no notion at the time of granting belligerent rights to the Rebel forces. The adoption of neutrality could only apply to civil wars where belligerency was recognized. To have recognized a state of belligerency would have meant granting the rights which sovereign nations have when engaged in international war. For the Rebels, such rights would include, among others, establishing blockades, visiting and searching ships of third powers on the high seas, and seizing and confiscating contraband goods. The Spanish government, of course, would have received the same rights although it already had the right to "close" the nation's ports simply by municipal decree. Granting belligerent status could have increased the likelihood of complications involving American ships in the Mediterranean. The State Department continued for the duration of the conflict to refer to it as a civil strife, to avoid the term "neutrality," and to refuse to grant belligerent rights.[8] In fact, no nation officially accorded belligerent status while still recognizing the Spanish Republic, although a few nations did recognize the Rebel government as the legitimate government of Spain.[9]

The situation was further complicated by the application of the principle of "nonintervention." Students of international law have found it difficult to be precise about what constitutes intervention or nonintervention.[10] While it is true, as became so commonly argued among pro-Loyalists, that an established government has the right to purchase arms abroad for protection against a civil insurrection, there is no commensurate duty requiring other states to sell it those arms. Norman Padelford, a student of the subject who favored the American policy, regarded the withholding of this privilege by the American government more as a corollary "of a basic policy of cooperation with Britain and France" than as a necessary deduction "from a basic policy of non-intervention and non-interference." But to withhold this privilege, he added, was "quite within the bounds of propriety."[11] It is still arguable, however, that a subversion of international law occurred in the difficulty which the Spanish government faced in purchasing arms compared to the ease which the Rebels had. In due course, under these tangled circumstances, the State Department was regularly compelled to deny charges that its policy was intended to effect any particular result in Spain.

It was apparent that if Secretary Hull, and those advisors present at the August 5 meeting, chose to adopt the policy as expressed in the proposed declaration, there would be nothing which would legally bind American citizens to that policy. The

State Department would by that statement place an embargo on both parties to the Spanish conflict—but not a legal embargo, simply a "moral" embargo.[12]

It was decided at that meeting that the substance of the proposed statement should be given "to the correspondents for background purposes" only, the conclusion being that it was not yet time to issue a formal statement. The decision was also made to send a circular telegram, instructing American diplomatic and consular officers in Spain.[13]

This instruction, issued by Acting Secretary Phillips on August 7, was markedly like the statement discussed at the Departmental meeting two days earlier. Indicating that the Neutrality Law was only applicable to war between or among states, Phillips added: "On the other hand, in conformity with its well-established policy of non-interference with internal affairs in other countries, either in time of peace or in the event of civil strife, this Government will, of course, scrupulously refrain from any interference whatsoever in the unfortunate Spanish situation." He concluded with a reference to the Department's belief that American citizens "are patriotically observing this well-recognized American policy."[14]

While this decision was of far greater consequence than that regarding the Tangier Zone, it was in some ways still similar to the earlier one. In both cases the policy adopted was simply the application of the principle of "nonintervention"; for the United States was not bound to such a policy either by its own statutes or by any international agreement. Since the decision was in neither case enforceable by law, Americans who chose to violate the policy could not be legally punished. Still further, since the United States was bound by no international agreement, the decision was in each case "independently" made, and in each instance it anticipated probable cooperative action on the part of other powers. There were differences, however, and these differences were substantial. On July 22, knowledge of the Spanish situation was still obscure. The positions of the European nations were yet to be defined, and no European power had inquired into official American attitudes. When, two weeks later, the State Department decided upon its policy of nonintervention in Spanish affairs, these circumstances had been radically altered. Furthermore, Spain was not, like Tangier, an international port under international control.

From the point of view of the State Department, there were advantages to acting independently and in anticipation of international cooperation. Not only was the Department disinclined to sabotage an effort at international cooperation before it had really begun; it evidently also wished to avoid being placed in the potentially embarrassing position of acceding to an actual request by European powers that an embargo be adopted by the United States. Had the United States not adopted what came to be known as the "moral embargo," the prospect of a European nonintervention agreement would have been gravely endangered. As it turned out, Europeans very shortly sought reassurances from the State Department that "nonintervention" was in fact the American policy.

Constantin von Neurath, the German Foreign Minister, told the French ambassador in Berlin that the attitude of the United States concerning the whole Spanish matter was very important to Germany and all Europe. There were even rumors, denied by the French, that the Blum government intended to ask the United States to join the proposed nonintervention agreement. Acting Secretary Phillips made it clear to the French that American participation in such an agreement was not necessary, for it was not American policy to intervene.[15] Armed with this assurance, the French were apparently able to dispel the concern of the Italians as well as the Germans. It was subsequently reported from the American embassy in Rome that a solely European agreement was envisaged "because the position of the United States was understood." Ambassador William E. Dodd in Berlin was similarly, although unofficially, informed on August 18 that the German Foreign Office did not consider necessary American participation in the proposed agreement.[16]

The adoption of the "moral embargo" by the United States helped make it possible for the French to obtain German and Italian "cooperation," and made it unnecessary for the French and the British to ask openly for American cooperation. In large part the moral embargo was an extension of the principles of international cooperation and nonintervention which were evident in the earlier decision regarding Tangier. But it became increasingly clear in the ensuing months that these principles assumed a secondary importance compared to the feeling of Secretary Hull that it was necessary to act in concert with the

French and the British. While the American government in one sense appeared driven to its policy by the force of international circumstances, it was already an advocate of those general principles of international conduct which it applied in the moral embargo. If some American officials later felt themselves to have been victims of circumstance, they became so not altogether unwillingly or unwittingly.

There were yet two problems regarding nonintervention with which the State Department had to deal in the days immediately following Phillips' circular telegram. The first was that of inquiries from American firms which received offers for the purchase of war materials to be shipped to Spain. The second was that of making public the text of the circular telegram and the Department's policy concerning the sale and shipment of arms and ammunition to Spain.

The first inquiry was made by the Spanish ambassador, and it occurred before the Phillips telegram. On August 6, Don Luis Calderón called upon Phillips and asked about obtaining 10,000 cartridges "of a certain prescribed size for the use of a particular type of machine gun." Phillips referred to American neutrality legislation, which did not provide for an embargo on the export of war materials in the case of civil conflicts; but he added that "of course the Ambassador understood that the whole problem was one of extreme embarrassment to the Administration because of the widespread feeling in this country against the export of war materiel to a foreign country for use in actual conflict." This particular matter was then dropped by the Spanish embassy.[17] It is likely that Calderón did not present the Spanish case forcefully; he shortly resigned from his position because he was out of sympathy with the Loyalist cause. There was anyway something curious about an inquiry concerning such a small sum of ammunition.

Four days later a more serious question arose. The State Department's Office of Arms and Munitions Control was asked by the Glenn L. Martin Company what its attitude would be toward the sale of eight bombing planes to the Spanish government. The inquiry was passed on to Moore and then to the Acting Secretary. Hull was, at the time, resting in Hot Springs, Virginia, after attending his brother-in-law's funeral. Phillips was even more concerned than Hull about the dangers of the Spanish situation. In Phillips' own words, the Loyalists had "what amounts to a communistic government." Less than a week before the Martin Company's inquiry, he had written: "The critical part of the situation in Spain is that if the Government wins, as now seems likely, communism throughout Europe will be immensely stimulated." He was concerned that the United States would be placed in an "embarrassing situation" if the European powers denied the Spanish government arms; for then it would turn to the United States. Phillips also feared that the Italian and French governments would collide if their division over the Spanish issue were permitted to continue.[18] Now he was in a position to draft the document which would, for all practical purposes, make American policy public, and he was well aware of the importance of the task.

Perhaps out of that habit so common among some of Hull's subordinates, Phillips first telephoned the President. He then proceeded to draft his reply to the inquiry, which he subsequently read to Hull over the telephone. Phillips mentioned in his daily journal that opinion was strongly divided in the Department, but he recorded only the views of Moore and the President. Moore, wanting to avoid specific references, preferred a simple reiteration of the government's general policy of nonintervention in the domestic affairs of other nations. "The President wished to go further and to intimate that any such sale would not be in line with the policy of the government, etc. etc." Roosevelt received Phillips' final draft about six o'clock that same evening, later approved it, "and then had considerable doubts." There is no evidence as to what these doubts concerned. Phillips, waiting for the President to telephone him, finally called Roosevelt at half past nine. He then persuaded him not to wait any longer and to let the letter go out. It was mailed an hour later.[19]

The Phillips letter to the Martin Company drew attention to the American policy of noninterference in the internal affairs of other nations and to the circular telegram of August 7—a copy of which was enclosed. Phillips then concluded from the above that "it seems reasonable to assume that the sale of aeroplanes, regarding which you inquire, would not follow the spirit of the Government's policy." The successful application of the Department's policy thus depended upon the patriotism of American citizens. The letter was made public the following day, against Phillips' wishes, when Roosevelt "let the cat out of the bag" at a press conference. The President afterward apologized for the mistake, saying he did not know how he got the impression it was to be made public.[20] Hoping against hope, the Acting Secretary probably wanted to postpone as long as possible widespread, official publication of the moral embargo policy—for the precise reason that it could not be legally enforced. The President's error forced his hand, and newsmen rushed to the State Department.

At the time Phillips sent the final draft to Roosevelt for approval, he was aware of its crucial nature. In the covering letter, he remarked: " 'in the absence of the Secretary I feel the responsibility in regard to the precise words to be used . . . since it forms a far reaching precedent.' " And, whether or not Phillips, the President, or Secretary Hull realized it at the time, the policy expressed in the letter to the Martin Company had an added importance. Once having chosen this path, the Department could not deviate from it without grave risk. To do so would cause a political controversy in the United States, once again raising in Congress and in the press the question of American policy toward foreign disputes. It also would cause serious embarrassment for Great Britain and France.[21]

The possibility that it might later be found desirable to lift the embargo seems not to have been discussed. Perhaps it was believed that the Spanish conflict would very soon be over. Perhaps it was believed that a European nonintervention agreement would be reached and would be effective. It is far more likely, however, that these were circumstances which the policymakers hoped their embargo would help to bring about.

The exact date upon which the State Department became aware of the real aims of British policy is not known. It would seem to have been on August 20 after the British confided in Bingham. According to the ambassador, the Foreign Office believed that the conclusion of a nonintervention agreement "*in principle* with the European powers, including Italy and Germany, would be most effective possible means at the present time [for] localizing the conflict in Spain, and *this statement was made with all reservations as to the practical difficulties of full enforcement in some countries.*" The Foreign Office, Bingham continued, "is hopeful that the British declaration of yesterday of a complete arms embargo in advance of full commitments from Germany and Italy will give practical evidence of British good faith and besides strengthening the hand of the French Government. . . ." Bingham added that the British believed French "weakness" to be "an international danger."[22]

This seems to have been the first concrete indication that the British would not press for an effective enforcement of a nonintervention agreement, that they were not especially interested in *preventing* foreign involvement in Spain as much as they were in *limiting* foreign interference. Certainly they desired to prevent the conflict from spreading over Europe. Existing evidence would indicate that, when Phillips responded to the Martin Company, American policy-makers could only have known British intentions inferentially. It is unlikely, however, that the possession of this information even before August 5 would have altered the judgment of those who favored the moral embargo.

There were other considerations which to the policy-makers made the adoption of the embargo seem the "natural, wise and inevitable course to follow." It was felt that such a policy fitted well with "the prevailing opinion" among Americans toward foreign disputes and the public's increased fear of another great war. And there is no evidence with which to dispute the opinion of one analyst that the public first responded to the embargo policy "either indifferently or with that matter-of-fact approval customarily given to policies which seem so right and so routine that there is no reasonable alternative." It was only later, when the Spanish issue was more clearly defined in the minds of many Americans, that major objections to the policy were made. In August 1936, American attitudes toward the Loyalists and the Rebels were only beginning to form, and the ultimate effect of the American embargo on either side was still speculative.[23]

As if to stamp approval on the Department's chosen course, those who stood to profit most from violating the "spirit" of American policy cooperated with the government. Inquiries were being received from several companies. R. F. Sedgley, Francis Bannerman & Sons, Bellanca Aircraft, Federal Laboratories, and Fairchild Aviation all notified the government about offers for the purchase of war materials for shipment to Spain, "but on being informed of the Department's policy, declined the offers received."[24] Considering the popular image of the "merchants of death" it was probably the better part of business wisdom not to anger government officials who would not lack public support. Bannerman's, for example, already derisively known as "the Sears Roebuck of the arms merchants," might feel particularly susceptible to public indignation. And manufacturers were apprehensive over periodic congressional threats to nationalize the arms industry. For whatever reasons, those who formulated the moral embargo must have been relatively certain that they could count on the cooperation of those businessmen who dealt in implements of war. The first direct challenge to the moral embargo did not come until more than four months after the policy was made public.

The embargo also met with a favorable press. Editorials from several metropolitan newspapers across the country indicated a variety of reasons for not interfering in Spain. The State Department's release of the circular telegram and the letter to the Martin Company was treated as though nothing else could have been expected. What seemed to interest some editors was the rumor that the French intended to invite the United States to join the nonintervention pact (followed by the alleged rebuff by the American government). In a Hearst paper it was demanded that the United States government "reject all suggestions" of American participation in a nonintervention agreement. The *Times-Picayune* of New Orleans indicated that the purported refusal "will be commended by most Americans," since membership in such a pact might result in "our participation in an 'airtight blockade' of a country with which we are at peace." On the other hand, the *San Francisco Chronicle* lamented the apparent necessity to refuse the "invitation." But all three papers agreed with the central idea of the circular telegram that the United States should remain aloof from the war.[25]

The *Boston Evening Transcript* expressed the common public view that the prospect of "Americans profiting through such human slaughter" was not pleasant, and implicitly endorsed the policy. But this editorial did question the State Department's notion that an American embargo would help shorten the conflict. The *New York Times*, which had been pressing for American participation in international affairs since 1921, agreed with both the French plan of nonintervention and American policy, but saw neither as a guarantee for avoiding international war. The *Christian Science Monitor* indicated that "a positive determination to remain neutral in thought and act is required." No complication arising out of Spain—"however unfortunate—can justify a general European war today."[26]

It was chiefly this fear of a general war which prompted editors to agree with American policy.[27] The President's speech at Chautauqua, on August 14, appealed to this anxiety: "I can make certain," he said, "that no act of the United States helps to produce or to promote war." Harold Ickes, Secretary of Interior and later a staunch supporter of the Loyalist cause, had before this speech thought that such a statement would be advisable. Ickes, at this time, expressed no distress whatsoever over the embargo policy. Thinking in terms of the presidential campaign that fall, he believed that not enough had been done to emphasize the administration's peace record. Ickes was not alone in his suggestion. Senators Gerald Nye and Elmer Benson, plus a number of congressmen, urged the President to announce in his Chautauqua address that everything would be done to prevent the shipment of arms to Spain. Obtaining Nye's support for Roosevelt was one of Ickes' objectives.[28]

Democratic campaign advisors could be expected to be pleased with the embargo policy. Any other course of action might have endangered some of the Catholic Democratic vote, and there was the far greater concern for the isolationist and pacifist vote in general. These considerations are nowhere evident in the recorded discussions which led to the formulation of the policy. But it is hard to believe that they did not enter Roosevelt's thoughts—maybe that evening when he relaxed in the White House swimming pool, mulling over the Phillips letter, and wanting to wait another day to give more thought to the matter. Still it is doubtful that, when the policy was actually determined days earlier, Secretary Hull was influenced by anything more than his reticent, conservative disposition, the weight of past policies and current public attitudes, his preferences for certain principles, and his desire to act in concert with Great Britain and France.[29]

That the policy was acceptable to opposing groups was undoubtedly beneficial to Democratic candidates, but Hull was pleased by the embargo's "political" rewards for the State Department. As Walter Lippmann wrote, and Hull later echoed, "isolationists like Mr. Nye saw it as a protection against entanglement, and the believers in collective security saw it as a form of practical cooperation with Britain and France."[30] This convergence of otherwise diverse groups continued for several months until judgments as to the goodness of one side in the Spanish war and the evil of the other became commonplace. Both isolationists and internationalists then began to quarrel among themselves.

Whether or not the Secretary had ill feelings toward the Spanish government before American policy was formulated is a question not clearly answerable. He certainly was not sympathetic toward extremists. And it was regularly reported by American officials in Spain that radical elements were increasingly influential. On July 25, and again on August 1, the Department was informed by the American embassy in Madrid that extremists were gaining control of the government.[31] It would have been surprising had Hull not been dismayed by the fact that moderate elements were losing their strength. The disintegration of moderate influence very likely made his decision for a moral embargo an easier one. But there is no evidence to indicate that the Secretary favored one side over the other at that time (as Phillips did), or that the moral embargo was adopted *because* of the changing character of the Spanish government. The embargo, however, was only one aspect of American policy. There was another and more fundamental diplomatic problem—that of protecting American citizens and property.

II

The arming of radical elements by the Spanish government early complicated the State Department's efforts to protect American citizens. On July 23, Hull consulted with Admiral William H. Standley, Chief of Naval Operations, to determine evacuation procedures. That same day, Hull wirelessed the President, who was then on a cruise off the New England coast: "The reports which we are receiving indicate that the situation is, if anything, becoming much worse and it seems like a fifty-fifty chance as to which side may come out on top, and, furthermore, with an equal chance that a completely chaotic condition may arise in Spain which may continue for some time." Hull went on to indicate that "one of the most serious factors in this situation lies in the fact that the Government has distributed large quantities of arms and ammunition into the hands of irresponsible members of left-wing political organizations."[32]

Troubles arising from inexperienced armed citizens were reported as early as July 20, and such reports continued with increasing gravity for many weeks. A month later Bingham communicated a British informant's opinion that "there was no effective government in Spain, and that the so-called government was completely at the mercy of its violent left-wing supporters."[33] For a time, that observation did not appear exaggerated. On August 25, Eric Wendelin, in charge of the Madrid Embassy in Bowers' absence, telegraphed that in the capital the situation was "getting out of hand. Wholesale cold-blooded assassinations of persons suspected of rightist tendencies [are] increasing rapidly. Looting of private residences increasing. Anarchists daily becoming more dominant and Government apparently dares not forcefully oppose their increasing reign of terror. A complete breakdown of authority with all it implies may occur at any time."[34] Bowers, who had gone from San Sebastián to St. Jean de Luz, passed along similar reports. In August he wrote that there might be rioting and arson by irresponsible mobs should the Rebels prevail in places like Madrid. He added that should the Rebels be defeated the influence of moderates like Azaña might be so weakened that they would be pushed aside by extremists.[35] Throughout September, October, and November, reports from the major Loyalist-held cities repeated the Spanish government's inability to control its own apparent supporters.[36]

The danger to American citizens,[37] a problem largely due to the terrorism of armed groups not controlled by military or civil authorities, was far more serious in Loyalist than in Rebel territory. Most of this difference must be attributed to the fact that a far greater number of Americans were located in areas held by the government. The problem was most challenging in the capital, where embassy officials received the cooperation of the Spanish government in their efforts to prevent injury to Americans. Dozens of American citizens—many of them Filipino and Puerto Rican—were housed in the embassy;

additional police protection was provided by the Spanish government; and an attempt was made to minimize injury by certifying American residences and property. These measures, and others, met with considerable success. Despite occasions of forcible entry, indiscriminate firing upon hotels and homes, the cross-fire of street fighting, and military bombardments, there were almost no injuries to American citizens.[38] The danger to Americans was easy to exaggerate, but there is no reason to question the State Department's praise of the work of embassy officials.

The Department soon found that mere encouragement to leave and the provision of ships in which to depart were not enough for many Americans. Some of them had what amounted to permanent residence in Spain, and some were married to Spaniards. Many of these Americans did not have the funds with which to depart and settle elsewhere. Others simply preferred to remain in Spain, despite the danger. The day was to come, however, when the embassy staff would be withdrawn from Madrid, and without this protection many Americans would depart with it.[39]

Attempts to protect American-owned property were not so successful. Here, problems ranged from the seizure of private automobiles to the taking over of a General Motors assembly plant and warehouse. The issue assumed far greater importance in government-held territory, but this was again probably due to the fact that government forces held both Madrid and Barcelona, where most American interests were located. Americans owned stocks of products of many kinds, the most important of these being cotton stocks worth about $800,000. There were also interests in banking organizations, and in the manufacture of automobiles, shoe machinery, automobile tires, cork products, sulphur products, olive oil, "and a number of miscellaneous products." The Western European Division claimed that "the total amount of American capital invested in these stocks and the various enterprises is roughly estimated at about $80,000,000."[40] This estimate seems to have excluded International Telephone and Telegraph, plus a number of far less important business concerns.

General Motors, Ford, and Firestone Rubber Company, because of the military value of their products, were among those American companies facing particularly difficult problems. The same was true of International Telephone and Telegraph, which had the additional liability of possessing the tallest building in Madrid—making it both an excellent post from which to direct artillery fire and an excellent target. It was finally shelled in November during a Rebel bombardment.[41] In the case of the Firestone Company, its officials feared they would be compelled to deliver secret formulas if they did not make the tires desired by the Spanish government. The company officials decided to comply.[42] Shortly afterward the Ford and General Motors plants were taken over. The main difficulty in these cases appears to have been the inability of Madrid to control the actions of the Catalan government in Barcelona, which in turn was incapable of controlling radical elements there.[43] During this time it was not the policy of the United States government to judge the propriety of confiscation of American-owned industries. The policy was first to insist that American property be protected; when that failed, full compensation was expected.[44]

This policy was only minimally successful. It worked best under Wendelin's guidance in Madrid and when the property or enterprise involved had no military use. As the Singer Company was to find out, even sewing machines serve a military function. Confiscation was to be expected because of the exigencies of war, particularly one as furious as the Spanish strife. Difficulties were compounded by the existence of powerful anarchist and syndicalist elements and by the inability of the Spanish government to control regional authorities. Further, as in the case of the confiscation of American-owned cotton lying on the docks at Barcelona and Tarragona, the Catalan government claimed inability to honor the provisions of original contracts. The American owners of the cotton demanded payment by the establishment of dollar credits in New York, according to the terms of purchase. The best that American officials believed the owners could hope to receive from the Catalan authorities was the deposit of pesetas. While assurances were given by Spanish officials, the requisitioned cotton was never paid for.[45]

A number of American controlled firms chose not to authorize the American embassy to present claims, even though they did not receive indemnification for requisitioned materials. These companies operated previously as Spanish companies for tax purposes and their directors feared that the presentation of claims would result in assessments of back taxes in excess of the value of goods requisitioned. Early in September, the American consul general at Barcelona indicated that caution was necessary: ". . . it is questionable if we can go far in protecting such American interests as have been incorporated under Spanish law and have none or little stock registered in American names. To do so is likely to prejudice the protection of American interests which have chosen not to obscure their status in this manner."[46] Such problems continued throughout the war. But the basic difficulty of obtaining indemnification for those Americans who had legitimate claims was never generally solved with the Spanish government.

Confiscation of American property by the Rebels was rare. The opportunities were fewer, as were the needs. Rebel requirements were far better met by the Germans and especially the Italians than Loyalist needs were met by the Russians. In October 1936, when it appeared possible that the Rebels might soon gain their victory, Bowers wrote to Hull and estimated the treatment American interests were likely to receive at the hands of a Franco Spain. Referring to American industries in Spain, the Telephone Company, the International Banking Corporation, the General Electric, General Motors, and Ford plants, Bowers predicted that the United States would probably have no trouble with a Franco regime.[47] It is highly doubtful, however, if this kind of information decidedly influenced American policy. The State Department, for example, avoided the kinds of financial and commercial relationships which British and French officials later developed with Rebel representatives. In addition, whatever hopes Franco offered in the economic field, Rebel treatment of American citizens more and more annoyed the State Department. The increasingly inhumane conduct of the war on both sides violated the sensibilities of American officials. But these were problems which reached their maximum later in the war. In the meanwhile other points of irritation arose.

Whenever there was a matter involving injury to Americans, Hull proceeded with that patience and firm language which characterized his actions throughout his years as Secretary of State. This approach, while it generally made for smoother relations, did not always bring the desired results; but then not all difficulties were resolvable. Such apparently was the case with an incident which occurred on the morning of August 30, when an unidentified plane made three attacks upon the American destroyer *Kane*. As in the *Exmouth* incident, no damage was done. The *Kane*, clearly identifiable from the air, was proceeding from Gibraltar to Bilbao to evacuate American citizens. Representations were immediately made to both Spanish parties through American officials in Madrid and Seville. Hull requested "that both sides issue instructions in the strongest terms . . . to prevent another incident of this character" and that investigations be made to determine the responsible party. Consul Charles Bay in Seville was further instructed to avoid the impression that the American representation implied recognition of the Rebels. Each side responded that after investigation it had no reason to believe that the responsible plane was one of theirs. No more surprisingly, each found reason to believe that the plane belonged to the other. Characteristically, the one weapon which Hull used to threaten both sides in the *Kane* affair was public opinion. It is difficult to imagine what effect the threat of an incensed American public could have had except to encourage further cross-accusations and make the responsible party even more certain that the United States would never know the answer to the mysterious bombing.[48]

His handling of the *Kane* affair did not prevent further incidents of the same character. The U.S.S. *Erie* and a tramp freighter, the S.S. *Wisconsin*, were later attacked by the Rebels. In 1938, the *Nantucket Chief* was captured by the insurgents while running petroleum from the Soviet Union to Loyalist Spain, and was compelled to discharge its cargo before the crew and ship were released. Representations were made because of the attack on the *Erie* and the incarceration of the crew in the case of the *Nantucket Chief*. But no protest was made in the *Wisconsin* incident, apparently because the ship was bombed (in the harbor at Barcelona) after running war materials from France to Spain.[49]

In September 1936, as the military situation became increasingly serious for the government forces and the insurgents pressed on toward Madrid, the State Department began to consider the necessity of withdrawing the American embassy and consulate from the capital. Such action had to be taken cautiously, for it probably would be interpreted as a political gesture against the Spanish government, particularly through association with governments which had already removed their embassies from Madrid. When the arrival of the Russian ambassador and the departure of the German and Italian embassies took place within a few days of one another, Wendelin had observed that it was all "clearly for political reasons and may herald important international developments."[50] Shortly thereafter, Wendelin reported that Portugal, Denmark, Finland, and a few Latin American countries had also withdrawn their embassies from Madrid.[51] Hull considered doing likewise when he began to fear that the insurgent advance might isolate the capital and further endanger American officials there.

On September 22, he telegraphed Wendelin that "the Embassy has now no mission so important that the presence of our officers in Madrid is indispensable at this time. We are aware that it is the intention of certain American nationals having large financial interests in Spain to remain in Madrid come what may and in spite of all urgings to leave." "We do not," he continued, "consider this sufficient reason for keeping our Embassy and Consulate staffs in Madrid in the face of serious danger. Neither do we feel that our property interests in Spain are sufficient warrant needlessly to endanger our officers." The Secretary concluded that in view of "the unpredictability of the situation in Madrid should the Government forces suffer further reverses we desire that you give immediate serious consideration to the desirability of closing the Embassy and, of course, the Consulate, and departing to a place of safety. . . ."[52]

Wendelin opposed immediate action as being premature. The military situation was grave, he responded, but not desperate; and should the embassy staff withdraw and the government forces win a military advantage, the diplomatic position of the United States would be weakened. Second, to withdraw while the French and British embassies remained would be a blow to the Spanish government and would associate the United States with Germany and Italy. Third, Wendelin feared that withdrawal "would destroy much of the goodwill now enjoyed both by Embassy and Consulate and Americans in general and resultant hostility would endanger American interests now receiving favored treatment." He added that Colonel Sosthenes Behn, president of International Telephone and Telegraph, "now in

Madrid insists that our withdrawal would probably cause seizure of the telephone company by the Government which thus
far has permitted Americans to retain control."[53] Hull did not
pursue the matter further.

Here the situation stood when, on November 7, the Secretary
and several assistants boarded the *American Legion* en route to
the Inter-American Conference for Peace at Buenos Aires. Before Hull even arrived at the Argentine capital, Wendelin was
reluctantly arranging for the closing of the embassy under the
orders of Acting Secretary Moore. The manner in which this
decision was made and finally carried out was important, for it
reflected a good deal on Moore's ability to run the State Department during Hull's long absence. At seventy-seven, Moore
was still an energetic man, and one with a full sense of the
importance and power of his position as Acting Secretary.

Despite a fair measure of urbanity, Moore had the appearance of a successful country lawyer—assisted by his very bald
head, heavy jowls, paunch, watch fob, and Paisley tie. A charming man, he did not lack for friends. He was not, however,
popular in all quarters of the State Department. That Moore
was considered by some of his colleagues to be "out of his ilk"
was a problem he probably encountered in subtle ways, but the
difficulties were much more complex than that. His duties as
Assistant Secretary had never been clearly defined, and both
Carr and Phillips complained of his interference in their work.
Hull purportedly "found it impossible to control Moore," and
spoke with him "two or three times" about it. Moore also had a
running feud with Sumner Welles, particularly after Phillips
was made ambassador to Italy late in August. Each man desired to be Under Secretary, and Hull was reported by Carr to
have said that "he had left the quarrel between Moore and
Welles to the President."[54]

The Acting Secretary was a hard man to describe.[55] What
seemed to set him apart from most others in the Department
was his optimism concerning current world affairs—an optimism which appeared in part real, in part contrived. To the
extent that it was real, it gave him a certain sense of security
concerning his isolationist tendencies. At times, he expressed
anything but despair about the course of European politics.
The basic problem, he felt, was the German demand for raw
materials and for colonies with those raw materials. The solu-

tion lay with Britain and France, who possessed the common sense to meet that demand. Europeans apparently would solve their problems peacefully if for no other reason than necessity. On the other hand, one sees in his isolationism an occasional trace of pessimism. He would sometimes write that there was nothing the United States could do to alter the dangerous course of events on the continent. Moore's desire to remain aloof from European problems must have gone deep.

Contradictions appear elsewhere. Moore went about his decision-making with an air of confidence, only to follow these decisions with numerous self-justifications. He was extremely sensitive to criticism, and his correspondence occasionally reveals unrestrained anger against critics and dissenters. His occasional excitability, a quality he deprecated in others, led him to exaggerations and simplifications which marred his judgment. All these characteristics were made worse by adverse conditions in the State Department. The top officials commonly overworked themselves. Some were divided by personal squabbles left unresolved by the Secretary. And all were ultimately troubled by a President who ran a frightfully loose ship.

Moore differed from Hull in many ways, but it is doubtful that the policy would have been essentially different had the Secretary been in Washington for those two crucial months. Moore desired to avoid involvement in the Spanish affair because of his preference for noninvolvement, while Hull went beyond this in his desire to act in concert with Britain and France. This was an important difference in emphasis. Whatever alterations in policy might have resulted from Hull's presence, and no one can be sure where they would have led, they probably would have been due to the Secretary's attention to details and his habitual caution. That Moore sometimes lacked these qualities was first shown in the way he handled the removal of the embassy from Madrid.

On November 18 and 19, immediately before Moore began to press the idea of evacuating the embassy staff, disturbing reports were received by the State Department. Several hundred Germans, probably of the 7,000 who had recently arrived at Cádiz, were said to be moving north from Seville; and Madrid was being heavily bombarded by insurgent artillery and aircraft. Italy and Germany seemed to be making General Franco's cause their own by giving formal recognition to the Rebel government at Burgos. In addition, Wendelin reported that there was a general need for food and clothing in Madrid. This would naturally affect the welfare of those in the American embassy.[56] Despite the fact that the embassy and the consulate were located in a designated safety zone, or "nontarget" area, the danger of bombardment constituted a second reason for giving serious consideration to immediate evacuation. In September, under less threatening circumstances, Hull had raised such a possibility. Now Acting Secretary Moore responded with a plan which went beyond the requirements of the situation in one important way.

On November 20, Moore telegraphed Wendelin and informed Bowers of the text of this telegram at the same time. Basing his decision on reports of the inadequacy of food supplies and the impracticability of trying to provide them (because of the military situation), Moore instructed Wendelin to give "immediate consideration to the desirability of closing the Embassy." The idea was to take the staff, and such Americans as would join it, to "whatever port you can most easily reach." "Arrangements," Moore concluded, "will be made to evacuate you and your party from this port by one of our naval vessels."[57]

The following morning, Bowers telegraphed his objections to Moore's plan. His most telling complaint regarded Moore's intention to evacuate the embassy not only from Madrid but from Spain. As Bowers viewed the situation, the closing of the embassy in "the immediate wake" of German and Italian recognition of the Burgos government could have "most disagreeable results." This was particularly true as long as the French and British embassies remained not only in Spain but in Madrid.[58] At five o'clock that afternoon, the State Department telephoned the American embassy.[59] The conversation between James Dunn of the Western European Division and Wendelin ranged from the number of Americans in Madrid to Departmental praise of Wendelin's work. They discussed some details of evacuation procedure, problems of protocol, the protection of Spanish employees who would remain in Madrid, and the feeling of urgency which both Moore and Dunn felt—particularly for the safety of the embassy and consulate staffs. It was during this conversation that Moore's plan to evacuate the Embassy staff from Spain was altered.

Dunn: If you evacuated the Americans and went to Valencia, we would send a ship of course to Valencia to pick you all up in that case.

Wendelin: Carry us to France?

Dunn: Yes. That is understood. Would you consider it advisable for yourself to remain at Valencia?

Wendelin: Yes. I think it might be advisable for the time being.

Dunn's response indicates that he, at least, was not determined to order the complete withdrawal of the embassy. Certainly Wendelin was not enthusiastic; at one point he expressed his continued opposition to withdrawal from Madrid. In this respect he achieved a momentary postponement, arguing that circumstances did not yet necessitate departure. But two days later, in another telephone conversation, Dunn informed Wendelin of the Acting Secretary's order to proceed with the evacuation according to instructions simultaneously being telegraphed to the embassy. Once again, Wendelin appeared reluctant, although his manner may have been affected by the poor telephone connection.[60]

The removal of the embassy to Valencia was wise in one major respect. The Spanish government, only two weeks before, had temporarily moved the capital to that Mediterranean port. And while many embassies remained in Madrid, there were advantages to staying near the Spanish government. Dunn had, in fact, instructed Wendelin on November 21 that in the event of evacuation he was to "give the impression" that he was "following the Government." Perhaps it was because Moore had not yet been informed of the change of plans, or maybe Bowers' objection was under consideration, but Dunn twice told Wendelin—"give the impression" that you are going where the Spanish government is. Later, for the purpose of having it "on record," Wendelin telegraphed that "every American member of the staff is entirely willing to continue on duty in Madrid and that their evacuation is not at the request or the intimation of a desire to leave on the part of either myself, Consul [Hallett] Johnson, or the Military Attache."[61]

On the same day, Frank C. Page of International Telephone and Telegraph in Madrid wired President Roosevelt that Colonel Behn wished him to express "his great regret at the action of the State Department." Behn, after indicating that Wendelin did not want to leave Madrid, added his own feeling that the withdrawal of the staff "will lower the regard for the United States Government throughout the world and particularly in Spain and South America. . . ." In addition, he felt that it would increase the danger for Americans in many Spanish cities, and that it would "jeopardize American commercial activities in Spain." He gave additional emphasis to the idea of injury to American prestige and good will, "especially in Latin American countries." It is not clear if Behn was referring to the possibility of aggravating the division among those Latin American nations already in disagreement over the Spanish issue. What probably troubled him most was the fear that in Wendelin's absence the Spanish government would take control of the telephone company, an action which might subsequently encourage confiscation in some Latin American countries. The answer to Page referred to the advantages of being in closer contact with the Spanish government at Valencia and expressed the opinion that everything that could be done to protect American interests in Madrid had already been done. It is not known if the President had anything to do with drafting this response. Months later Page was still talking about how bitter Behn was over Moore's order to move the embassy.[62]

The Acting Secretary's conduct during this entire week raised some troubling questions. When he presented the situation to the President on November 21, he colored it with exaggerations, saying that, for example, "anyone in Madrid is now in danger of starvation." Being so informed, the President did not interfere with Moore's actions. Four days later, while the President himself was en route to Buenos Aires, Moore wrote to him, attempting to justify the evacuation decision. He mentioned how the death of an American official would probably have subjected the State Department to a "howl of criticism." "So far as American property is concerned," Moore added, "most of it, against our protest, was some time ago taken over, by the Spanish Government, both at Madrid and Barcelona." The Spanish ambassador, with whom Moore had just conversed, "thought we had taken a sensible course."[63]

This "sensible course," however, was not the one first intended by Moore. Despite German and Italian recognition of the Burgos government on November 18, Moore two days later had encouraged complete evacuation from Spain. What Moore apparently failed to consider was that total withdrawal would associate the United States with the Fascist states and would invite, by reprisal, that which he wished to avoid—further danger to American citizens and property. Additional importance must be attached to the haste with which Moore dealt with the problem. Wendelin told Dunn on November 21 that Madrid had been quiet for four days. He telegraphed the following day that the embassy possessed enough food and fuel for two weeks, and that while fuel was scarce more food could be acquired. He further reminded the Department that the embassy was located in a neutral zone.[64] Also, the Department already knew what nations were still represented in Madrid. In spite of all this, Moore acted hastily. The Acting Secretary wrote another letter to the President on November 27, explaining his reasons for not keeping Hull fully informed and not awaiting the Secretary's decision: ". . . the case had so many ramifications that it was simply impossible for me, at this distance to present it in detail to the Secretary and expect him to be able to reach a speedy conclusion."[65]

This urgency was not created by the serious circumstances in Madrid so much as by Moore's desire to act immediately. The Secretary was still aboard ship and readily available to the Department. But rather than let Hull decide whether immediate action was necessary, Moore took the full measure of responsibility available to him and failed even to inform the Secretary of the immediate developments in Spain or of Moore's own proposed course. After the final decision was made, Moore wrote to Hull hoping that he approved of it and then offered justification.[66] While there is no record of a response by Hull, there is no reason to believe that he objected to the action which was finally taken.

The decision to remove the embassy to Valencia was really a matter of prudence and involved no serious diplomatic consequences. Yet Moore, perhaps conscious of the error of his initial decision, was rather excessive in his attempt to justify the Valencia move to the President. He characterized Bowers' view of the situation as "unduly theoretical and political" and "without sufficient concern as to the serious trouble to us that would result from a lot of Americans in Madrid being killed."[67] Only one justification was required for the moderate action that was finally taken—the safety of American nationals and officials—and Bowers did not question that. It was not the

decision to relocate the embassy at Valencia which boded ill for
the future. Rather it was the manner in which Moore handled
the entire problem. There was his haste, his exaggeration of
conditions, his failure to inform the Secretary fully, and his
misrepresentation of the views of one who dissented. When, two
months later, in January 1937, Moore once again rushed head-
long into a decision, no one corrected his judgment; and the
consequences were not unimportant. In the next instance he
helped handcuff the President by his inadequate planning and
by failing to consider all the ponderable consequences of his
actions. It was not a question of Moore's basic integrity, nor
even of his administrative ability. He was an intelligent and
talented man. He was simply in the wrong executive department. He was not adept at handling such international problems, because he did not fully understand them as being international. In this instance, confronted with a problem of how to
protect lives, his almost instinctive response was that of an
isolationist.

American policy toward Spain during 1936 was not guided
as much by a clearly defined set of intentions as by inertia
joined with hope. It was hoped that the Spanish strife would
not bring all Europe to war, that it would soon end, that the
intervening nations would find it necessary to drop their
schemes, and that Spain would not have a government controlled from Moscow, Berlin, or Rome. That the realization of
its largest hopes was placed in the care of the British and
French foreign offices was not particularly troubling to the
State Department, as long as the Anglo-French approach did
not kill those hopes.

An idea which was obviously not entertained by the policy-
makers was that the Spanish civil war could end in a victory for
democratic government. This was reflected in the reception
accorded a report by the American vice consul at Seville, who in
September wrote a paper entitled "The Future of Liberty in
Spain."[68] He interpreted the statements and actions of President Azaña, an admirer of the British parliamentary system, as
acknowledgment of the Spanish people's "antagonism to a democratic form of government" and as recognition of the necessity
for "state direction." Turning to the Rebels, the report attempted to dispel the idea that insurgent leaders had no con-

cern for the welfare of the worker. This was accomplished by references to the speeches and actions of the fiery Rebel general, Quiepo de Llano. Further emphasis was placed on the character of Spanish Fascism, in which there was an insistence upon the "spiritual as well as material values of the individual." After observing that the "present majority" of the membership appeared to be persons of "quite modest means," the vice consul felt that this group would "play a part in determining the final character" of the Fascist organization. It was concluded that Spanish Fascism would "develop a character all its own." The vice consul also dwelt upon the historical Spaniard, in whom "individualism, love of liberty, and a trace of anarchy are inextricably woven. . . ." But the Spaniard had not developed the capacity for limited antagonism.

Spain's failure, according to this report, was its neglect of the masses—the failure to provide education, equal opportunity, and fulfillment of man's most basic material needs. All this "has made it impossible at this day to grant universal suffrage without introducing communism or anarcho-syndicalism into the body politic." The vice consul closed with an historically illogical, but familiar, contrast: The future of liberty in Spain "does not appear difficult to predict. When liberty makes its reappearance the approach will be different than in Anglo-Saxon countries. Whereas we began with liberty and successively imposed discipline to restrain its free use to the injury of others, Spain will have to start with discipline and gradually relax it to permit free expression." This consular report, read by the most important men in the State Department, received a rating of "excellent"—an infrequent occurrence.

While this report was incompatible with the expectations of the ardent democrat, its major points conflicted in no way with the hopes of American policy-makers. They were not concerned with the internal character of Spain, unless that should endanger world peace. The mild concern of the British government over the prospect of a Franco Spain hardly went unnoticed by American officials.[69] If Britain and France—both having great commercial and strategic interests in the Mediterranean—were not going to attempt to prevent a Franco victory, then they must have reasonable doubts that his victory would necessarily threaten European peace.

More important, there were reasons during 1936 to believe

that the Anglo-French strategy might yet work. The three major powers intervening in Spain were encountering difficulties. It was doubtful how long each would be able to sustain its commitments. There was likewise doubt in some quarters as to the seriousness of these commitments. Interpreting Anglo-French policy as one of postponement, the State Department agreed with the strategy and awaited a favorable turn of events. In the meantime, a number of important questions were going unanswered. How long would Britain and France be able to wait for that "favorable turn"? Would they temporize indefinitely? Where else would they make accommodations? To what extent should the United States follow this lead? Would Spain be, and should Spain be, a special case? During the first week of 1937, the American policy of nonintervention would become sealed by law. And largely because of this, it became increasingly difficult to escape the drift into further appeasement.

4

FROM MORAL
TO LEGAL EMBARGO

THE MORAL EMBARGO could not remain effective indefinitely. It was clear that some American citizens seeking profits, or simply determined to aid one side against the other in this civil war, were going to ignore the request of the government to abstain from traffic in arms. Incredibly, no one directly challenged the moral embargo until the last week of December 1936. The government was, in fact, saved a good deal of embarrassment for five months; for continual, sizable shipments of American arms to Spain would certainly have caused a crisis for the foreign offices in London and Paris. During these months, however, there were numerous attempts to violate government policy indirectly by exporting small quantities of war materials to both Mexico and France for ultimate shipment to Spain. When the first direct challenge finally came, preparations were already being made in the capital for the opening of the first session of the Seventy-fifth Congress. Little more than a week later it was no longer simply "unpatriotic" to sell and ship arms to Spain; it was illegal. In a race against the first open violator of American policy—who hurriedly shipped some airplanes, aircraft engines, and assorted parts out of New York harbor—Congress passed a hastily and carelessly drafted embargo act.

I

From all indications, there had been little debate in the State Department concerning the enunciation of the moral embargo. And there is no evidence that extensive thought had been given to the very probable result that some Americans would violate the government's wishes. The one person known to have taken exception to the policy was Stanley Hornbeck, a highly experienced officer who headed the Far Eastern Division. On August 11, the day after the Phillips letter to the Glenn L. Martin Company, Hornbeck presented a dissenting memorandum with a three-pronged argument. If the executive branch felt that it was desirable to embargo the export of arms to both parties to the Spanish civil strife, Hornbeck argued, then it "should be prepared to feel that the same attitude should be taken in case of civil conflict in countries other than Spain." Hornbeck pointed out that the government took no such attitude toward civil strife in other nations, "conspicuously China." Second, from the point of view of political considerations and potential effectiveness, prohibition by process of persuasion is a "very unsatisfactory and dangerous procedure." Finally, such a policy had within it "great potential unfairness," since it would favor "the citizen who is indifferent to or hostile to the government and its policies and who is intent upon making profits for himself."[1] It was on the latter two points that the policy was particularly defective. Only by persuasion and public condemnation could the government hope to prevent the determined dealer in arms from shipping implements of war to Spain. It was simply a matter of how long it would be before the State Department and the President would find both policy and prestige under attack with no adequate defense. Whatever the merits of Hornbeck's argument, his colleagues obviously did not think that it presented an acceptable alternative to the policy they so recently decided upon. Given his Asian duties, at a time when specialization was beginning to fragment the Department, Hornbeck's dissent was probably interpreted as having less to do with Spain than with China.

Those who favored the moral embargo appeared for a time to be justified—that is, as long as the policy was challenged only indirectly. The problem in these instances was essentially one of trying to prevent the transshipment of American arms and planes through other countries to Spain. The civil war was hardly a month old when the British discreetly inquired about the possibility that American arms were reaching Loyalist Spain via Mexico. Since the State Department's Office of Arms and Munitions Control licensed arms exports, the Department was well aware that there had been—up to that time—no increase in exports of this sort.[2] There was the possibility, however, that planes could have been flown illegally across the border for transshipment to Spain. In the months that followed, the Treasury Department tracked down several cases of planes flown to Mexico to be sold without having been licensed. Several others were legally sold to various parties but fell quickly into the hands of Felix Gordon Ordas, the Spanish ambassador to Mexico. By December 1936, so many planes of American manufacture had come into his possession that one officer in the State Department later referred to them as "the Spanish Ambassador's collection."[3]

Well before these problems arose, the Mexican Minister for Foreign Affairs, General Eduardo Hay, called upon Josephus Daniels. Hay suggested to the American ambassador a plan whereby the United States government would permit the sale of bombing planes to the Mexican army, which would, in turn, sell its present planes to Loyalist Spain. Daniels responded that this indirect method would not be in accord with American policy. A few weeks later, through Ambassador Castillo Nájera in Washington, the Mexicans asked if the State Department would simply permit the reshipment of American arms through Mexico. The ambassador was "politely informed" that this would not be allowed; and, at least in theory, Washington could prevent it by refusing export licenses to anyone whose application contained false information. In practice, there could be (and would be) some difficulty uncovering a falsification before the items were exported—especially in the case of unarmed aircraft.[4]

Because of the number of planes coming into the possession of Gordon Ordas (and coincident with Washington's determination to prevent the first attempt at a direct shipment of planes to Spain), Acting Secretary Moore asked the American embassy in Mexico City to approach the Cárdenas government concerning the reexport of American planes. It was clear that any cooperation that the Mexicans might give would have to be voluntary. There was neither a treaty nor a statute to which the United States could refer in order to compel the Mexican government to prohibit the reshipment of these planes to Spain. But President Lázaro Cárdenas responded favorably by saying that his government would not authorize the reshipment to Spain of war materials from the United States. It was later found that the Mexican government was excepting from this stricture American planes already in Mexico.[5]

Mexico was not the only country through which Americans attempted to ship planes ultimately destined for Spain. Of the many attempted transactions, the most complicated involved the sale of airplanes to a Dutch corporation for delivery in France. The episode began on September 22, when Charles H. Babb, a San Francisco dealer in second-hand planes, applied for permission to export nine used Vultee transport planes to L'Office Général de l'Air, in Paris. His application was granted, but Babb did not export the planes. In November it was found that Babb had sold these planes to one Rudolf Wolf of New York City. This information was obtained from General R. C. Marshall, who called upon the State Department requesting permission to export the Vultees. At the end of November, both Marshall and Wolf appeared at the State Department to request a license to export ten other planes to Le Havre, France, the purported purchaser being a Dutch corporation with offices in The Hague. "Mr. Wolf declared that he did not know the ultimate destination of these planes but that he had no reason to believe that they were going to Spain."[6] In an effort to satisfy the State Department's demand for assurances, Wolf presented a telegram from an attorney for the Dutch corporation which indicated that the planes were being purchased for "speculative resale" in France. "After examination and consideration of all the known facts," Wolf's license to export the ten planes was granted under Moore's instructions. Then, on December 4, Wolf applied for a license to export the nine Vultee transports earlier purchased from Babb, and along with this was another telegram from the Dutch corporation's New York attorney. This time the State Department held up its decision until it could attempt to verify the details of the transaction through the American embassy in Paris. Apparently nothing conclusive was learned. Then, with none of the nineteen planes having yet left the United States, Wolf suddenly died. Only a few days later, his widow applied for two export licenses covering all nineteen planes. These were granted her, and by the first week in January all the planes were en route to Le Havre, accompanied by two American test pilots.

The planes remained at Le Havre for about a month before an attempt was made to export them "ostensibly to Bulgaria but presumably in fact to Spain." The American legation in Sofia found that no purchase had been made by anyone in Bulgaria, and this information was passed on to the French government. The French thereupon refused permission to export the planes. Eventually ten of them were successfully flown to Spain, four crashed en route, and five others were unacceptable to the Spanish government—which must have paid a dear price. It is likely that the failure of the French government to prevent the planes from reaching Spain was due to some officials in the French Air Ministry who did not favor Blum's nonintervention policy. Throughout the remainder of the Spanish strife, additional American planes, arms, and munitions were to reach Spain through third countries. Both the exporters and government officials were compelled to be more persistent and ingenious in their endeavors. But before this game of wits resumed there was a bold, open attempt to defy the moral embargo.

Agents acting in behalf of the Spanish government decided to alter tactics in an effort to purchase war materials in the United States. The decision was made during December to challenge the moral embargo head-on by applying for licenses to export airplanes directly to Spain. Up to that time, the kinds of evasion which had been practiced to purchase and ship arms from the United States could not have been entirely stopped by any conceivable embargo legislation. Even the most thorough screening of applications could not prevent some arms from reaching Spain eventually by one or more transshipments. And even a total ban on the export of arms could not have prevented occasional clandestine shipments or flights across national borders. Until there was a direct defiance of the moral embargo policy there was no need for a legal embargo to replace it. The problems of which Hornbeck warned in early August were four months in coming.

Those who were acting in behalf of the Spanish government appeared to face two alternatives. If they challenged American policy, they might provoke legislation. American policy sealed by law would be less likely to turn in their favor at a later time. On the other hand, Congress would be back in session during the first week of January, and it might enact an embargo anyway. Perhaps tired of playing cat-and-mouse with the Office of Arms and Munitions Control and agents of the Treasury and Justice Departments, the responsible parties decided to attempt direct defiance before Congress opened its next session. Thus, on December 29, the name of Robert L. Cuse, "Jersey City junk dealer," was spectacularly splashed across the front pages of American newspapers. On the previous day, the State Department had announced the granting of two export licenses to Cuse for items valued at nearly $3 million. The licenses covered 18 airplanes, 411 completely assembled aircraft engines, and sufficient parts to make about 150 additional engines.[7]

Cuse, president of the Vimalert Corporation of Jersey City, was a mysterious and inaccessible figure. Contradictorily referred to as "the country's leading buyer and seller of used planes and equipment" and as "a shoestring dealer in airplanes and aviation accessories," Cuse caused all kinds of speculation regarding the nature of his business. The *Washington Post,* for example, pursued the possibility that the Soviet Union was behind the sale, since Cuse was of Russian birth and because records of a 1930 Senate investigation reported that a "Vimelert" Corporation had sold and shipped aircraft engines to the Russians under concealment.[8]

Cuse first called at the Office of Arms and Munitions Control on October 19, and discussed a transaction he desired to make involving the sale of arms and planes to the Mexican government, which would in turn sell some of its planes to the Spanish government in the manner which the Mexican Minister for Foreign Affairs had earlier described to Daniels. Contact had been made with Cuse in Paris by a person under an assumed name who had previously been connected with the Soviet Amtorg Trading Corporation, and through this source he was introduced to the Spanish consul general in New York. The

State Department made it clear to Cuse during his visit that the proposed transaction would be an evasion of the moral embargo policy. For reasons unknown to the Department, Cuse dropped the matter.[9]

On December 24, Cuse returned to the Office of Arms Control with two applications for licenses to export—directly to Spain —$2,777,000 worth of airplanes, engines, and parts. "The planes were of outdated types and the engines and parts had been taken from scrapped planes." Incapable of doing anything else, the State Department would grant licenses. But Cuse's timing was not good. December 24 being a Thursday, he was compelled to wait until Monday before the licenses were granted. Those four days should have provided the much needed time for the State Department and the President to plan a course of action.

Without difficulty, the administration made full use of the press for attacks upon Cuse. When announcing the issuance of the licenses on December 28, Joseph Green made it clear that in his opinion Congress could legislate to stop the shipment from leaving the United States.[10] Acting Secretary Moore, at his regularly scheduled press conference the following day, was even inspired to quote from *Paradise Lost*:

> Mammon, the least erected spirit that fell from Heaven,
> For even while in Heaven his looks and thoughts were
>   always downward bent,
> Admiring more the riches of Heaven's pavement, trodden gold,
> Than aught divine or holy.

On the same day, the President was said to have referred to the Cuse transaction as a "thoroughly legal but unpatriotic act."[11]

The administration was careful not to offend exporters and manufacturers of war materials who had cooperated with the State Department. Green pointed out that one party turned down an advance commission of $450,000 after the Department explained to him its policy, and that "in at least twenty cases representatives of companies of high standing have sought advice at the State Department. . . . And, in every case, except that of Mr. Cuse, the manufacturer or broker refused to make the deal." Even more important, the Department made it clear that the Cuse transaction was "most unfortunate" coming at a time when Great Britain, France, and other European powers were striving to strengthen the nonintervention agreement.[12] These days were, in fact, critical ones for French and British diplomatists.

Since early December, Anglo-French policy toward the Fascist states had been stiffening with apparently favorable results; the strained internal conditions in the totalitarian nations possibly had something to do with this. The British then hoped to take advantage of the situation. They met with the Italians for the purpose of reaching an accord concerning their mutual interests in the Mediterranean. Such an accord had been talked about for weeks. It was finally concluded on January 2, 1937, and as far as the Spanish civil war was concerned there was one passage of particular importance in this "Gentleman's Agreement": both governments disclaim "any desire to modify or, so far as they are concerned, to see modified the status quo as regards national sovereignty of territories in the Mediterranean."[13] But, in the context of the Spanish strife, and the recent efforts to curb foreign intervention, the statement solved nothing. In this it only reflected the utter confusion of the two weeks surrounding the signing of the agreement. What was apparently understood, but not stated in the accord, was the British hope for the withdrawal of at least some of the Italian "volunteers" then in Spain. There were reports of Italian withdrawals, but also of Italian arrivals. On the other hand, there were even reports of the departure of 4,000 volunteers of various nationalities from France to Barcelona, these intending to serve the Loyalist cause. While the British seemed hopeful around Christmastime, they were dejected soon after the new year began.[14]

The key to the increasingly critical situation was the uncanny timing of Hitler, who, earlier seeing the possibility of an accord between Mussolini and the British, decided to act boldly and compel Mussolini to go along with him. Ignoring the advice of many of his generals, as well as his economic advisor, Hjalmar Schacht, Hitler sent more troops, airmen, and engineers to Spain at the end of December and early January. Then a crisis broke which brought threats of outright war between the Spanish and German governments. Hitler so succeeded in confusing the situation that Mussolini found his own prestige at stake. Seeing Hitler's boldness, Mussolini was unwilling to slacken his commitments to the Spanish Rebels. At the same time, Hitler had come to terms, although ambiguous ones, with the Catholic hierarchy in Germany. The bishops, while stressing reservations concerning past actions against Catholics and dangers that might yet develop regarding Nazi activities and doctrines, instructed German Catholics to join with the National Socialists in the latter's anti-Bolshevist campaigns. This provided further pressure on Mussolini to assist the insurgents in their war against "Red Spain." He was now straining to maintain his policy of playing between Germany and Great Britain. He apparently succeeded to some extent by the signing of the vague "Gentleman's Agreement" while continuing his support of Franco. All parties attempted to keep the doors of negotiation open with pronouncements of good will and fine intentions. But during the first week of the new year, European diplomatists were working in a fog.[15] All this was going on while the Roosevelt administration was attempting to deal with the problems raised by Robert Cuse.

In London and Paris, responses to the announcement of the Cuse licenses indicated some concern that the United States government "was indifferent to the efforts that Great Britain and France are making to inject some honesty into the non-intervention policy of European powers in the civil war." But the news of probable legislation to deal with the Cuse shipment appeared to cheer them up.[16] Meanwhile, Berlin cited the granting of the licenses as justification for continuing intervention. And in Rome, the press featured reports that Great Britain was thinking of making representations to the United States concerning the shipment of American arms to Spain. The British and French were, in fact, consulting on the best method by which to approach the United States government should the Americans do nothing on their own initiative to prevent these shipments.[17] It was hardly possible to ignore these European developments as the administration sought the necessary legislation to deal with direct violations of the embargo policy.

II

Panic and confusion characterized the developments which led to the Spanish Embargo Act of January 8, 1937. Between December 24 and January 5, when the administration made its final decision as to the form of legislation it believed necessary, there arose some fundamental differences of opinion among top governmental figures in Washington. There was no doubt in their minds that legislation was necessary; the disagreements developed over its form. Should presidential discretion be protected? Should an attempt be made to stop the Cuse shipment with no concern for executive discretion? Should this legislation be kept apart from all other "neutrality" acts? Until January 4, the President moved in the direction of broad, discretionary legislation. On January 5, under the advice of Acting Secretary Moore, Roosevelt reversed his opinion. The enactment by Congress of the administration's final proposal would have been anticlimactic had not part of the Cuse cargo been leaving New York while debate was still in progress.

If the State Department prepared for the day when the moral embargo would meet open defiance, the evidence is lacking. On December 15, Moore had prepared a memorandum for the President concerning legislative matters upon which the State Department held decided views. One section of it dealt with neutrality legislation, but almost exclusively with the mandatory versus discretionary debate and without a single reference to the Spanish situation.[18] The first indication that the administration was concerned with the moral embargo problem was reported in the *New York Times* on December 26, two days after Cuse applied for the licenses and two days before the licenses were made public: "The administration already is studying a proposal to permit the Chief Executive to extend the present policy to civil wars, such as the one now raging in Spain."[19] The lack of newspaper reports of such proposals before this time is not necessarily surprising. Had the State Department been considering legislation applying to the Spanish conflict, it might have been a mistake even to hint at the possibility—since the slightest suggestion could have provoked a rash of applications for export licenses. The lack of evidence showing that there had been discussions of this aspect of the Spanish problem might only indicate that no particular course of action had been decided upon. But the fumbling manner in which the Roosevelt administration tackled the Cuse challenge would indicate that there was a failure of some kind.

Much the same would have to be said for congressional leaders. On December 26, the *New York Times* itemized the proposed changes in neutrality legislation which congressional leaders were currently discussing. There was no mention of embargo legislation concerning either the Spanish conflict or civil wars in general. Two days later the *Times* indicated that proposals to plug the civil conflict loophole in existing legislation "already have been discussed in congressional circles, where the deficiency in the law had been seen and recognized."[20] Congressional leaders had by that time undoubtedly been informed of the Cuse applications.

The most decisive factor in the events which followed was the growing determination to enact legislation by which the government could deal *immediately* with the export of arms to Spain. When Green announced the granting of the licenses, it was said that several weeks' preparation would be necessary before the Cuse cargo would be ready for shipment, which led the *New York Times* to surmise that this would leave plenty of time to draft amendatory legislation and still stop Cuse. Information suggesting an opposite conclusion was reported in the London *Times:* men had been working day and night in "recent weeks" on the "packing of the machines" at Floyd Bennett Field in Brooklyn.[21] This information must have been about as long in reaching the State Department as in reaching the London *Times* correspondent, for it was not until December 29 that the administration and congressional leaders threw themselves into the problem wholeheartedly. Much of the action of the next few days centered about the White House.

The President at first kept sight of his primary aim. While he was determined to check Cuse's efforts, there is no doubt that he wanted this done through executive action and not by congressional mandate. In a press conference on December 29, he emphasized that the President should be vested with discretionary powers to handle problems arising out of internal strife in foreign nations. In this respect the situation remained as reported three days earlier. On the day of the President's press conference, Senator Key Pittman, chairman of the Foreign Relations Committee, consulted with the State Department. Afterward, he indicated that he would propose an amendment to existing legislation which would authorize the President at his discretion to impose embargoes on arms shipments to countries involved in civil conflict. That evening, Pittman drew up a memorandum for the President which he sent to him the following morning. This spelled out Pittman's proposed amendments. As he pointed out to Roosevelt, the way in which his proposal qualified a state of "civil war" only showed "the intent but would in no way legally limit the discretion of the President." The civil conflict had to be found by the chief executive to be of such magnitude or conducted under such conditions as to "threaten the neutrality or peace of the United States. . . ." This proposal was in keeping with the President's idea. Of special importance to Roosevelt was the closing paragraph of the memorandum: "The present suggested amendment is not controversial and probably could be passed through both branches of Congress within a very few days."[22]

Pittman was certainly in a position to know more than what was reported in the newspapers, and press reports indicated that his conclusion was justified. The Democratic majority, for example, was said to be in sympathy with a "free hand" policy for the administration.[23] And, should anyone question the extent to which the State Department could be trusted with discretion, the latter need only refer to the five-month period during which it successfully held off direct challenges to the moral embargo. Of additional importance, two hidebound isolationist Republicans supported Roosevelt's position. Borah, along with Senator Arthur Capper of Kansas, both on the Foreign Relations Committee, switched over to the "discretionary school." The support of the less well-known Capper may have been considered more valuable, for the shaggy-haired, unpredictable Borah had by this time lost much of his influence over his colleagues. Still, being the more newsworthy of the two, it was the senator from Idaho who received the press notices when he declared that the Cuse episode pointed up a weakness in mandatory legislation: the President needed freedom, he now maintained, to deal with unanticipated problems.[24] Senator Arthur Vandenberg, leading spokesman for the mandatory position, persisted in his views; but a legislative proposal, which he made public the day before the announcement of the Cuse license, left him open to ridicule. Vandenberg, at this late date, still failed to account for direct violations of the moral embargo against Spain. Since the antimandatory people had consistently argued the need for discretion on the basis that it was impossible to foresee what the future would bring, the weakness of Vandenberg's position was now embarrassingly exposed.[25] It seemed that the administration possessed all the weapons it needed to attain its goal.

On the afternoon of December 30, Roosevelt, Moore, Pittman, and Sam McReynolds, chairman of the House Foreign Affairs Committee, met at the White House to discuss the form the legislation ought to take. The President, already in possession of Pittman's memorandum, inclined toward the senator's views. The decision was made to "rush a simple resolution through Congress extending neutrality prohibitions on arms shipments to civil conflict of the Spanish type, with the President granted wide discretion. . . ." When Pittman and McReynolds afterward met with reporters, it was clear that there had been an important disagreement. Upon questioning, Pittman admitted that the matter of discretionary power was foremost in the discussion with the President, and he added, vaguely: "That's just it; what are discretionary powers?" And McReynolds cast some doubt on the form of the legislation Congress would pass. He indicated that it would either be a joint resolution amending existing legislation in order to allow the President discretionary powers to meet the Spanish situation or perhaps an entirely new resolution applicable only to the Spanish crisis. This notion of separate legislation applying only to Spain was Moore's. He felt that it would be less likely to cause extended debate in Congress.[26] Moore, most clearly, was anxious to put an immediate stop to direct violations of the moral embargo. As in the past, Moore was not committed to the principle of executive discretion in all aspects of neutrality and embargo legislation.

Things were not going smoothly for those determined to obtain executive discretion, despite Pittman's previous claim to the President that his proposal would not be controversial. Vandenberg, upon learning of the discussion at the White House, fulminated against discretionary legislation, calling it "the first cousin to sanctions." Here he played upon the fear of many congressmen, who believed that sanctions were provocative acts all too likely to lead to war. "The cure," Vandenberg added, "is not to abandon mandates, but to extend them." During the next few days, the President's position seemed less secure. References were now made to a "considerable minority" group demanding mandatory legislation and to the embargo proposal as a "controversial subject" which might require "some days of debate." But both the *Washington Post* and the *New York Times* held fast to the notion that the discretionary forces would prevail.[27] Then, news reports on January 5 indicated that something had occurred the previous day which had thrown the administration and its congressional spokesmen into a state of confusion.

Pittman disclosed on January 4 that he was considering an alternative resolution specifically authorizing embargoes in the Spanish situation. He apparently feared that his earlier proposal, while it would have no trouble passing through Congress, would meet sufficient opposition so that its passage might be held up "for a day or so."[28] The developments which brought about confusion and began to upset the original plans of Roosevelt and Pittman were: first, a new set of applications by Richard L. Dinely for the export of arms to Spain to the value of $4,507,050; and, second, the hurried preparations of Robert Cuse to ship at least part of his cargo out of New York harbor.

The Dinely applications, the licenses for which were granted on January 5, contributed to a state of panic and to a belief that emergency legislation was drastically needed.[29] This, combined with Cuse's quickened preparations, would explain Pittman's concern over the prospect that his original proposal would be held up in Congress "for a day or so." It would also help to explain his alternative plan for special legislation applying to Spain only, a plan which concurred with that presented by Moore at the White House on December 30. But it was not so much the facts of the Dinely case and of the Cuse preparations which led to this change of plans as it was Moore's alarmed response to these events. This alarm quickly spread to others.

There is little doubt that Dinely's actions would have to be numbered among the most brash acts of intimidation ever performed by an American citizen upon the State Department and also among the boldest swindles ever attempted by an American citizen upon a foreign government. But despite this, his actions did not justify the panic which characterized the next few days. Dinely first telephoned the Office of Arms and Munitions Control from Kansas City on December 31. Stating that he had been in contact with the Spanish ambassador to Mexico, Dinely indicated that he could obtain from the Spanish government a contract for $9 million worth of assorted implements of war.

He said that he would obtain payment for these as soon as he obtained an export license. He then suggested to Green that as soon as he obtained payment the State Department could revoke his license, and Dinely, $9 million richer, would not violate the Department's embargo policy. Green had his next opportunity to be shocked when, a few days later, Dinely put in a personal appearance. He was without a doubt an unwelcome sight. (The Department was already familiar with a $77,000 deal which Dinely was thought to have put over on a group of Cuban revolutionaries earlier in the year.)

Dinely proceeded to advance the same proposal "in considerable detail." When Green charged Dinely "with an attempt to swindle a friendly government," Dinely said that he only wanted the $9 million and did not wish to violate government policy. But, he added, should the State Department refuse to go along with his scheme, he was prepared to follow through with the transaction and ship the arms. On January 4, Dinely carried out part of his threat and presented 19 applications covering 1,000 machine guns, 7,000 rifles, 40 million rounds of cartridges, and 47 airplanes. These licenses were granted the next day, and the State Department immediately informed the Spanish embassy of the risks of dealing with Dinely. These licenses might have justified drastic and immediate action by the State Department, if it were not for one significant fact. The majority of the items described in Dinely's applications were unobtainable at that time and probably very little if any of the materials were actually in his possession. At four o'clock on the afternoon of January 4, bearing the information on the Dinely case, Moore and Hackworth went to the capitol to see Senator Pittman.[30] From that time, the original Pittman proposal for discretionary legislation was pushed aside.

That the chairman of the Foreign Relations Committee would swing over to Moore's position was predictable. Pittman was notorious for refusing to extend himself for any cause except that of silver interests. Recognizing now that Vandenberg could marshal at least enough support to cause a contest over discretionary legislation, Pittman might even have been delighted to see the controversy disappear. The tall, lean senator from Nevada was a hard-drinking man who had already, in an earlier neutrality hassle, proved "that he was not capable of withstanding the emotional pressures allied with leadership."[31]

Still, the responsibility of what was about to happen was not really Pittman's. If the State Department was not going to stand up for itself, why should he? Pittman might wonder at Moore's attitude and his tactics, and he might even want to leave his own mark on the bill, but he would go along.

When Pittman asked for Moore's opinion, the Acting Secretary replied that legislation concerning Spain ought to be kept apart from general neutrality legislation in order to be able to deal with the Spanish situation "at once."[32] Moore thereupon presented Pittman with a draft resolution along these lines. That evening, Moore telephoned Roosevelt and informed him of the proposed changes. The President must have at least tacitly agreed. The next morning, Moore sent Roosevelt a note indicating that he and Pittman had arranged to meet in order to discuss the "emergency resolution." "Unless he has changed his mind," Moore wrote, "the resolution simply provides an embargo on shipment to Spain of arms, ammunition and implements of war including airplanes and cancels licenses heretofore issued for shipment of airplanes. If that is the resolution I will assume it has your approval and will furnish McReynolds a copy." Moore concluded his message to the President: "I urged Senator Pittman and he finally agreed to deal with the matter as an emergency and not complicate it with general neutrality legislation."[33] Moore thus won his earlier argument for quick and separate legislation, even though such legislation would deal a blow to executive discretion by allowing Congress alone to deal with the Spanish problem. It was not until after Dinely applied for licenses and after Cuse began to load part of his cargo aboard the *Mar Cantábrico* that the President and Pittman were drawn over to Moore's position.

Pittman, disagreeing with some of the details of the emergency resolution drafted by the State Department, drew up a similar one of his own, and then requested a meeting at the White House with Moore and McReynolds present.[34] It appears that Pittman's draft came out of this conference of January 5 unscathed. The Senator afterward "told reporters a resolution banning further arms to Spain and annulling all present licenses (those of Cuse and Dinely) would be passed by unanimous consent . . . without debate."[35] On the same day, in a note to the President, Moore outlined his objections to Pittman's draft. He specifically disliked its preamble, which he felt might be so interpreted as to raise the question of whether or not Germany and Spain were at war. There had been talk in some quarters that embargoes should be placed upon arms shipments to both countries. Moore again stressed his belief that "the resolution should be spoken of as an emergency measure, in disconnection from general neutrality legislation. That there is an emergency," he continued, "is shown by the fact that already licenses have been granted to the New Jersey man . . . and that another man is applying for licenses to cover shipments of planes [and other war materials] valued at $4,500,000."[36]

The President was thus convinced, on the advice of Moore, that it was worth while to sacrifice executive discretion in order to attempt to stop that part of the Cuse cargo which was ready for shipment. If the President was fully informed about Dinely and the items described in his applications, it is unlikely that the licenses granted him had much to do with Roosevelt's decision. His applications should not have been cause for immediate anxiety. The question arises as to how much Moore actually told the President and Senator Pittman about Dinely. A third factor, of unknown importance, was the extent to which even a partial shipment by Cuse would adversely affect British and French efforts to bring about agreements with Germany and Italy. Press reports on the morning of January 6 indicated a heightened sense of urgency, the situation being characterized as a race between Cuse and Congress.[37] It was curious that no one in the government publicly noted how slim were the chances for preventing some of the Cuse cargo from leaving New York.

III

Congress opened its session on January 5, but the form of the emergency resolution was not decided upon until late that afternoon at the White House. For that reason Moore suggested the introduction of the resolution be delayed until the next day. It was Moore's opinion that this would "not create any embarrassment, since the House Committee is not yet created."[38] In light of his desire to drop the already prepared discretionary proposal because of the need for haste, and in light of the final failure of the government to stop the Cuse shipment, this one-day postponement proved to be ironic. The debate in both houses of Congress did justify Moore's opinion that a discretionary amendment would be too long in passing to prevent the export of some of the planes and engines. But even the emergency resolution was not passed in time to accomplish that.

The resolution was first introduced in the Senate on January 6 by Pittman, who spent most of the morning session providing superficial answers to questions concerning the terms of the resolution. Once he went so far as to deny knowing to which Spanish party the licensed exports were intended. In answer to the question of why a simple amendment extending existing legislation to civil wars had not been presented, Pittman responded that "information has come from various Senators and from certain Representatives particularly, indicating that they do not desire to have the subject of the general law opened up at this time."[39] Pittman had hardly presented the actual resolution when it was time to recess in order to hear the President's message to a joint session of Congress. Roosevelt, quickly passing over the Spanish strife, directed his remarks toward the domestic situation. At 2:30 the Senate returned to its chambers and resumed debate.

For another hour, until the resolution came to a vote, Pittman, Vandenberg, and Nye did most of the talking. Some of the debate was directed toward the preamble, which made several points, the most important being references to the efforts of some European nations to contain the war and of others to give military aid to one side or the other. Vandenberg's attack upon the preamble led Pittman to withdraw it with the comment that it was "no longer" needed. It had only been inserted to demonstrate the existence of an "emergency" and "for the purpose of inducement." Vandenberg found one reason for contentment—the legislation was mandatory. From that time on, it was a matter of trying to get the floor away from Nye, who, after first seizing the occasion to plead for the nationalization of the arms industry, dwelt upon the idea that the administration was endeavoring to cooperate with France and Britain. What will happen he asked rhetorically, if "next week, or the following week" those two nations should decide to sell arms to the Loyalists? A few moments later, Nye argued that the embargo would work to the advantage of the Rebels. Then, in order to make it clear why he was going to vote for the measure, Nye commented: "If this action this afternoon is to be conceived, as I am going to conceive it, in the light of an effort to keep the hands of the United States clean and removed from the danger of being drawn into that war or strife in Europe, I am quite unwilling that it should be done in the name of neutrality, for, strictly speaking neutrality it is not."[40]

Pittman denied charges that the resolution favored the Rebels by indicating that the Spanish government would have difficulty receiving shipments, for the only ports it freely controlled were Valencia and Bilbao. (It was interesting to note that a few days later General Franco praised the United States for the enactment of this resolution.) He added that "tomorrow" some other "junk dealer" could attempt to sell arms to the insurgents —a remark indicating he did know for whom the Cuse shipment was intended. Senator J. Hamilton Lewis of Illinois concluded the debate with what might accurately be called the President's viewpoint. Lewis would have preferred a congressional declaration of "the policy of neutrality," leaving its details "to the Executive order of the President, and for that," he added, "I shall contend at a later time. I shall not now attempt to defer action. . . ."[41] The Senate then passed the resolution unanimously. It would have been difficult to conceive another measure at that time which could have drawn all the votes from both the supporters of the administration and the adherents of mandatory legislation.

The Senate's resolution was quickly sent to the House, which was already discussing the question. There Maury Maverick of Texas dominated the floor, and during the course of the afternoon he raised in one form or another almost all the objections mentioned by other congressmen. This resolution, he argued, would mean a "reversal of a policy of the United States Government for 150 years," and "a reversal of international law of four centuries." "This is not neutrality," he complained, "it is against neutrality. We are taking a stand against a democratic government, the parliamentary Government of Spain. . . ." He later added, "I am in favor of neither side in any foreign country. But we must face facts. . . . We talk for hours, days, and weeks on matters which are unimportant, and we rush through matters of such grave importance as this." Maverick was applauded when he stated: "If we are going to have neutrality, let us have it for the whole world." He then added, "and if we do not have it for the whole world, let us not have it at all." Maverick, Hamilton Fish, and Gerald Boileau all complained about the limitation of debate, especially with no right to amend. Shortly after, there arose another objection to McReynolds' rush tactics. If this is an emergency, it was asked, "why was not a rule brought in yesterday?"[42] But it was still Maverick who dominated the debate.

Maverick repeatedly dwelt upon what he considered the break from traditional American policy and international law, the narrowness of the resolution, and its ineffectiveness in dealing with the problems brought about by the munitions industry. It was the second point which disturbed him most: "So we sell munitions to Germany, but refuse to sell munitions to Spain. Is that not a fine diplomatic pickle?" Maverick, along with other objectors, held the floor for such a period that Edward Creal of Kentucky charged McReynolds with opposing the resolution because he "allots time to men who offer various thoughts and reasons why the legislation should not be passed."[43] As with so many debates on the floor of Congress, there was as much indirection as direction. John T. Bernard (who was finally the only one in either house to vote against the resolution) raised a technical objection requiring the House to proceed according to a special rule which extended debate—a tactic which permitted the *Mar Cantábrico* additional time to sail out of New York harbor. Most of the resulting discussion consisted of efforts by various congressmen to set their general positions on neutrality legislation before the House. When the resolution was finally passed, 411 to 1, there was not enough time remaining for the President to sign the act and stop the *Mar Cantábrico*. The latter, after proceeding to Veracruz to take aboard more arms, was eventually captured by the Rebels on March 3, 1937. Pittman was ironically justified.

If Cuse was pleased at having the profits from at least a partial shipment of his cargo, Dinely was disturbed: "After we've been working on this deal for months, the President starts shooting off and the thing gets all screwed up."[44] Roosevelt finally put his signature to the Spanish Embargo Act on January 8. Meanwhile, Dinely was planning in vain to ship arms and planes through Mexico. On January 7, he expressed bafflement over the attitude of Spanish officials. He said of Gordan Ordas,

who had flown to New York from Mexico, "I don't know why
he's stalling me now. Seems like a fine running around after the
way I worked on this deal."[45]

If there was a potentially troublesome inflexibility and a
potentially dangerous sacrifice of principle resulting from the
President's acquiescence to Moore's arguments, there was, from
another point of view, possible merit in Moore's tactics. In the
first place, the State Department now possessed a political
weapon. With only one dissenting vote in both houses of Congress, the Spanish Embargo Act could hardly be referred to as
a controversial measure. (At the time of its passage, the resolution did not even generate much debate in the press.[46]) The
State Department, in later days, would repeatedly answer demands for a change of policy by recalling the unanimity of
congressional opinion. Second, because the embargo was ef-
fected by congressional mandate, the State Department and the
President could plead helplessness to those demanding that it be
lifted. Any merit in these two points, however, rested upon the
idea that the administration would never care to alter its policy
toward the Spanish conflict. How much consideration the President gave to this question is not known, but he did have the
habit of conceding a point now with the hope of picking it up
later. Comprehensive neutrality legislation was still to be enacted later that session, and perhaps Roosevelt had the hope of
gaining at that time discretionary powers over the Spanish
embargo. If so, this was in spite of all the obstacles brought
about by having once let Congress gain ultimate control over
the policy.

Calculating the general consequences of a mandatory resolution on the one hand, and of a comprehensive discretionary
resolution on the other, was not impossible. The extra time
necessary to enact a discretionary resolution should have been
little cause for concern. If one small shipment of second-hand,
unarmed, American planes would have endangered the plans of
Britain and France, then their efforts had little chance for
success anyway. What was immediately important to the British and French was that the American government display its
determination to stop shipments of arms. Moore's desire to
have, right now, the power to thwart a single challenge apparently clouded this whole question. As in November, during the

days preceding the removal of the American embassy to Valencia, it was Moore's determination to remedy an evident and
impending difficulty that caused him to put aside the more
subtle and removed problems. Those on Capitol Hill who favored executive discretion encountered two obstacles in addition
to the vocal minority among their colleagues—the Acting Secretary of State, and a President lacking the resolve to battle
for what he professed to want. The prodiscretionary forces
were left without a leader.

As far back as 1933, when he first came to the State Department, Moore expressed reservations concerning some areas of
executive discretion in neutrality legislation. It should not,
perhaps, have been expected that he would extend himself to
protect executive discretion in what he considered an emergency
situation. The President, since his first days in the White
House, permitted the State Department and Congress to determine foreign policy. Not yet confident of his own analyses of
foreign affairs, the President once again yielded his position
under pressure. Moore, unlike the President, was extremely
confident. The day after Congress passed the embargo resolution, Moore wrote to his friend, Ambassador Dodd: "I believe I
can say to you as a friend, very confidentially, and I hope you
will believe without any trace of vanity, that I now have perhaps more knowledge about the operations of the Department
here and abroad than any one individual has had in a recent
period."[47]

On January 13, Secretary of State Hull returned from his
extended stay at the Buenos Aires conference. It was later
claimed that, upon returning to Washington, Hull pronounced
the embargo resolution "the worst act of the Roosevelt Administration."[48] While there was not much reason for him to be
delighted, it is unlikely he put the problem in language quite
like that. If he did, he left no personal record of it. What is
really important, with respect both to the Secretary and to the
State Department as a whole, is the lack of evidence that
officials were making predictions and calculations in order to be
prepared for a variety of possible eventualities. A fear that the
civil war would erupt into a general war, and a conviction that
the Spanish strife was Europe's business and not that of the
United States—these two attitudes were no proper substitutes
for intelligent, even if difficult, calculation. The aphorism

"Don't cross bridges before you come to them" adequately describes the development of American policy toward the Spanish strife. If it occurred to the policy-makers that the future might provide important alternatives, imperatives different from existing ones, or developments which would make policy changes desirable, it would seem these thoughts were not sufficiently compelling to be committed to writing. Whatever the case, the State Department, between January and August 1937, encountered a new set of problems for which it was again unprepared.

5

NETWORK OF APPEASEMENT

THE STATE DEPARTMENT confronted two decisive developments in May 1937, with respect to the Spanish crisis. One of these was Neville Chamberlain's rise to the prime ministry in England; the other was the failure to wrest control of the Spanish embargo from Congress. The effects of these two developments all but eliminated the faint, and as yet neglected, possibility that the embargo might be abandoned before the civil war ran its course.

The British, who so largely determined the foreign policies of the other Western democracies, had been groping for most of the decade. During the winter and spring of 1937, with the abdication of Edward VIII and the retirement of Stanley Baldwin, there came a further period of "muddling through." Baldwin, who was already uninterested in foreign affairs, exerted even less influence in the months before the coronation of George VI. And Chamberlain, Baldwin's obvious successor, did not yet have the power to determine policy. On May 28, all this changed, when Chamberlain became Prime Minister after the King's coronation. Even during these awkward months, American policy closely followed that of the British. By July 1937, officials in Washington discovered a practical difference between the "accidental" appeasement of the Baldwin ministry and the purposeful appeasement of Chamberlain. The State Department found itself tied more than ever to the British

Foreign Office, with a consequent decline in alternatives. So determined was Chamberlain to carry out his policy that the Americans feared what would happen should they ever attempt to disentangle themselves from the network of appeasement in Europe. What would Chamberlain do should the United States somehow provoke the Fascist nations? The new Prime Minister's policy helped clarify the Spanish situation in one sense. It had never been considered more "unthinkable" for the United States to consider the sale of arms to the Spanish government.

If developments in Britain made a continuation of the existing policy appear necessary and further limited the freedom of American policy-makers, there was also the passage of the Neutrality Act of May 1, 1937. What went on behind the scenes remains a mystery; but while the President was granted some discretion in the application of "neutrality" provisions by this new piece of general legislation, he was specifically prevented—not so much legally as politically—from taking the Spanish policy out of congressional hands. Whatever the case, there was a conspicuous attempt to keep in effect the Spanish Embargo Resolution of January, instead of having it superseded by the new legislation which granted more executive discretion.

During the months leading up to the passage of the Neutrality Act, European diplomacy was in turmoil. The military situation in Spain added to the confusion; for Loyalists and Rebels were alternately reported to be justified in their claims of ultimate victory, and the Spanish conflict was still the continent's major crisis. A growing sense of foreboding, a feeling of inexorable drift into general war, meanwhile spread over Europe. What precise relationships the uncertain Spanish situation had to the increasing fear of world war is difficult to assess. But the mere recollection of "that incident" at Sarajevo, twenty-three years before, was sufficient to cause anxiety every time an international complication arose out of the Spanish strife. This constant uneasiness gave rise to pessimism, and American officials were not immune to it. While not everyone believed that world war was unavoidable, many would have agreed with John Cudahy, then ambassador at Warsaw. "None of the optimists," he wrote, "have any argument except their unquenchable optimism." According to Bullitt, the European situation was "tremulous."[1] That was on January 8, the very day President Roosevelt put his signature to the Spanish Embargo Resolution.

The dubious military and political situation in Spain, and the growing apprehension that general war was on the horizon, contributed to the paralysis of American foreign policy. Earlier decisions to follow the British lead in policies toward Europe seemed to be choices which, having been made, could not now be rejected. Caught in the tide of old decisions, American policy began to drift, often reluctantly, behind that of Downing Street. If the freedom to choose among viable alternatives, to make real decisions, is what makes a diplomatist's job fascinating, American foreign policy was already well into a dull phase.

A look at developments in Europe which preceded the passage of the Neutrality Act (and Chamberlain's assumption of power later that same month) provides some indication of why American policy-makers brought less resolution to their tasks. Baffled by events abroad, restrained by the public's distrust of them at home, they had long been too little determined to protect their freedom to make policy. Now, as far as Spain was concerned, the force of events nearly crowded that freedom out altogether.

I

Estimates of the military situation in Spain fluctuated more than actual conditions did, mainly because of the unexpected ability of the Loyalists to hold off Rebel offensives. During the Nationalists' Jarama Valley offensive in February, for example, experts in Washington predicted the imminent fall of Madrid and, shortly thereafter, a Rebel victory. But the resistance which the Loyalists demonstrated at Jarama, and during other campaigns that winter and spring, periodically led some observers to the speculation that the Loyalists' staying power would be decisive. In April, for example, Bowers estimated that the government had "every justification" for its optimism. Hardly a month passed before this judgment also proved erroneous.[2]

The tenacity of the Loyalists early in the year made a prolonged war more probable. This was of special importance when taken in conjunction with the policies being pursued by

Germany and the Soviet Union, for a quick conclusion of the
Spanish strife was now of no great benefit to either power.
Stalin's European policy, Spain included, began to enter one of
its more puzzling phases with the approach of spring, 1937.
Yvon Delbos provided one interpretation of it during a conversation with Bullitt, late in February. He believed that Stalin
was moderating his international policy and added that the
Soviet Union had become convinced that a victorious Spanish
government would not establish a Communist state. Delbos
further believed that the Russians consequently preferred a
Franco victory for purposes of propaganda. Stalin was also
"deeply afraid of the Trotskyist movement, especially of its
strength among the youth and army." It might have been more
accurate to say that Stalin did not really expect the Loyalists
to win, and did not want a Communist regime in Spain to suffer
the onus of the defeat. (This would help to explain the Communists' reluctance to increase their representation in the Loyalist
government, when they had the opportunity in May 1937.)[3]

Years later, George Kennan elaborated upon an interpretation of Russian policy consistent with either of the above theo-
ries. Stalin, once he regained the flagging support of the Communist Central Committee, resumed his purges. The ax fell
heavily upon those Communists who had been sent to Spain, for
Stalin believed these people were dangerous to him. The cause
of the Loyalist government had become, in Kennan's words,
"the repository of the hopes and enthusiasms of the West.
People read into this Spanish struggle the epitomization of all
the liberal hopes and dreams which the early part of this
century had fostered—dreams which had suffered one major
frustration in the economic crisis, and were now suffering another in the march of European fascism." However unsound
was this liberal interpretation of the Spanish strife, it was
sufficiently convincing for Stalin to fear the "Western" influence it had upon those Communists who were sent to Spain.
Nothing could have been more destructive to his plans than a
return to Russia of an idealism similar to that of the early days
of the Bolsheviks. For this reason, he purged the Russian participants and cut down Soviet aid to the Loyalists, maintaining
only enough "to prolong the conflict in order to engage German
and Italian energies there as long as possible."[4] If in 1937, or
even in 1938, officials in Washington carried Delbos' theory to

similar conclusions, it made no difference in policy. Certainly, British and French policies did not change on account of it.

One of the ablest descriptions of German policy during the same period was written by A. J. Drexel Biddle, then in Oslo. Biddle argued that Germany could not then support a general war. Hitler was therefore turning to "pin pricking"—a policy which could be expected "to have an important bearing on the Spanish situation." Hitler, under the urging of the General Staff, decided to cut down aid to Franco, and so prolong the Spanish strife. This conflict would "provide an ever-ready spark when necessary . . . and a constant menace to the allies."[5] The State Department was thus informed that neither Hitler nor Stalin was as interested in Spain as they were in keeping the Spanish struggle going. The same could not be said of Mussolini, however; for the Italians threw troops and materials into Spain recklessly. In the end it proved costly to the Italian war machine, especially in terms of equipment.

The whole of February was filled with reports of Italian aid to Franco and Italian reluctance to adhere to the so-called spirit of the Anglo-Italian accord of early January. The State Department regularly received estimates of the total number of Italian troops in Spain: 40,000 in early February; 60,000 later that same month; 70,000 in April. Italo-French relations further deteriorated, and the British Government had to contend with a public which increasingly opposed the Foreign Office's "Italian flirtation."[6]

The international brigades had also grown, particularly during January; but consistently thrown into the front lines, they were, in Bullitt's apt phrase, "shot to pieces." In April Bullitt was told that there were some six to ten thousand foreigners fighting for the government.[7] This provided good reason for assuming the futility of any attempt to reach an agreement on the departure of foreign troops from Spain. Franco, who had at the time probably some 80,000 Italians and Germans, in addition to thousands of Moors, would virtually have been sending away his army—even had the Fascist powers permitted it.[8] The Italians and Germans gave the British and French some hope, periodically, that troops would be withdrawn, but nothing was really accomplished until the outcome of the war was definitely decided.

The notorious lack of respect Hitler and Mussolini paid to

the Non-Intervention Committee was a continual source of anxiety to the Blum Government. Every Fascist violation of the agreement made it more difficult for Blum to continue a nonintervention policy himself. A few concessions were made to the French left—for example, the Government's failure to prevent foreign volunteers from entering Spain through France—but Blum continually drew back from outright aid to the Loyalists. As a French official reported in February, the Blum Government had "no desire nor present intention" of abandoning nonintervention. Claude Bowers, whose sources of information on French policy were sometimes very good, meanwhile reported developments of the greatest consequence concerning French attitudes toward Franco. Believing that the Rebels would ultimately win the war, and that satisfactory agreements might be reached with Franco, the French began to pursue a more calculated policy of expediency.[9] This information could only have confirmed Cordell Hull's opinion that the United States was pursuing the appropriate course.

Implicit in French policy was the notion that, should Franco be victorious, he would not remain tied to Germany and Italy. This idea was more evident in British policy, and with little effort at concealment they increased their contacts with the Franco government.[10] What seems to have caused the most concern in London was the possibility that the Blum Government would not be able to withstand left-wing pressure for providing extensive aid to the Loyalists. In light of Hitler's and Stalin's most recent decisions, and the notion that Spain would not end up under foreign control, this would seem to have been the best time for the French to test their position by providing some assistance to the Loyalists. The most telling answer to this proposition came from Delbos, as reported by Bullitt: "In the end Spain would come out with a government which might be either somewhat to the Right or somewhat to the Left. It was certainly not the part of wisdom which would make a European war about the nuances of a future Spanish Government."[11] Once more the State Department must have felt its policy of noninvolvement justified, for it had far less reason to care about "the nuances of a future Spanish Government" than did the French.

The fact that Secretary Hull could be little concerned for the particular future of Spain—except for the hope that it not be tied to the Fascist bloc or to the Soviet Union—permitted him a degree of detachment. When, for example, Bowers once suggested that the American commercial attaché be sent to St. Jean de Luz so as to be closer to Rebel functionaries, Hull was concerned that this action would result in a charge that the United States was abandoning neutrality. Bowers later made it clear that he was not suggesting trade arrangements, but only friendly contact with Rebel commercial interests. The commercial attaché was sent.[12] For similar reasons of propriety, Hull refused the opportunity to place a military observer with the Rebel forces.[13] Reports from Bowers certainly gave the State Department reason to believe that American policy was successful with respect to maintaining the good will of both Spanish parties. "It seems significant and certainly gratifying," Bowers wrote, "to observe both sides in the bitterest of controversies uniting both in praise of the United States and in their desire to maintain cordial relations with us."[14]

This achievement was clearly accomplished with the Rebels by the embargo on arms shipments to Spain, and with the Loyalists by observing important proprieties. Roosevelt, for example, did not fail to send President Azaña his felicitations on the sixth anniversary of the proclamation of the Spanish Republic. Even while the Loyalists complained about the embargo and would have liked to have an American of ambassadorial rank in Valencia itself, their protests were always most "proper," and they continued to speak highly of Eric Wendelin.[15] It is probable that the Spanish government realized that the United States could not be won over to its side unless Britain and France were first converted. There was little sense in departing from diplomatic niceties—the neutrality of the United States was much more valuable than its opposition. And American officials, unlike the British and the French, were not developing expedient business relationships with the Burgos government and its representatives. During the winter and spring of 1937, the State Department thus continued a policy which might be described, despite technical objections, as "neutrality with propriety."[16]

For the Rebels the ultimate meaning of American policy could only have been uncertain. Without success, they queried Americans about the prospects of postwar relations with the United States. The Franco representative in Rome, for instance, spoke to Ambassador Phillips about postwar credits,

loans, and relief.[17] But there is no evidence that the Americans
replied to such talk. Even the commercial attaché who was sent
to St. Jean de Luz proved unhelpful to the Rebels, because he
was instructed simply to evaluate economic conditions in insurgent Spain. For the Loyalists, the prospect of good postwar
relations with the United States was almost as vague. What
both Loyalists and Rebels could expect was at least "official"
good will—provided the postwar Spanish government were free
of foreign control.

The attitudes of American officials did not change during the
first six months of the year. European diplomatic developments
did not appear to warrant an alteration in American policy.
The possibility of some day wanting to lift the embargo was
still not even considered. And this in part would explain the
administration's easy acceptance of a peculiar stipulation attached to the Neutrality Act of May 1937.

II

The Spanish embargo resolution of January 8 had
hardly been enacted before officials in Washington were compelled to consider the formulation of general neutrality legislation. Members of the administration, leaders of Congress, and
pressure groups turned to the issue long before the approach of
the May first deadline, when existing legislation would expire.
For the first time since the outbreak of the Spanish strife,
important pressure groups devoted to one or the other of the
Spanish causes began to organize.

The results of a Gallup poll in January could hardly have
been satisfying to proponents of either side. Almost two-thirds
of those people questioned favored neither side in the Spanish
strife; 22 per cent favored the Loyalists, 12 per cent the
Rebels. Despite an intensive effort to mobilize public opinion,
these pressure groups failed miserably. A *Fortune* poll in April
showed almost 24 per cent pro-Loyalist and almost 12 per cent
pro-Rebel—hardly a change since January. Another poll in
May, shortly after the enactment of new legislation, showed
that the percentages favoring each side were cut just about in
half from the April figures. Despite all the space and promi-
nence given to the Spanish civil war in the American press, not

until the last three months of the conflict did a majority of
those polled favor either party in Spain.[18]

The desire to remain aloof from the horrors of the war, a
feeling of general disgust due to the excesses committed by
Loyalists and Rebels alike, the confusion caused by exaggerated
claims for and against both sides, added to a surprising record
of public indifference—all these factors helped to account for
the failure and refusal of so many Americans to take a stand.
Even while the real and imagined issues of the Spanish strife
broke up families, caused Red scares, incited religious antagonism, converted men and women to and from Communism, split
and splintered parties on the left, created strange bedfellows on
both left and right, and turned dedicated pacifists into volunteers in the international brigades, the majority of Americans
—if the results of the numerous public opinion polls are accepted—remained uncommitted until the war was almost over.

The Spanish war had a lasting impact on many thousands of
Americans who passionately identified themselves with one
cause or the other. The point, however, in the context of neutrality legislation, is that the majority of the American people
never came close to desiring intervention in the Spanish civil
war.[19] Another point is that, among those who favored one side
or the other, it is clear that sympathies were much more
strongly with the Loyalists. It was because of this last attitude
that the administration was so careful in the way that it publicly explained its policy. In late January, in answer to a letter
from Norman Thomas, the Socialist leader, the President simply mentioned the view that American policy developed independently of foreign pressures, discussed certain legalisms concerning embargoes, pointed out the explosive dangers in the
Spanish situation, and referred to the desire of the American
people to remain aloof from that European strife.[20]

The President was only then beginning to develop his interest
in foreign affairs, and there is no doubt that his sympathies on
the Spanish issue lay with the majority of "opinion holders."
Fascist leaders infuriated him, and his impotence in dealing
with them exasperated him. Most of all, the President was
perplexed. Early in February, he wrote to his friend, William
Phillips, in Rome:

What a confusion it all is. Every week changes the picture and the
basis for it all lies, I *think,* not in communism or the fear of

communism but in Germany and the fear of what the present German leaders are meeting for or being drawn toward.

. . . I am 'watchfully waiting' even though the phrase carries us back to the difficult days from 1914 to 1917.

I would not dare to say this out loud because sometimes it is better to appear much wiser than one really is.[21]

Hardly anything seemed more confusing than the issue of neutrality, which was so intimately tied to the Spanish strife. The need for especially flexible and discretionary legislation was evident. During March, Ambassador Joseph Davies wrote to Secretary Hull from Moscow: "Changes are sudden, even violent, indicative of the shifting national realistic interests. There is no firm ground," he continued, "upon which a foundation can be laid with any security. All seem to be playing their own games and nationalistic interests are running riot." The British, meanwhile, expressed "considerable anxiety" over the prospect of new American neutrality legislation, fearing that it encouraged the Germans and disabled the United States as a deterrent to potential aggressors. Two months before Chamberlain actually became Prime Minister he wrote to Secretary of the Treasury Henry Morgenthau, "earnestly" hoping that "some way may be found of leaving sufficient discretion with the Executive to deal with each case on its merits."[22] But these British overtures need hardly have been made; the President and the Secretary of State were already convinced of the necessity for greater discretion. Their problem was to mobilize sufficient congressional support.

Secretary Hull decided to forgo the presentation of an administration proposal, preferring to pursue the Department's ends by working through congressional leaders.[23] Hull even declined the opportunity to appear before the Senate Foreign Relations and House Foreign Affairs Committees. Moore, Hackworth, and Carlton Savage met with Senator Pittman's committee on February 13, and during the questioning barely touched upon the Spanish civil war. Hackworth, along with Joe Green, met with McReynolds' House committee three days later, and again one week after that (with Charles Yost replacing Green). Neither time was the subject of Spain more than touched upon. If it had not been for the appearance of representatives of pressure groups, the Spanish issue would have been bypassed. Those represented were the Socialist Party, the American League against War and Fascism, and the American Friends of Spanish Democracy. Members of the House committee were plainly unconvinced by the pro-Loyalist arguments presented.[24]

With regard to Spain, the only certainty in the weeks before the passage of the new legislation was that there would be a more comprehensive amendment covering civil wars in general and providing for presidential discretion in the application of the legislation to civil wars. Yet it later became clear that something else had been decided behind the scenes which may well have sealed the Spanish policy for the remainder of the war.

As early as the end of January, Moore apparently felt that Key Pittman and Sam McReynolds were not entirely in accord with the President's views on the coming legislation. If it were not already clear to the President, Moore informed him that the support of those two congressional leaders would determine the defeat of "any undesirable legislation."[25] Neither the Pittman resolution which passed the Senate on March 3 nor the McReynolds resolution which was later passed in the House gave the President cause for rejoicing—although Moore claimed that Pittman's measure was "a fairly liberal" one and "the best that anyone knowing the situation could expect the Senate to pass. . . ." The McReynolds resolution provided somewhat more presidential discretion, and Roosevelt, favoring it, asked Senator Joseph Robinson to "persuade Key to yield just as far as possible to the House bill."[26] None of this concern seems to have been directed at the relationship between the new legislation and the Spanish issue. When the bill was finally passed by both houses on April 29, it was "a curious mixture of mandatory and permissive features."[27] And while the President was given the power to determine an embargo in cases of civil war, his power to do so with regard to Spain was taken away only minutes before the House agreed to a conference report completing the passage of the Neutrality Law. Exactly what caused the exclusion of the Spanish embargo from presidential discretion is not known. It is possible that some influential people feared that the President's anti-Fascist feelings might sometime get the better of him and so decided that the Spanish policy ought to be kept out of his control. Whatever the reason, it was McReynolds who took, or was given, the job of curtailing the President's power.

Shortly before the conference report was voted upon, McReynolds addressed the House:

The Spanish resolution, which was passed on January 8, 1937, of this session is not repealed by this act. The previous act repeals itself when a certain proclamation is issued, but this legislation extends the provisions of the resolution of January 8 and gives the President authority to prohibit the exportation of arms, in addition to those covered by a previous former resolution, and includes provisions in regard to loans, credits, and solicitation of funds not covered by the resolution of January 8. I make this statement so that it will be in the *Record*.[28]

The President's power to reverse the Spanish policy was considered to have been eliminated. The mandatory "emergency" resolution which Moore so hastily threw to Congress in January was still in effect and would remain in effect until Congress removed it or the civil war ended. Even if McReynolds' statement were not legally binding upon the President, it was politically binding. To ignore this public pronouncement at any time could be politically disastrous. If Moore earlier carelessly limited the power of his Chief Executive, McReynolds acted deliberately.

With characteristic attention to detail, Secretary Hull informed Roosevelt of the meaning of McReynolds' statement and elaborated upon each provision of the new bill applicable to Spain. At the same time, he enclosed a proclamation to be signed by the President. It extended the list of articles whose export to Spain was illegal, prohibited certain financial transactions, and prohibited American citizens from carrying war materials to Spain. Of further importance was a provision requiring the registration of humanitarian organizations sending funds or goods to Spain, and the submission by such organizations of periodic reports and audits to the Department of State. Only the Red Cross, already required to submit similar reports to the Secretary of War, was exempted from this requirement.[29]

In his letter of April 30 to the President, Hull pointed out that some provisions concerning arms embargoes had already met the President's objection and that other features were not "entirely satisfactory." But the Secretary anyway recommended approval. Obviously neither Hull nor Roosevelt felt that the necessary battle for a better bill was worth it; and it is not beyond possibility that Hull, knowing the President's sympathies, actually approved of McReynolds' last-minute remarks before the House. But if Hull knew of it beforehand, in all likelihood the President was informed about it. It was not Hull's practice to deceive the President. The simple fact is that, once having assumed control of the Spanish embargo, Congress did not relinquish it. In the meanwhile, new pressures upon the Spanish policy developed at home and abroad.

III

The failure of pro-Loyalist organizations to make a dent in the large uncommitted majority of the American public led them quite naturally in another direction. Instead of pressing the virtues of the Loyalist cause, they began to take advantage of growing anti-Hitler and anti-Mussolini sentiment. Much of this campaign went on concurrently with the debate over neutrality legislation, and its aim was to have embargo restrictions extended to Germany and Italy—on the ground that these nations had invaded Spain. This program broadened the base of "pro-Loyalist" support in Congress. The American Friends of Spanish Democracy, for example, kept in touch with Maury Maverick, that stalwart isolationist, who was in sympathy with the idea of prohibiting arms shipments to Portugal, Germany, and Italy (really, all nations).[30] More important, this new emphasis on anti-Fascism stood a greater chance of receiving the President's support.

Toward the end of March, when Roosevelt returned to Washington from a vacation, he instructed Secretary Hull to probe British attitudes in the event that Italy made an avowed official move in Spain. It was the first indication that the President was considering the possibility of an embargo against the Fascist states. Perhaps no single event persuaded him to consider this course, but doubtless a very recent resolution by Senator Nye did help provoke the President. The resolution called for the application of existing embargo restrictions on shipments of war materials to Germany and Italy. For once, a passionate (and influential) isolationist was demanding a policy change which coincided with Roosevelt's sympathies. Nye's action did move Hull to call a meeting in the State Department on March 25. It was there "agreed that there was no existing state of war between nations. . . ." A check by the Office of Arms and Munitions Control found that "Germany and Italy were importing only an insignificant quantity of war products from the United States. . . ." Hull concluded that an embargo might, instead of having a "sobering effect" on Germany and Italy, "on the contrary, seriously endanger the success of the conciliatory efforts of Britain and France and thus increase the likelihood of a general war."[31] But, under Roosevelt's orders, Hull probed the British through Ambassador Bingham in London.

Four days later, the State Department was informed by Bingham that the hypothetical situation of an official Italian move in Spain would probably not result in any appreciable change in British policy.[32] The matter was then dropped—but only temporarily. During the last week of April a series of events began which provoked great cries of humanitarian indignation in the American press and gave renewed strength to those calling for an extension of the embargo to Germany and Italy.

In what will long be remembered as a great atrocity, Rebel planes bombed the city of Guernica, in staunchly Loyalist and devoutly Catholic Basque country. It was the world's first real experience of civilian bombing, and the American press responded in horror. Little more than a month later came the *Deutschland*-Almería incident. The four major powers—Britain, France, Germany, and Italy—had in mid-April put "into effect" a naval control scheme to "prevent interference" in Spain by foreign powers. Late in May, one of the German patrol ships, the *Deutschland*, was bombed, a score of sailors being killed. The Germans, under orders from Berlin, two days later retaliated by shelling the defenseless city of Almería. In an act of solidarity, Italy then joined Germany in its departure from the Non-Intervention Committee—a departure which turned out to be temporary after discussions among the four powers.[33] It was charged in some quarters that the planes and pilots involved in the bombing of the *Deutschland* were Russian (just as the planes and pilots in the bombing of Guernica were allegedly German).[34] Chamberlain, having become Prime Minister only a day before the *Deutschland* incident, must have felt that the revolutionary powers were bent upon giving him a sad welcome. In the United States the effect of all this was to stir up much anti-Fascist feeling.

Secretary Hull immediately spoke to the German ambassador and expressed his "earnest hope" that the German government would "see its way clear to make a peaceful adjustment of its difficulties. . . ."[35] Later in June, the Germans charged that another ship, the *Leipzig*, had been attacked by a submarine but had not been hit. Following this alleged incident, Germany and Italy permanently left the naval control scheme while remaining on the Non-Intervention Committee. May, June, and July were very tense months on the continent, and across the Atlantic the pressure to extend the embargo to the Fascist states increased.

The State Department, deluged with indignant anti-Fascist letters and telegrams, was also under the pressure of a group of congressmen. The principal figure was Representative Jerry J. O'Connell, who has been described by one writer as a "Communist sympathizer who effectively exploited his [Catholic] religious ties in his campaigns and while in office."[36] Whatever O'Connell's political sympathies were, a case could be made for embargoing arms shipments to the Fascist states. German and Italian troops were, after all, making war against what the United States recognized as the legitimate government of Spain. The situation was, however, terribly confused by the existence of the Non-Intervention Committee and by the recognition accorded the Rebel government by several other nations (including a few in the Western hemisphere). More to the point, the Spanish government itself did not recognize a state of war with Germany or Italy—it obviously was in no position to do so. This more than anything undercut the strictly legal basis upon which to apply the embargo provisions of the neutrality act against the Fascist states. An embargo under these conditions could only be considered as something of a provocative act, even if it were in defense of a friendly government so far as the United States was concerned.

Despite this, President Roosevelt did not discard the notion. Late in June the President granted an interview to Norman Thomas,[37] a meeting which encouraged the idea that Roosevelt was leaning toward an embargo against shipments of war materials to Germany and Italy; for this is what Thomas had been advocating. On June 24, it was reported in Valencia that "President Roosevelt has adopted an attitude resolutely favorable to the Spanish cause. . . ."[38] Roosevelt was favorable to the Loyalist cause, but not resolutely. On June 29 in a memorandum to Hull, the President wrote: "For many reasons I think that if Mussolini . . . or Hitler . . . have made or make any official admissions or statements that their Government armed forces are actually taking part in the Spanish war, then in such case we shall have to act under the Neutrality Act." He wrote of "precedents and the future" and of compounding "a ridiculous situation" wherein "no proof" is said to be had; and then he added that Hull should check the situation abroad and telephone the findings to him at Hyde Park on the first or second of July.[39]

From Rome, Phillips advised against any such action: "it would be unwise for us to inject ourselves into the picture and thus create a wholly new situation." He feared that complications arising out of an embargo applied only against those nations supporting one side could "spread the conflict beyond the Spanish frontier." After probing Anthony Eden, Bingham reported much the same view: "any departure from the spirit of the legislation which is one of strict neutrality would be regarded by Europe as a gratuitous intervention in continental affairs"—especially since no European government considers that a state of international war exists. Eden told Bingham that an extension of the embargo would be, " 'to say the least, premature' and intimated that it would complicate his task." Hull, with these opinions in hand, telephoned the President, who then "readily agreed to continue our position unchanged."[40]

Even before the President requested Hull to investigate the situation, the Office of Arms and Munitions Control prepared a lengthy memorandum[41] on the knowable (or "immediate") and the probable (or "secondary") effects of applying the neutrality legislation against Germany and Italy. Those provisions relating to an embargo would seem to have been least effective, for Germany had purchased only some $440,000 worth of war materials from the United States since January 1, 1937; Italy, almost $169,000. Of the total, about $443,000 worth consisted of engines and propellers which they installed in airplanes to be exported to South Africa, Denmark, Bolivia, and Yugoslavia.

An arms embargo was therefore an ineffective measure. Concerning loans and credits, the restrictive prohibitions of the legislation would not affect Germany or Italy since they were already prohibited from loans and credits by the Johnson Act of 1934. As for the freezing of securities, this action might well injure American investors more than the Germans and Italians. Next, trade in products other than war materials would certainly be hurt. Finally, the provision of the Neutrality Act which would ban American travelers from German and Italian ships would bring about a sizable loss of revenue to those nations. In short, the many provisions of the neutrality act would have brought confusing immediate results.

It was in the discussion of "secondary" effects that the memorandum was most revealing, for here its authors drew upon past experience as well as upon current conditions. First the "Ethiopian experience" suggested that an embargo would impel Mussolini, and probably Hitler as well, "to hasten to push their Spanish adventure to a successful conclusion in order to save their faces, to escape more onerous restrictions, and to lift as rapidly as possible those already imposed." Second, the attempted Hoare-Laval Agreement of 1935 suggested that the proposed action by the United States might induce England "to come to a quick compromise with Germany and Italy in order to remove the growing menace of a general war, for which she obviously does not believe herself to be prepared at this time." Third, "the effect on France would be complex," for the Government had only that week left the hands of Léon Blum (Camille Chautemps being the new Premier). Either the Popular Front Government would give in to an encouraged left wing and aid the Loyalists, or refuse and risk the break-up of the Popular Front through the withdrawal of the Communists. Finally, the Spanish Loyalists might be encouraged to take provocative action against the intervening Fascist powers, while the Rebels would hasten their offensive "lest the present balance, which is favorable to them, should change." In sum, the memorandum expressed the fear that the application of the neutrality law to Germany and Italy might have uncontrollable results and "might increase the likelihood of a general war." Then, as if to close the door on the whole question, the memorandum concluded that an extension of the embargo "might precipitate the very catastrophe which we seek to avoid and injure most those people—the Spanish Loyalists—on whose behalf the action has been sought."

While there was in the State Department no more complete analysis of the complicated nature of the Spanish strife than this one, the memorandum was clearly not written for the purpose of further, open discussion. The reason for this stands squarely on the fact that no consideration was given to the ponderable consequences of extending the embargo to Germany and Italy in conjunction with the adoption of other theoretical policy changes. A number of explanations are possible. First, the men who prepared the memorandum might have been instructed to limit their considerations. Next, it is possible that they were predisposed to avoid an anti-Fascist policy in Spain. And finally, they might have believed that other options would be ineffective, politically unrealistic, or diplomatically unfeasible; and therefore they decided against even mentioning them. None of these possibilities necessarily excludes the others, but the issue raised by the third one must be considered central in importance. Even if the Office of Arms Control did not at least explicitly deal with the broader issue, others in the State Department shortly would.

Probably the most revealing part of the above memorandum was the recollection of the attempted Hoare-Laval agreement, for Chamberlain's open professions of appeasement (of "reasonable discussion and compromise among reasonable men") were causing concern in the State Department. All during Chamberlain's ministry, the Americans were uncertain where his discussions with *un*reasonable men would lead. Early in July, the Division of European Affairs submitted its own memorandum on the Spanish situation in which the British position was amply discussed.[42] Again, as in the earlier memorandum, an expression of suspicion is mixed with an appreciation of the harsh realities the British confronted. Above all else, the British were not prepared to fight a war, "and the Chamberlain government without any doubt will do everything in its power —even compromise—in order to avoid a drift toward overt hostilities." There was a concern over what Chamberlain's words of good will—"caution, patience, and restraint"—meant in terms of concrete action. The memorandum pointed out that "the City of London" was "predominantly in favor of an agreement with Franco, who seems to be on the winning side, in order to protect British investments and with a view to being 'in early' on any favors Franco grants." The British preferred Franco, but not under the control of the Germans and Italians. American officials could hardly neglect these developments: "Any action on our part, then, which may tend to accentuate the differences between the nations and forces engaged in the Spanish affair may have the effect of precipitating the English into a position where they will make broad concessions to the German-Italian-Franco group." So far as the policy-makers were concerned, the question of an embargo against Germany and Italy was closed—especially in combination with other anti-Fascist moves. Chamberlain's policy of appeasement posed an additional, and apparently an insuperable, obstacle to a change in policy toward the Spanish strife.

There were thus two developments during the first six months of 1937 which all but guaranteed continuation of the existing policy. The first, internal, was McReynolds' politically (if not legally) binding statement that the embargo resolution of January 8 was still in effect. This kept the "noninterventionist" basis of the Spanish policy ultimately under the control of Congress. The other, external, was the State Department's fear that a provocation of the Fascist nations would only lead to further appeasement by the British. A policy which seemed so "right" in August 1936, proved one year later to be "irrevocable."

6

EMBARGO: "UNCHANGEABLE" POLICY

I N MAY 1938, a year after the passage of the third Neutrality Act, the Spanish embargo policy came closer than it ever would to being reversed. On May 2, that "uncompromising isolationist," Gerald P. Nye, placed before the Senate a resolution calling for the repeal of the arms embargo on Spain. For a few critical days, a majority of the top-level officials in the State Department advised Secretary Hull not to stand in the way of congressional action. Had Hull accepted this advice, it is conceivable that the repeal resolution would have passed through Congress—although it is also possible that the dangers of a serious political fight on Capitol Hill would have killed the movement right there. Of additional importance was the fact that, since the initiative for this change was developing in Congress, the so-called "McReynolds dictum" of the year before was of no consequence. As for the fear that repeal of the embargo would lead to further appeasement by Great Britain, this attitude gave way momentarily to other considerations among most of the Department's important personnel. Significantly, Hull's attitude did not change.

It is far easier to explain the State Department's rejection of this repeal resolution than to explain the fairly widespread willingness to stand aside while Congress acted. It is clear, however, that within one faction of the Department there developed a frame of mind which might readily have lent itself to a sharp change in foreign policy. What it needed was a catalyst, and for a short time it appeared as though all that was required was congressional initiative. But there is no evidence that this group, whose most able spokesman was Assistant Secretary George Messersmith, was very enthusiastic about reversing the Spanish policy. Its real importance in the spring of 1938 was that it created within the Department an antiappeasement atmosphere. With respect to the other faction within the State Department, there developed much more suddenly another attitude which lent itself even more readily to a change in policy— and in this instance, specifically the Spanish embargo. This group—comprising Moore, Dunn, and Hackworth—simply collapsed under the crush of intense pro-Loyalist pressure and was willing to let Congress repeal the embargo in order to shift the burden of a controversial decision to other shoulders. In short, those who for a brief time were willing to let Congress alter the embargo policy did not act out of firm conviction. Rather their decision was characterized by an uneasy, uncomfortable defiance of a cautious past, of Chamberlain's appeasement policies, and of Fascist aggression.

The growing opposition toward appeasement policies was the more subtle of the two changes. Two developments between June 1937 and May 1938 helped to shape this new frame of mind. One was related to the policy adopted toward the Sino-Japanese conflict which broke early in July 1937. The other was the growing frustration the President and some of his advisors felt, due to their inability to turn the course of events toward peace. And this had very much to do with the feeling that Chamberlain's general policy of appeasement would have disastrous consequences and that the democracies must pursue a firmer course.

I

In terms of its impact on the Spanish strife, the Far Eastern policy was the more oblique of the two developments which helped to produce more aggressive attitudes. The link between the Far Eastern and Spanish policies was the changing opinion toward neutrality legislation among some congressional leaders. The conflict between China and Japan quickly caused complications in Washington, where a decision had to be made with regard to the application of the neutrality law.[1] The government decided to pursue a cautious policy of postponement. Because China was almost totally dependent upon foreign sources for war materials, it was believed that the enforcement of the "neutrality" provisions would indirectly aid the Japanese. The long accumulated reservoir of pro-Chinese sentiment in the United States, plus the fact of Japanese aggression, led to a domestic situation which the State Department had not experienced concerning the Spanish strife; for the American public was very strongly sympathetic toward one party in the Sino-Japanese war.[2] The failure to apply the neutrality law was, therefore, not unpopular. It was generally believed, although in the end difficult to prove, that the purchase of American war materials by the Chinese was of greater consequence than the purchase of American petroleum and scrap iron by the Japanese.

From the beginning of this conflict there were demands in some quarters for the enforcement of the neutrality law, but the general public's acquiescence to the government's continual postponement of such action weakened the position of those congressmen who were stalwart advocates of mandatory neutrality legislation. The President's stand was made somewhat easier by the fact that the war remained undeclared. The indirect result of this policy was to undermine the sanctity of neutrality legislation and help pave the way for revision or repeal. But the change in attitude was not wholesale. In the spring of 1938, it did not appear sufficient to cause a radical revision of neutrality legislation, although it did appear for a short while as though it might be sufficient to bring about the repeal of the Spanish embargo and thereby bring the policy toward the Spanish strife into harmony with the policy toward the Sino-Japanese conflict.

The second development—which manifested itself in the attempt to bring the United States out of isolation and toward more active involvement in the international arena—began midway through 1937. The President moved hesitantly and without measurable success. He was first of all frustrated in his attempt to have Chamberlain visit the United States as a symbolic gesture of solidarity between the two democracies. The Prime Minister refused on the ground that it would raise false hopes of an important agreement between the two governments. Hull, in August 1937, appears to have discarded the idea of a visit by Léon Blum for the same reason.[3] Two months later, in Chicago, the President made his first public move in his well-known "quarantine" speech. Although he forever remained publicly silent on the exact meaning of his words, he called for a "quarantine" of aggressors, a "concerted effort" among nations to restrain those few who were "creating a state of international anarchy and instability." Apparently dismayed by what was believed to be an antagonistic response, he immediately dropped whatever plans he may have had. And it does appear that he had in mind something more than the encouragement of an international consciousness in the American people, as has sometimes been claimed.[4]

In the same month of October, Sumner Welles, by this time Under Secretary, brought to the President a plan he had conceived for an international conference for peace. All during the Spanish civil war, rumors were widespread abroad that the President would indeed call for such a conference. Welles' plan was to have a White House meeting of diplomatic representatives on Armistice Day, on which occasion the President, without warning, would spring his plan for peace. It was to be founded upon three international agreements—one on principles of international conduct, another on disarmament, and a third aimed at achieving economic stability. Secretary Hull, shocked by its unrealistic hopes and its tactics of surprise, and dismayed by the welcome reception which the President accorded it, smothered Welles' proposal. The Secretary later wrote of his conviction that it would have resulted in even further appeasement, "probably under the leadership of our friend, Prime Minister Chamberlain."[5] The President dropped this particular plan but continued to harbor the idea of sponsoring an international gathering.

Early in January 1938, Welles once again presented a plan for a conference, this time incorporating some changes arising out of Hull's earlier objections. The most fundamental of these was that the British were to be confidentially probed for their views before anything was divulged. The inquiry was made and then this project, too, collapsed. Its only immediate result abroad was to encourage the resignation of Foreign Minister Eden, the one member of the British Cabinet who was turning away from appeasement. Chamberlain, hastily answering the President's inquiry as had been requested, failed to consult Eden (who was then in France). Chamberlain felt that such a conference would "excite the derision of Germany and Italy" and endanger British conversations with those governments. Eden was opposed to the conversations which Chamberlain was then planning with Italy and which concerned an Italian promise of gradual withdrawal of troops from Spain in exchange for recognition of Italy's Ethiopian empire. Shortly after finding out the Prime Minister's negative answer to Roosevelt, and his intention to proceed with the Italian conversations, Eden resigned.[6] As for the effect of Chamberlain's action upon Anglo-American relations, Lord Halifax later wrote that he was "satisfied" that it is not possible to "maintain the argument" that "the President felt resentment" at the rejection of his initiative.[7] But this is questionable. In answer to Chamberlain's first rejection and subsequent letter of clarification, the President sent a lengthy note drafted by the State Department. It mixed "understanding" with words of concern for the course of British diplomacy. It even suggested the adverse effects which appeasement in Europe would probably have upon the Far Eastern situation. Recognition of the Italian empire, for example, might fire the hopes of the Japanese on mainland Asia.[8] American concern over the British policy of "determined appeasement," a concern which was evident as early as June 1937, became more intense when it was feared that the policy would have repercussions in an area of more direct American interest.

Since the outbreak of war between China and Japan, the attention of American statesmen had been focused primarily upon the Far East. In March 1938, the Austrian situation broke open and attention turned toward new and ominous developments in Europe, as well as toward the struggle still raging on the Iberian peninsula. Following the Anschluss, it was feared that the Germans might next attempt to "absorb" Czechoslovakia and that general war would follow. Only a month later, the British concluded a pact with the Italians. In the words of Winston Churchill, the agreement was a "complete triumph for Mussolini, who gains our [British] cordial acceptance for his fortification of the Mediterranean against us, for his conquest of Abyssinia, and for his violence in Spain."[9]

France was meanwhile laboring through several internal crises, and the Government during March and April passed from Camille Chautemps, to Blum, and then to Daladier. On March 20, Bullitt reported that the French evidently proposed to England "the ending of the scandal of Non-Intervention," and that Chamberlain, rejecting the proposal, was "ready to break with France and to pin his faith on the good will of Germany and Italy."[10] Time and again French leaders expressed to Bullitt their lack of trust in the Chamberlain ministry. Then only two weeks after the Anglo-Italian accord, France and Britain concluded a military agreement. Even that was not entirely pleasing to the French, for the British refused to put teeth into it for fear of causing difficulties with Germany.

These continental developments in the late winter and spring of 1938 were interpreted in the State Department primarily as the results of appeasement. The rising dissatisfaction with the fruits of British policy led to a growing belief that a stronger course should be pursued. No one was more capable of presenting this case than George Messersmith, who had been brought home to Washington from Vienna in 1937. He was made Assistant Secretary when Moore was promoted to the recently re-created position of Counselor. Messersmith was an experienced and able diplomatist, very much admired for his detailed analyses of European affairs. The dominant theme of his interpretation at this time was that "a temporizing policy . . . will almost certainly bring war in the end." It is probable that Messersmith opposed the world conference plans of Welles on the ground that they would end, as Hull believed, in further appeasement, and also because of his conviction that according to Hitler "agreements are valid only as long as he believes they should be kept." In one memorandum he elaborated on this idea, arguing that "certain groups in England should have learned how utterly futile and fatal" is the idea that Germany will make lasting agreements "under present conditions."[11]

During the spring of 1938, Messersmith's pessimism—at least momentarily—turned to fatalism. On April 6, he wrote to his friend J. Flournoy Montgomery, then stationed in Budapest: "It looks to me . . . as though war in the end is inevitable and I am one of those who have felt that it would be better now than later. It is a horrible thing to think that we live in a world where war is still the only instrument with which one can meet certain situations, but when one is dealing with men drunk with power there is only one thing to oppose to them, that is superior power." Messersmith would argue at length on the dangers of Fascist expansion. In February 1938, he expressed his conviction in a memorandum that continual appeasement would lead to German control of the continent, followed by the disintegration of the British Empire, and an eventual threat to the United States through German and Italian penetration of South America. This memorandum, which analyzed the current situation and its probable results in some detail, was transmitted to the President.[12]

These dire prognostications did not constitute Messersmith's actual contribution to the changing attitudes in the State Department. Bullitt was writing that continued appeasement would result in German control of all central Europe. Joseph Davies, ambassador to Moscow, wrote that the democracies were taking a tremendous risk. And concern over Fascist influence in Latin America was very common. Furthermore, Messersmith, just as the others, seems to have failed to present a plan of action. His real contribution was the sense of immediacy which he brought to his analyses, for it was in stark contrast to the State Department's previous attitude of postponement. Messersmith argued that the democracies would do better to resist *now*, and this was the first time such thought had been given serious consideration in the State Department. Dodd and Bowers might well argue positions close to this one, but lacking Messersmith's cool temper, his professional training and experience, his grasp of details, and his logical exposition, their impressionistic reports were looked upon as those of amateurs. Messersmith was the most eloquent official spokesman for the rejection of "watchful waiting."[13]

How much influence Messersmith exerted upon Hull at this time is difficult to estimate, but Stanley Hornbeck—who occasionally held views akin to those of Messersmith—is known to have had some influence upon the Secretary. According to Moffat, Hornbeck convinced Hull early in 1938 that public opinion had swung around enough to support a more active foreign policy and that only minorities were vociferously isolationist. During this same period Hull purportedly worried some congressmen "by the intensity of his feeling that we must stand for the maintenance of law and order everywhere or international anarchy will engulf the entire world." That there was a rift developing within the State Department (and this was true to an extent within Congress, as well) is clear from Moffat's diaries. Moffat himself did not fit as neatly as did some others into what he called the "realist school," but he did oppose the assumption of a more active role by the United States. And as Anglophobic as he was, Moffat inclined toward the views of those who did not want to complicate current British policies. When Hugh Wilson departed for his new embassy post in Berlin, for example, Moffat lamented the loss of an ally by the "realists" in the Department and the corresponding strengthening of the "messianic school" of activists. When the pro-Chamberlain Joseph Kennedy attended a Departmental meeting at the end of January, Moffat reported that he came in "like a breath of fresh air." Kennedy apparently took up an argument with Hornbeck over the issue of isolationism.[14]

The so-called "realist school" outnumbered the so-called "messianic school"—at least in the upper echelons of the Department. Among top-level assistants, division chiefs, and important special advisors, the "messianic school" could not count even a scarce handful of advocates. But the strength of this minority during the early months of 1938 was not to be measured in numbers. The plain fact was that during this time they had greater influence upon both the President and the Secretary than did men like Moffat, Dunn, Hackworth, Moore, and Green. The problem faced by Messersmith and Hornbeck, who were occasionally joined by Welles and later by Adolf Berle, was that Roosevelt and Hull were inclined to be influenced in the last analysis by the views reported to them from the major European capitals. These embassy posts were firmly in the hands of the "realists"—with Kennedy in London, Bullitt in Paris, Phillips in Rome, and Wilson in Berlin. Joseph Davies in Moscow simply did not have much influence, nor had his views taken definite shape. As for Bowers, even those (like Messersmith) who sympathized with his views were not enthusiastic about him.

The activists still had much working in their favor despite

those difficulties. They had the President's sympathy, and at least Messersmith and Hornbeck had the Secretary's respect. Additionally, none of the "realists" in the Department was close to the President (as Welles was, for example). Finally, and most significantly, the course of events in Europe and the shifting attitudes of some congressmen toward neutrality legislation could be used to justify the views of the "messianic school" that appeasement was a failure and that isolationist attitudes were on the decline.

With the rise of this internationalist, anti-Fascist, anti-appeasement group, pro-Loyalist organizations became increasingly hopeful of a reversal of the Spanish policy. Yet it was easy for pro-Loyalist groups to misunderstand these developments, since even the "activists" in the Department did not view the Spanish crisis as the key to the deteriorating European situation, while pro-Loyalist groups generally argued that it was. Adopting an "active role" meant, to them, adopting an active role in Spain. As they would find out during the spring of 1938, however, the Spanish embargo policy was not of primary interest to the ardent opponents of appeasement in the State Department. Would the repeal of the Spanish embargo lead toward the repeal, or substantial modification, of general neutrality legislation? Would it stiffen the French and ultimately the British? Would it result in a Loyalist victory? Had the "activists" convinced themselves, and then Hull as well, that these questions could be answered in the affirmative, then the Department most probably would have labored for the repeal of the embargo during this period. But affirmative answers were not forthcoming. And the only change which really took place in the Department—and in the White House, too—was that it became more susceptible to pressures calling for new departures. Under certain conditions, even Moore and Moffat might be drawn over to a more aggressive policy: Moore, if Congress inclined in that direction; and Moffat, if his Anglophobia were fired up. These two possibilities were of the ponderable variety. What no one could predict, even as late as March 1938, was the enormity of the pressure which would shortly be exerted upon the Department by pro-Loyalists—and which would push Moore, Dunn, and Hackworth momentarily out of the pro-embargo camp.

II

For several reasons the initiative for a change in the policy toward the Spanish strife had to come from outside the State Department and the White House. In the first place, the executive branch did not have the unquestionable power to repeal the embargo. Second, the conviction was still prevalent in the Department that any significant policy changes could only come as rapidly as Congress willed them, for the key to American policy was the existence of neutrality legislation. Third, the President's popularity had been slipping steadily— along with the state of the American economy—since late 1937. Under these unhappy circumstances, to take the initiative on an explosive question, particularly during an election year, could be disastrous. Finally, in spite of the growing spirit of defiance against Fascism within the State Department, there continued to exist a reticence to challenge British leadership and a fear of setting in motion a series of events which would lead to a general European war. While the Department was more susceptible to pressures calling for change, it was not ready to part company with Congress, to ignore domestic political realities, or to take the initiative in Europe.

Pressures leading toward a reversal of the Spanish policy began to build up during the winter of 1938, even if in a fitful way. Late in January, sixty members of Congress sent their blessings for democracy to the Loyalist Cortes. Some of the congressmen quickly repudiated their signatures or explained them away after being pressured by a number of Catholic leaders—among the latter, the irate David I. Walsh, Democratic senator from Massachussetts.[15] This stir had hardly subsided when sixty prominent citizens sent a petition to the President, urging him to revise the Spanish policy. Among the signatures were those of former Secretary of State Henry L. Stimson and ex-Ambassador Dodd (who, having recently left the Berlin post, had returned to private life).[16] Letters from various pro-Loyalist organizations steadily arrived at the State Department, which dutifully responded with lengthy explanations of the Spanish policy—always mentioning in some way that the policy was actually in the hands of Congress.[17] One development which gave additional strength to the repeal movement was the Anglophobia which increasingly characterized it. The editors of *The Christian Century* accurately diagnosed it: "A year ago the blanket embargo was accepted in this country as a proper complement for the nonintervention policy promoted by Great Britain. Now, however, it is felt that Mr. Chamberlain has manipulated the nonintervention policy to make it in actuality a policy of intervention on Franco's behalf and that by adhering to its arms embargo the United States becomes a direct contributor to a fascist victory." Anglophobia affected official circles as well. After being told by Norman Davis that the British were convinced that within two years after a Franco victory the general would be "eating out of Britain's hands," Moffat recorded in his diary: "Methinks I have heard that kind of talk before." Observing British efforts to "form some agreement with Germany and Italy," Sam McReynolds concluded that this "should satisfy the people of this country that we have to go alone." Ambassador Daniels, viewing Britain's policy toward Franco, remarked that the philosophy of modern British rulers was "philanthropy and five per cent." But it was Senator Nye who expressed the attitude most vividly, when he said that he wanted to end "the policy of coming to heel like a well trained dog every time England whistles."[18]

Perhaps encouraged by the movement to repeal the Spanish embargo, the State Department, late in March, did an about-face and decided to test its strength in Congress on the issue of general neutrality legislation. The Department was at least spurred by a belief that Congress was sufficiently less committed to neutrality legislation that revision might be possible. As one commentator described what happened: "The Administration marched up Capitol Hill to reopen the neutrality issue, but it promptly marched down again to avoid fresh trouble."[19] During the same week, the State Department made public its response to a letter from Raymond Leslie Buell of the Foreign Policy Association. Buell argued that the President should lift the Spanish embargo. Secretary Hull gave his opinion (prepared in large part by Moore) that there had been "no change in the situation in Spain to warrant the President revoking his Proclamation of May 1, 1937. . . ." He added that even revoking that proclamation would leave in effect the congressional resolution of January 1937. Simultaneously, McReynolds announced that the House would not hold the hearings on neutrality legislation it had contemplated. A prorepealer, Congressman Melvin J. Maas of Minnesota, said that he was satisfied to drop the subject at that time "because of the state of world affairs."[20] For a while it thus appeared that all paths leading toward both neutrality revision and repeal of the Spanish embargo were blocked.

During March and April, as a victory by the Franco forces appeared more likely than ever, pro-Loyalist groups increased their pressure upon the President and the State Department. The most notable change in some of these pressure groups was the continual addition of prominent individuals who had acquaintance with government officials. On March 24, Breckinridge Long, former ambassador to Italy, went to the President, who sent him to see Hull. Long was then shunted to Moore, Dunn, and Moffat—none of whom could be expected to be very sympathetic to his views. During the last conversation, it turned out that Long had been consulted by the Spanish authorities. In other words, recorded Moffat, "he was really presenting a brief on their behalf." Long fully recognized that a political fight would result from the repeal of the embargo, but he was hoping that the Department could find "some way to wink at transshipments of military equipment." The four of them went "round and round" until the "realists" convinced Long that unless Congress took action nothing could be done which "would not be a violation of the law." Four days later, Donald R. Richberg (previously known as "the number one boy of the White House") brought a copy of a prorepeal memorandum to the President's son and private secretary, James Roosevelt. At the same time Richberg informed him that Long was going to present another copy to Hull either that day or the next. Along with the memorandum to Hull, there were galley proofs of an article by John C. DeWilde, entitled "The Struggle in Spain," which would appear in the next issue of *Foreign Policy Reports* (published by the Foreign Policy Association). One of the more revealing comments in this memorandum was that the repeal of the Spanish embargo "would harmonize the policy of the United States and place the neutrality of the United States toward Spain on the same basis as the neutrality of the United States toward China." Another point emphasized in the memorandum was necessary to a "proper" interpretation of DeWilde's article. The former concluded that a Franco victory would have dire effects in Latin America; DeWilde stressed that the British were making their calculations in accordance with a Franco victory and that a Franco Spain could possibly "remain essentially independent." On the face of it, DeWilde's article might have been interpreted as a good case for following British policy in Spain. But Richberg and Long, and perhaps Buell (who in his letter to Hull had earlier stressed the ill effects upon Latin America of a Franco victory), apparently believed that in conjunction with the attached memorandum DeWilde's article showed that the United States should break with British policy: dependent or independent, a Franco Spain would damage the cause of democracy in Latin America.[21]

One week later, on April 3, the counselor of the American embassy in Spain reported that he had been visited by Foreign Minister Alvarez del Vayo. Del Vayo said that the Spanish government had been told that both President Roosevelt and Secretary Hull were favorably disposed toward the abolition of the neutrality law, but that Hull was not acting because he felt the Spanish government's cause was "nearly lost." Del Vayo attempted to dispel any reasons for that notion. The counselor reported his own opinion, and that of the military attaché, that the Loyalists were in fact facing "virtually irresistible" Rebel advances. The repeal of the embargo would greatly strengthen the Loyalists and "might affect the outcome of the war," he added, but it would also be construed as an act of intervention by Germany, Italy, and Nationalist Spain. Should Franco then win, it might endanger American investments in Spain. On the same day that the Department received these opinions, the Spanish ambassador left a communication with Hull protesting the embargo. Hull subsequently telegraphed the American embassy in Spain that the repeal of the embargo was "not in prospect."[22] Only a few days before, however, Moore informed Congressman Jerry O'Connell that, contrary to some press reports, Hull had not said that he did not desire Congress to reconsider neutrality measures.[23] The way was thus apparently left open for congressional initiative. Whatever were Hull's real desires, Representative Byron Scott, who had worked closely with O'Connell, presented a resolution for the repeal of the Spanish embargo on April 5. Only the day before, Moffat recorded that "the organized pressure of the Left Wing surpasses belief." (On the other hand, business interests were also active—for a different reason. Representatives of the National Foreign Trade Council, for example, now renewed an earlier plea that Franco be recognized "while he will still be grateful" for it.)[24]

For the next three weeks, while the Anglo-Italian accord was being concluded and Mussolini was planning for Hitler's forthcoming visit to Rome, there is, surprisingly, no evidence that the Spanish issue was extensively debated in the State Department. On Capitol Hill, meanwhile, there was more and more agitation. On April 27, Marvin McIntyre, secretary to the President, informed Roosevelt of reports that Senator Pittman and others were disposed toward some action on the Spanish question. On May 2, the embargo wall began to crack. Senator Nye presented a resolution to repeal the arms embargo on Spain; the movement that began in the House spread to the upper chamber and was now led by the isolationists' most renowned senator. A good many people, within the government as well as outside it, quickly set about to test Senator Vandenberg's tart comment that Nye's resolution "was not worth the energy to take seriously."[25]

During the controversy wrought by the repeal resolution, some credence was attached to a report of administration support for the measure. It seems safe to say, however, that the administration only appeared to acquiesce in Senator Nye's initiative. What proved surprising was that the so-called "realists" prepared the way for genuine acquiescence. The Secretary of State, himself, stopped this movement. The confusion—with Moore at the center of it—arose out of a series of conferences on May 3. The Counselor first met at different times with Hackworth, Pittman, and Hull. In the early afternoon he was involved in further meetings—the one of greatest consequence being that attended by Dunn, Hackworth, and Green. At 3:30 Moore again visited the Secretary and this time informed him that he, Dunn, and Hackworth agreed that the Secretary, in response to an inquiry from Senator Pittman, could safely say that he found "no objection" to the Nye resolution. Moore added: "I do not think that we should feel any particular concern about the terms of the Resolution. . . ."[26]

There was no statesmanlike reason for this reversal by these advisors. All three were concerned about attacks being made against them in the liberal press. Moore was probably additionally influenced by the fact that Congress was taking the initiative. (With respect to Hackworth, it should be noted that in his capacity as legal advisor he could have no real official objection to the resolution.) But it was an article by Drew Pearson, in which the "career boys" were charged with blocking the repeal of the embargo, that set most of the Department on edge. Moffat, whose diary provides the only detailed account of this brief period, claimed that the story on which the article was based came "perilously close to a breach of confidence by Breck Long." Dunn, over the next few weeks, became a favorite target of pro-Loyalist pundits. Max Lerner sniped at him on one occasion, declaring that he was "a favorite of Hull, who found him arranging place cards as chief of protocol, and stepped him up until he became political adviser."[27] The ganging-up tactics applied by influential pro-Loyalists provide the best explanation for the "change of heart" by Moore, Dunn, and Hackworth.

Hull responded quite another way to this same pressure. (While he was not charged with "Fascist inclinations" as some of his subordinates were, he was nonetheless attacked as a captive of Chamberlain.) Returning to the Department from a vacation on the very day that Nye presented his resolution, Hull immediately decided that "he must make some sort of a statement outlining our policy throughout the crisis and defending his subordinates against the charges of radical leaders which in effect were charges that he could not keep order in his own house." Moffat was asked to find out the exact circumstances under which the resolution of January 1937 was passed, so that a statement could be prepared for Hull's scheduled press conference. Moffat, like Hull, had not been in Washington in January 1937; and discovering now that Green's and Hackworth's memories were "decidedly at variance," he advised Hull not to say anything about Spain until the facts were gathered.[28]

On May 4, the day after receiving the Moore-Dunn-Hackworth advice, Hull called his advisors to his office for what resulted in "a long conference." He had already delayed an

answer to Pittman, who wanted it in time for the Foreign
Relations Committee's meeting that same morning. Most of
Hull's advisors favored sending up an immediate response, neither approving nor disapproving of the repeal resolution, but
simply stating that if the embargo were lifted it ought to be
lifted for both sides—a gesture toward impartiality. (As Moffat so practically put it, "the pressure from the lobbyists pro
and con is gaining everyday.") But, once more with his characteristic attention to detail, Hull was determined "to mull over
the situation, talk about its origin, clarify his mind, et cetera."
Needing even more time, Hull telephoned Pittman to say that
he wanted "two or three days more to work out a reasoned
reply."[29]

At this point the course of events becomes somewhat
blurred, primarily because Senator Pittman's position at this
time is not adequately revealed. According to Moffat's account,
Pittman took Hull's desire for more time to mean that he was
trying to draft an explanation for a policy change. Such an
interpretation would have seemed reasonable, since Hull would
likely need more time to put together a careful statement of a
policy change than to draft a justification for a continuation
of policy. "At any rate," Moffat continued, Pittman "gave the
impression to newspaper people that the Administration was
behind the Nye Resolution and that it would pass overwhelm-
ingly." Yet Moffat reached his conclusion from the premise
that Pittman himself desired to repeal the embargo. If Pittman
were acting in a manner consistent with his behavior in the past,
it should rather have been concluded that he did not much care
what the Department decided as long as it would remove him
quickly and safely from the scaffold. Pittman complained that
political pressures were building up to a rare peak. If that was
the case, then he should have been the last person to tell a
newsman for publication that the administration was behind the
embargo when he was not absolutely sure of it. Furthermore,
William Stone, of the Foreign Policy Association, shortly afterward told Moffat that Pittman should be absolved from "dou-
ble-dealing" charges, although Stone had not been able to trace
the actual source of the sensational story which was first
printed in the *New York Times* on May 5.[30]

From the day he returned to the Department, Hull became
increasingly perturbed by what was happening. On May 4,

when he was better informed about what had taken place, he lit into Moore "for having said the State Department disinterested itself in whatever legislation Congress chose to pass." (For Moore, it was a discouraging day. He was also charged —again accurately—by Drew Pearson as the central figure behind the embargo resolution of January 1937. Generously pouring salt on this wound, Pearson concluded, "thus the whole map of Europe may have been changed by the ambitions of one old man.") During that day's conference, the Secretary clearly rejected the majority opinion of his advisors.[31] Instead of "giving in" to pro-Loyalist pressure, Hull decided to defend his subordinates publicly from press attacks and to draft a statement disapproving of the Nye resolution. A vigorous defense by the Secretary was apparently all that the defectors from "realism" needed, for they fell back into line.

When, on May 5, the *New York Times* erroneously reported that the administration had "thrown its support" behind the Nye resolution, the story was not too difficult to believe; first, because the President's sympathies for the Loyalist cause were well known; and second, because Hull's desire to have Fascist aggression stopped in Spain was too often placed in a misleading context. In reality Hull simply would not move the United States in that direction unless France and Britain did so first (in that event, somewhat ironically, American arms might not have been needed by the Spanish government). The Secretary of State's attitude toward this matter should by this time have been clear, even by implication, but the *Times* article expressed no awareness of it. It reported uncritically, but still understandably, from another point of view. As a reason for the purported policy change, it cited the embarrassment caused by different policies toward the Sino-Japanese conflict and the Spanish strife. The administration, the article continued, had recently failed in its indirect attempts to have the neutrality law modified or repealed. The "opposition in Congress . . . has subsided in the face of the developing Spanish situation, so that the Administration is encouraged to try again." A canvass of the Senate showed that a "majority will vote for the Nye resolution with the Administration supporting it. Furthermore, House leaders have sent word that they can obtain approval for any measure passed by the Senate." The article concluded that the embargo would probably be lifted against both parties (as opposed to the original intention to lift it only with respect to the government) and that cash-and-carry provisions would be invoked (to prevent American involvement should ships carrying war materials to one side be sunk by the other).[32]

From Hull's point of view, matters were now far out of hand. He had to contend with the results of Moore's irresponsible comment about the Department's lack of interest in neutrality legislation, the rapidly increasing attacks against Dunn, Moore, Hackworth, Green, and Moffat (alleging that they were "harbouring secret pro-Nazi leanings"), and now a sensational front-page article misrepresenting the official position of the Department. Making matters more difficult, the President had departed on a West Indian cruise on April 30, leaving the State Department (which was then not even tended by Hull) to face the coming crisis. At a press conference on May 6, the Secretary demonstrated just how testy he had become. He "blew up" and "had a passage at arms with Drew Pearson that those present will not soon forget." His anger did not easily subside, for he took the unprecedented step of authorizing for publication the whole stenographic transcript of the conference.[33] Having accomplished one of his goals—that of publicly defending his subordinates from attacks by the pro-Loyalist press—Hull began to turn the tide of rumors about a change in the Spanish policy. The United States had "enough to do," he said, "to look out for more immediate interests and affairs than to be watching opportunities to get into a situation fraught with danger. . . ." The same rumors were passing away on Capitol Hill, only a bit more gradually. There was increasing concern among politicians over the probable effects a debate on the embargo would have upon the upcoming congressional primary elections and those later in November; particularly worried were the Democrats, who already faced the prospect of substantial Republican gains. (This concern later proved justifiable: Bernard, Biermann, Boileau, Kopplemann, Maverick, O'Connell, and Scott—all very readily identifiable left-wing pro-Loyalists —were defeated in 1938.) There was a fear that the growing indignation expressed by many Catholics at the possibility of repeal might become infectious. As a consequence the "prorepeal stand" of the administration had hardly been reported when there was information "from the Hill" that Nye's resolution would never reach the Senate floor. On the very day Hull grappled with Pearson, it was learned that the prospect of a filibuster could prevent Nye's proposal from being debated.[34] Moreover, events abroad confused the Spanish issue for both the State Department and election-minded congressmen.

III

On May 3, Hitler arrived in Rome, and while welcomed by a massive demonstration organized by the Italian government, he was treated with scorn by the Pope. The Vatican went so far as to close its museums during the Fuehrer's stay in the Italian capital. At the same time, although known only in diplomatic circles until several days later, the Vatican was preparing to exchange representatives with the Franco government. (The exchange finally took place four days after the Roosevelt administration formally rejected the Nye resolution.) In London, meanwhile, Chamberlain stepped up his efforts at appeasement by extolling the "new vision" of modern Italy on the eve of Hitler's visit to Rome and by advising the Czechoslovakians to raise their proposals with the hope of satisfying German demands.[35]

Opinions in London and Paris regarding a repeal of the American arms embargo were of special interest to Hull, who wanted to be fully informed when the President returned to Washington. On May 5 and 6, he instructed Ambassadors Kennedy and Bullitt to question British and French officials regarding current plans, and prospects, of the Non-Intervention Committee. There had been rumors to the effect that the French would close the Spanish frontier entirely as soon as the NIC reached a proposed agreement concerning the withdrawal of foreign troops and the reestablishment of an international control scheme. Bullitt verified this on May 7; the French ambassador in Washington did likewise two days later. On May 10, however, Bowers reported that, since there were many technicalities to be worked out and since the required consent of the Spanish government could be withheld, the arrangement might never be concluded. A few hours before the arrival of Bowers' telegram, there was another one from Bullitt which indicated that Premier Daladier's attitude was stiffening. In defiance of Chamberlain's wishes, Daladier had "opened the French frontier as completely as possible." While it was not difficult to see that in all probability the proposed NIC arrangement would fail, it was difficult for the State Department to conclude anything definite about French attitudes from current French actions. On the one hand they were defying Chamberlain, on the other they were complying with his wish that the French attempt negotiations with Italy for the reconciliation of Franco-Italian grievances. On the more immediate issue of American arms shipments to Spain, there is no evidence that the French encouraged the repeal of the American embargo or discouraged it. The British were certain to disapprove of the Nye resolution, and when Kennedy reported to Secretary Hull on May 9, he closed with an opinion which reflected British attitudes: "With all its faults non-intervention has contributed towards the preservation of peace in Europe. . . . The injection of any new factor into this already overcharged and delicate situation, might have far-reaching consequences."[36]

Newsmen already reported that the NIC might discuss the Nye resolution and that in London, where the Committee met, the proposal was considered "another stone thrown into the troubled and leaky pond of non-intervention." In Geneva, where the League Council was preparing to meet, opinions were mixed. It was felt that the passage of the Nye resolution during the next week would "leave the British in a quandary that many league supporters would welcome." But the diplomatic importance of the sale of American arms to the Spanish government, it was believed, would depend upon the Loyalists' ability to get supplies in American ships. On May 11, Alvarez del Vayo, the Spanish representative to the League, successfully demanded continued discussion of his proposal to call an end to embargoes enacted against his government by League members. The Council decided to debate the matter further at its next meeting. This was considered an important step, for del Vayo "gained time for public opinion to react in London and Paris." More important, it gained time for public opinion to react in "a place that the British delegation fears most of all—Washington, where the Nye resolution, to do exactly what Senor Alvarez del Vayo asks the League to do, looms in Congress."[37]

That same day, in the House of Commons, Chamberlain was accused of trying to discourage the American government from lifting its embargo. The ambiguous wording of the accusa-

tion enabled Chamberlain to deny that there was "any foundation at all" for the charge levied against him. In truth, the
British Foreign Office appears to have done nothing more than
impress Ambassador Kennedy with its views, certainly a normal
diplomatic practice. The British acted more directly in Geneva
two days later when they led a reluctant League Council in the
rejection of the Spanish demands (the vote being four to two,
with nine abstentions). This was an unhappy time for the
Spanish Loyalists and those who sympathized with them; for
on the same day, Secretary Hull made public the decision not to
support the Nye proposal.[38]

It was reported in the press that the administration's
decision was reached after President Roosevelt's return to
Washington on Sunday, May 8. This was not exactly correct.
In fact it was only true to the extent that the President could
still have overruled his Secretary of State, as well as many of
the most prominent Democrats in Congress. On the day of his
return, the President declined to answer reporters' questions on
politics and diplomacy—specifically declining to do so with
regard to the Nye resolution. On Monday, Nye purportedly
claimed that the resolution "was as good as passed; that it
would be reported out of committee 4 to 1"; and that a roll call
vote could be blocked (to satisfy many senators who did not
want to have their votes recorded).[39] If Nye actually made such
claims, he was being far too optimistic. Sam Rayburn, in the
company of other congressmen, visited the White House that
same day. Rayburn afterward remarked that the neutrality
issue had been discussed "incidentally" and then offered a personal view: "I am opposed to taking up the question of amending the Neutrality Act now. It would be a funny thing if we
changed the Neutrality Law after a short operation." Although he evaded a direct reference to the Spanish embargo, his
meaning was clear. When McReynolds was asked for an opinion, he said that he had not seen the President about it, "but in
my opinion he will not ask for repeal of the act." Hull, after
conferring with the President, refused to comment. Actually the
Secretary already had his advisors working on a letter to Pittman opposing the repeal resolution. Pittman had just informed
Hull that only two senators, Nye and Borah, were now pressing

him. He also intimated that the Foreign Relations Committee would follow the President's lead. It would appear that Hull had only to sell his case to the President (who was presumably undecided, although Pittman believed very early that Roosevelt would not favor repeal). Upon his return from the White House, Hull ordered Dunn to prepare another revised draft of the letter to Pittman. It was then clear; Hull had won. The following morning, a *New York Times* editorial commented that "present indications are that the President will not yield to pressure to lift the embargo on the sale of arms to Spain." And with no little ambiguity, it concluded that "the Administration could hardly adopt a different attitude at this time, by lifting the embargo in advance of changing the law itself."[40]

On May 11, only eight days after Moore, Dunn, and Hackworth decided that there should be "no objection" to the repeal resolution, Secretary Hull forwarded to the President a draft of a negative reply to be sent to the Senate Foreign Relations Committee. It formally advised against lifting the Spanish embargo. The President gave his approval on the following day, and on May 13 the letter, addressed from Secretary Hull to Senator Pittman, was made public. The Foreign Relations Committee then tabled Nye's resolution indefinitely. One "influential member" of the Committee afterward privately said that "the Administration did not know its own mind on policy from day to day."[41]

In his letter to Pittman, Hull argued that even a repeal applicable to both sides "would still subject us to unnecessary risks we have so far avoided. We do not know what lies ahead in the Spanish situation. The original danger still exists." He then turned to the idea expressed to the State Department a few days earlier by Ambassador Kennedy: a reversal of policy would "at this juncture" offer a "real possibility of complications." "Our first solicitude," the Secretary continued, "should be the peace and welfare of this country," and the "real test" of the advisability of any changes should be whether they "would further tend to keep us from becoming involved directly or indirectly in a dangerous European situation." He concluded that any reconsideration of the neutrality law should be broadly based and not "in relation to a particular consideration." This led him to suggest that the matter be dropped during the closing days of that session of Congress and the problem of general neutrality legislation taken up at a later time.[42]

The press afterward continued its mistaken interpretation of what had happened inside the administration; yet there was a certain element of truth in a *New York Times* observation that the publication of "the fact" of administration support for the resolution "changed the fact." While this was misleading insofar as Hull never favored the Nye resolution, it was true that when Roosevelt returned to Washington he was impressed by "the storm"—and most likely he would have "directed a change of policy" had there been a change to be made. The "acrimonious controversy" did not play a role "in the final decision" exactly as was claimed, but it did help shape the manner in which Hull dealt with the problem. Finally, the administration and Congress certainly learned how explosive the issue was. Roosevelt, for example, may have confined himself to terms which Harold Ickes could best appreciate when he told him that members of Congress were "jittery" about the Catholic vote and that they wanted to drop the embargo issue; but there is no doubt of the accuracy of his remark.[43]

That there were other important considerations was evident in the manner in which the State Department dealt with the whole problem. The Moore-Dunn-Hackworth decision of May 3 was not calculated; there had been little, if any, preparation. British and French officials, for example, were not probed until days after this first "decision"; yet it was necessary for the Department to know if the French were willing to keep their frontier open for the passage of arms to the Spanish government, and also what plans were under way in the NIC. The announcement that the administration was supporting the repeal of the embargo was said to have taken Europe by surprise;[44] and it certainly would have been an aberration. Most of Hull's advisors, in this sense, appeared to be on a lark; for they decided upon a course for which they had made no plans. As press reports indicated, days before the President's return, there was some discomfort in the State Department over what had been done—or almost done.

With respect to the "activist" group among the policymakers, that sense of frustration and impatience, that nagging desire to pursue a stronger course in order to curb Fascist advances, had developed over the period of a year. But, significantly, there is no evidence that this group desired to initiate a firmer policy in Spain.[45] And the few advisers who momentarily left the "realist" camp early in May were clearly not interested themselves in pursuing such a course. They were interested primarily in escaping the bitter attacks by influential pro-Loyalists. It was the Secretary who put an end to this stand-aside, "prorepeal" sentiment within the Department. And there was obviously more than one reason why Hull blocked the Nye resolution. One cannot avoid the impression that he could get his back up if pressure groups pushed him too vigorously. He is also known to have objected to what he interpreted as another attempt by Congress "to take over the power of the executive" to make and to change policy.[46] But at the core of his objection to the repeal resolution was a firm belief that it could result in a European explosion. It must not be forgotten that even those who (like Hull) believed that ultimately Britain would have to side with France in the event of war, at the same time feared that Britain might well get into it too late. Any action which might embolden France to pursue a firm anti-Fascist policy in Spain, without concurrently pushing the British in the same direction, could be an invitation to disaster.

Still, had the European situation at that time not been so terrifyingly complex, Hull might well have been attracted to that course of action Nye and others were trying to achieve in Congress. The complications were so great that the prospects of bringing about favorable results by aiding the Loyalists were perhaps less than they ever had been. This was due partly, and paradoxically, to the fact that the Spanish situation of itself constituted a relatively less serious threat to world peace than it had for many months. If for a moment in May 1938, a few men in the State Department were willing to adopt a policy entailing some risk, that risk would have concerned Czechoslovakia more than Spain. For almost a year the State Department had been concerned about how far the British would pursue appeasement. On the evening of the very day when Moore presented Hull with the "no objection" memorandum, the Department learned that Chamberlain (and Georges Bonnet, the French Foreign Minister) was willing to go to great lengths to appease Hitler in Czechoslovakia. While the French were bound to the Czechs by a military alliance, they had shown themselves unwilling to move without the British alongside. On May 5, it was found, moreover, that the so-called Anglo-French military alliance constituted little more than staff conversations (contrary to claims made in sensational press reports). It was also learned that the French were being rebuffed in their desire to have the agreement made more extensive and more binding. The British feared the dire effects that a stronger military commitment would have upon German willingness to enter into "a general understanding with the other great powers."[47] What would happen should the United States counter the Fascist powers in Spain? How far would the British then go in their appeasement of Germany? And would Hitler seize the opportunity to follow through with his Czechoslovakian designs? Even in 1937, considerations of the same kind had led Hull and his subordinates to advise against applying the neutrality statutes against the Fascist powers. Matters had not been as delicate then, either. It was now, even more than before, a question of what the British—and then the Germans and the Italians—might do should the United States take an "unneutral" stand in Spain.

There was one possible way in which American aid to the Loyalists in 1938 could have resulted in success. It would have to stiffen at the same time the attitudes of both the British and the French against Fascist advances. There was certainly no evidence that the British were about to stiffen, nor was it likely that the French would give up whatever weak ties they had with the British in order to align their Spanish policy with a new one initiated by the Americans. For almost twenty years the French and British knew the Americans to be unsteady and unwilling participants in European affairs.

Cordell Hull was not begging the question when he expressed his fear of European complications arising out of American aid to the Spanish government. Even if American assistance could conceivably have provided the psychological uplift and, over a period of time, the required war materials to bring about a Loyalist victory, such a policy was not the way to prevent general war, nor even the way to postpone war (which is what the British and French believed they needed, at the very least). Hull was simply not prepared to take any action that might hasten appeasement or the coming of war, particularly for a cause which was so uncertain. The argument, like the one propounded by Messersmith, that the Fascist leaders must be opposed "now" with superior power was rejected. Neither the French nor the British believed that together they had the superior power with which to oppose Germany and Italy, and Hull was not about to reject their self-assessments. Further, as soon as the Russians were figured into a balance of power calculation (and Washington, Paris, and London hardly felt secure about doing this), so was Japan. As for the United States, there were no assurances of support that Hull could really give the British and French. Given the state of American public opinion in 1938, toward both European affairs and the New Deal, no meaningful, decisive promise from Hull or from Roosevelt would have been credible. If some Americans were concerned that, in the event of a general war, Britain would come to the aid of France too late, the British feared that American assistance might arrive too late. As long as the complications of the Spanish strife were tangled up with the possibility of a larger conflict, and as long as the democratic powers were not able to combine openly and with mutual trust, Germany and Italy would wield an effective (even if unwarranted) preponderance of power on the Iberian peninsula.

7

THE GOOD NEIGHBOR

ONE OF THE MOST complicated diplomatic problems created
by the Spanish civil war was the threat it posed to the Good
Neighbor policy. The conflict accented and aggravated the
divisions among American nations and within them as well.
Since the Good Neighbor policy constituted the Roosevelt administration's only successful foreign policy, Washington was
thus faced with the prospect of failure all around.

The threat presented by the Spanish strife was particularly
worrisome because it struck at the very foundation of the
United States' hemispheric policy—the ideas of "continental
isolationism" and "hemispheric solidarity." These were out-
growths of the "doctrine of the two spheres"—Old World and
New World—which, more than a century before, found expression in the Monroe Doctrine. During the 1930's, the prospect of
a European war and of Fascist cultural and economic penetration of Latin America brought about a resurgence in Washington of the two spheres idea. It was thought necessary to bring
solidarity to the hemisphere, and this was the task the Roosevelt administration set for itself.

It was not easy to break down the suspicion and distrust,
built up over decades, which Latin Americans felt toward the
United States. It took a good deal of convincing to bring many
Latin American leaders around to the belief that they had
common interests with the giant to the North. It was clear at

the time that the success of the Good Neighbor policy was only relative to the current failure of the democratic states to deal with the European and Asian crises and that, in fact, the limited achievements won in the Western hemisphere were largely due to the frightening developments abroad.[1] Many Latin American leaders were willing to see what the Roosevelt administration would and could do to insulate them from the unhappy course of events in Europe. The Good Neighbor policy was thus born out of and nourished by failures of the Old World. But the two spheres doctrine was still more idea than substance. The Latin American nations to varying degrees had strong ties with the Old World. And, culturally, this was especially true in regard to Spain, the mother of eighteen American nations. Many Latin Americans followed the Spanish strife with passionate involvement; and a growing desire among them to aid one side or the other in Spain menaced the Good Neighbor policy. It threatened to put Latin American governments at odds with each other. It threatened to involve the New World in the Old World. And, for these reasons, it created a delicate diplomatic situation for the State Department.

The persistence with which Secretary Hull pursued hemispheric solidarity contributed to Washington's steadfast refusal to aid the Spanish Loyalists. This was important not only of itself, but also because of the fact that Ambassador Bowers was ignorant of the State Department's appraisal of the Latin American situation. The Secretary's failure to inform Ambassador Bowers of the full reasons for American policy added to a growing misunderstanding between the two men which has since warped the history of the American policy toward Spain.

I

Cordell Hull, later writing of the Buenos Aires conference of 1936, said that "the Spanish Government would liked to have seen some Pan-American declaration of sympathy for its cause and some measure of assistance." One of the primary objectives of the Buenos Aires conference, he continued, "was to keep away from the Western Hemisphere the wars in which the European nations were involved, and the greater war toward which they appeared inevitably to be heading. This was in direct conflict with the desire of the Spanish Government to see the New World intervene in the affairs of the Old."[2]

In the new sense of the term suggested by the existence of the Non-Intervention Committee, some Latin American nations acted "unneutrally" toward the Spanish strife. Only a few of them, however, overtly expressed such commitments. Others sustained their "neutrality" with difficulty. Costa Rica, for example, refused to recognize either of the Spanish regimes. Colombia, under the anti-Fascist and progressive leadership of Dr. Alfonso López, pursued a nonintervention policy in the manner of the United States, although the Chamber of Representatives did send greetings of "fervent solidarity" to the Loyalist Cortes. The most boldly partisan nation, although legally neutral in the traditional sense of the word, was Mexico. The Mexicans sent war materials to the Spanish government for the duration of the conflict.[3]

The policies of most of the remaining Latin American nations were influenced by internal political developments. This was a period of "benevolent" strong men—with great variations both in benevolence and in strength. Many of the reforms inaugurated at this time were done in the spirit of necessity, for otherwise the dictator or ruling clique was in danger of losing his or its hold upon the people. In numerous countries this resulted in Fascist-like regimes in which the causes of the old conservative groups were united with some reforms, and occasional pageantry, to meet the demands of the masses. There was a foreign Fascist character to some of these governments, sometimes overt, sometimes not. In most cases the quasi-Fascist quality was more truly a native product, created without conscious imitation of European models. This generalization, while it does injustice to the distinctions among more than a dozen nations, reveals three facts. The Pan American system was not composed of democratic states (indeed, Secretary Hull certainly did not think that international organizations should be restricted to democratic states). Next, there was both open and concealed admiration for Hitler and Mussolini among many influential Latin Americans. And finally, a good deal of sympathy with the cause of General Franco had to be expected. Even where there was a horror of and fear of Nazism, there was that familiar distinction—most common among Roman Catholics—between Hitler on the one side and Franco (and sometimes

Mussolini) on the other. (The distinction was hardly unwarranted; but it was often used to obscure vital issues.) For these reasons, there were several governments whom Washington might very easily offend by pursuing a pro-Loyalist policy. United States aid to the Spanish government could have destroyed the Good Neighbor structure which was so laboriously being erected.

During 1936 alone, three Central American nations—El Salvador, Guatemala, and Nicaragua—recognized the Franco government.[4] The most notable problems in respect to pro-Franco sympathies, however, were naturally presented by the larger, more influential nations. The Argentines posed a particularly difficult problem, for they had long aspired to lead the southern hemisphere. In this respect they sometimes took advantage of the conditions brought about by the Spanish strife. It appeared in the 1930's that the Argentines had in Carlos Saavedra Lamas a foreign minister who was at least capable of *obstructing* North American leadership in the southern hemisphere. Secretary Hull did, in fact, find himself frustrated on strictly hemispheric matters at the Buenos Aires conference by the independence of Saavadra Lamas. The Argentine Foreign Minister was at the time riding the crest of international acclaim, being the President of the League Council and recently the recipient of the Nobel Peace Prize.

At the Buenos Aires conference, both the American and the Argentine government believed it would be unwise to do anything during the meeting that might constitute intervention in the Spanish civil war.[5] But this was one of only a few occasions when the two governments agreed on the Spanish issue. Before this time, there had been some differences of opinion over the actions of the Argentine ambassador to Spain, who was the dean of the diplomatic corps in the Spanish capital. On one occasion the ambassador called the corps together for the purpose of arranging an exchange of prisoners; and because of the relative importance of these prisoners to each side, the exchange would have been favorable to the insurgents. On a second occasion, the ambassador wanted to call the diplomatic corps together to consider the problem of the less-than-humane conduct of the war. Representatives of both Spanish factions were to participate—an arrangement which would have been tantamount to according Franco equal status with the Spanish government. The United States refused to participate in either scheme and thus contributed to the failure of both.[6] A third incident reflected more directly the hemispheric battle between the United States and Argentina. The Argentines had been declaring the unlimited right of asylum for anti-Loyalist Spaniards taking refuge in its embassy. Some other Latin American nations took the same position. (It was reported, for example, that Chile had some 1,300 "guests" at one time under the protection of its embassy.) The Argentines attempted to rally all other Latin American governments to make a joint representation to the Spanish government concerning the rights of asylum and protected evacuation for Spaniards unsympathetic to the Loyalist cause. For this purpose, they called a meeting in Buenos Aires in October 1936, but again the United States refused to attend, and again the project collapsed.[7]

The policies of the American states toward the Spanish strife were often characterized by indirection. The Uruguayan government, at that time under the repressive regime of Gabriel Terra, attempted to bring about the widespread recognition of Rebel belligerency—outwardly by the most honorable means. On August 17, exactly one month after the outbreak of the conflict, the Uruguayans proposed to all Pan American nations an attempt to conciliate the Spanish strife. Had this been tried, it would have resulted in the virtual recognition of Rebel belligerency—and there was no hope of successful mediation. Eleven Latin American governments accepted the proposal without reservation. The United States, Argentina, Brazil, and Panama rejected it. The Uruguayan government later announced that the proposal had been "postponed." Shortly afterward, the Uruguayans withdrew their representative from Loyalist Spain.[8]

A year later, the Uruguayans, turning to more direct means, proposed to other American states the joint recognition of insurgent belligerency.[9] This received the qualified endorsement of Venezuela, but was rejected directly or indirectly by the other American nations. Saavedra Lamas was reported to be "seriously annoyed" by the proposal, possibly because, as Chile argued, it would "hinder the work of the League of Nations" (which was cooperating, under the lead of the Argentine Foreign Minister, with the Non-Intervention Committee). In this case, several American nations had waited upon Secretary Hull's response to the Uruguayan government before they acted themselves. The anticipation of United States leadership in this instance was enough to upset the Italian embassy in Washington. A representative of the embassy told Harold Tittman of the European Division that Uruguay should not have included the United States in the circular demarche; for, having no historic ties with Spain, the North Americans did not "have the feel" of the Spanish situation.[10] While the State Department did not offend its pro-Franco neighbors in Central and South America, it did exert some influence against fuller diplomatic expression of their sentiments.

Throughout the Spanish strife, the United States, even with its policy of strict nonintervention in Spain, found itself at cross purposes with the governments of other Latin American nations. Chile tried in vain to obtain United States support for a complaint against the Spanish government concerning rights of asylum. Paraguay reportedly shipped a few arms to Rebel Spain through Buenos Aires, an act which might have been part of a Paraguayan arrangement with the Italians for the purchase of aircraft and the training of pilots. Brazil, under the opportunistic Getulio Vargas, courted (and was courted by) the Italians and the Germans, despite Nazi involvement in a 1938 revolt against the government. Cuba, in October 1937, raised the issue once more of mediation by the American nations, and only six governments (the United States included) refused to support it because of their policies of nonintervention. In April 1938, shortly after Congressman Byron Scott presented his resolution for repeal of the United States arms embargo on Spain, the Brazilian Foreign Minister, Oswaldo Aranha, proposed that the American states pursue a common policy toward the Spanish war—clearly this was not intended to bring about pro-Loyalist policies in the Western hemisphere. Upon the objection of Jefferson Caffery, the American ambassador in Rio de Janeiro, the United States, Brazil, Chile, Peru, and Argentina merely agreed to "maintain contact to follow war developments." As Caffery reported to the State Department, he was given the obvious hint that the United States should inform the others "whenever any change of policy is impending."[11]

II

Secretary Hull, while attending the Buenos Aires conference in December 1936, described the situation as it would remain throughout the war: "Sentiment in Latin America regarding the Spanish situation is highly combustible." Partly for this reason, the State Department was scrupulously "neutral" in the way it associated itself with events in Europe. The particular incident which prompted Hull's remark above was the Anglo-French demarche of early December 1936, calling for measures leading toward mediation. Hull instructed the State Department only to express its humanitarian concern for the Spanish tragedy, and Acting Secretary Moore subsequently did this—at the same time avoiding references to specific proposals.[12]

Time and again the Roosevelt administration refused to involve itself in plans for conciliation of the Spanish strife, some suggesting that President Roosevelt and Pope Pius XI mediate the conflict, and others (from outside the hemisphere as well as from within) suggesting that the United States and other American nations offer mediation.[13] The explosive character of the issue, the apparent impossibility of successful mediation, and the potentially destructive costs of failure dampened any enthusiasm for this course of action. But in November 1938 Washington reversed its policy. It not only was willing to participate in a Pan-American–sponsored mediation attempt, it was ready to encourage such a move.

During the fall of 1938, President Roosevelt was more than ever frustrated in his hope that something would be done to turn the course of events. With the Munich agreement at the end of September, the President felt a greater sense of urgency about Fascist expansion. In Spain, meanwhile, the victory of Franco was certain if the Loyalists failed to receive arms and food to survive the winter. Plans were laid in the United States and elsewhere to help combat the problem of starvation among Spanish civilians.[14] At the same time, within the State Department a plan was conceived—at the instigation of the President —which allowed for the possibility of easing the Loyalists' second problem, the purchase of war materials. It was first of all, however, a plan for mediation. As recorded in a memorandum by the new Assistant Secretary, Berle, an offer of mediation would be made during the Lima conference the following month. The Loyalists, facing defeat, could not afford to refuse it. Franco, on the other hand, would certainly not welcome it; but, if he did, well and good. If he did not, the United States might claim a "moral right" to sell arms to the Loyalists, who had been refused mediation by the Rebels. It appears that Hull at least approved of the offer of mediation. Whether he thought well of the alternative is not known, but it can certainly be doubted. That the White House and the State Department were serious in the attempt to bring about mediation and were not simply looking beyond it with the idea of aiding the Loyalists, would seem to be indicated by the adoption of two tactics intended to help guarantee the success of mediation. It was first decided to maintain as much secrecy as was necessary. Second, the State Department wanted to make sure of the support of the Vatican; this might of course act as an inducement to otherwise reluctant American governments which looked with favor upon Franco's approaching victory. The first tactic failed. The execution of the second one is impossible to document (Cardinal Mundelein was, however, visiting the Vatican during the time the administration was laying its plans and would have made an excellent intermediary).[15]

It was apparently thought that a unanimous act by the American nations, proffering mediation, might compel the Rebel government to accept the offer. There was some strength to this argument, although less than was probably believed in some quarters of the State Department. Hopes were predicated in part upon the idea that Franco was encountering more serious difficulties behind his lines than was the case during November and December. But it was still true that if unanimous Pan American support for mediation were mobilized before Franco grasped the intention, he would find it very awkward to refuse the offer. The real points of weakness in these mediation plans were: first, that Franco would most probably learn very soon what was happening and be able to state his opposition to mediation before it was offered; and, second, as Messersmith pointed out, that it was "almost impossible to get 21 governments to act as a unit"—especially when so many were already pro-Franco.[16] The Rebel government did not want to face a *fait accompli,* but it did not appear likely that it would have to confront one.

Whatever chances of success there were in this project, it was not helped along by the British or the French. The source of the problem was that the State Department did not maintain sufficient secrecy. The very day on which the Lima conference opened, the Havas Bureau in London announced that "the British Government has been advised by the Government in Washington that the American Delegation in Lima is going to propose that the Conference offer mediation of the Spanish conflict." Sumner Welles, the next day, telegraphed Hull in Lima, informing him of this news release; and with obvious concern over the leakage, Welles indicated that the subject had been broached to the British ambassador for his personal reaction before his recent departure for London. Welles reported that the ambassador had at the time "personally believed his Government would be enthusiastically favorable to such a step." If in fact the British did leak the story to the press, then they were most likely not in favor of mediation. A few days later, Welles warned the French ambassador in Washington that any publicity given to the fact that the French would favor mediation by the American nations would in all probability destroy the movement in its infancy; for Franco would announce beforehand that mediation was unacceptable. Joseph Paul Boncour, at the time French "cultural agent" in Latin America, went to Lima and for better or worse pressed the idea of mediation upon all the delegations—many of which were anything but favorable to the Popular Front in France or in Spain. By this time, the conference was nine days old, and despite these problems there still remained a "definite disposition to take some action on the part of many delegations." Then, two days later, Hull reported the movement virtually dead. The consensus within the committee on initiatives "was that nothing could be done as matters now stood though the matter was held open pending possible developments during the week. It was definitely determined not to open the matter for debate at least for the time being. Since such debate would probably emphasize the differences of opinion in the hemisphere this seems wholly advisable."[17] That marked the end of inter-American plans for mediation of the Spanish civil war.

III

Many aspects of the Good Neighbor policy disturbed the liberal conscience in the United States. This conscience found continuous expression in the dispatches of Ambassadors Dodd and Bowers. While they were proud of the self-denying principles of the Good Neighbor policy and complimented the efforts made by the State Department to bring about hemispheric solidarity, they believed that this "liberal" policy was making the United States party to the stabilization of numerous military dictatorships and other undesirable governments. Time and again Dodd would write that in Berlin many of the Latin American ambassadors seemed "to wish Europe to go Nazi or Fascist." At the same time, Dodd wrote, "they speak highly of the present policy of the United States" toward Latin America. Despite Dodd's readiness to label conservatives as "Fascists" or "Nazis," there was truth to his observation about the attitudes of Latin American envoys. On one occasion, President Roosevelt attempted rather feebly to dispel Dodd's concern by telling him of the crowds that hailed his arrival at Buenos Aires in December 1936: "The great shout as I passed was 'viva la democracia.' Those people down there were for me for the simple reason that they believe I have made democracy work . . . and that as a system of government it is, therefore, to be preferred to Fascism or Communism." Dodd, Jeffersonian that he was, believed that the people would prefer democracy given the encouragement and opportunity to bring it about. The problem was how the United States could help accomplish that. To men like Dodd and Bowers, an answer lay in the challenge presented by the Spanish crisis. The United States should aid the Spanish government and thereby give strength to liberal elements in Latin America. Bowers wrote the President that Spain was the testing ground for South America.[18]

It must be made clear that neither Dodd nor Bowers, before 1938, advised that the United States send aid to the Loyalists. Before that time their personal preferences were clear, but Bowers for one did not think that such a policy was possible in light of the strong isolationism of the American people. In

1938, Dodd returned to private life, and "advised" the government simply as a private citizen. Bowers meanwhile never left his post, and for most of the year stressed the dangers of a Franco victory in respect to the future of Fascism in Latin America. He was convinced that if democracy triumphed in Spain, Fascist movements in South America would be discouraged. Three days before the opening of the Lima Conference, he once more spelled out his position. He had no doubts that the Fascists and Nazis intended to use a Franco Spain as a spearhead against the United States' position in Latin America. And he expressed his conviction that American interests were patently on the Loyalist side.[19]

Bowers' position is of particular importance because it is out of his later testimony and Hull's memoirs that the historical debate over American policy toward Spain has largely evolved. Neither the ambassador's nor the Secretary's later accounts did much to clarify the issues behind their differences of opinion. Hull, as he wrote in his memoirs, believed that Bowers' views were narrowly conceived, that he did not appreciate all the complications caused by the Spanish situation. No doubt Hull was correct. But Hull never genuinely attempted to broaden the ambassador's perspective. It was no use complaining that Bowers failed to appreciate the full complexity of the problem, in regard to Latin America as well as to Europe. It would have been much more useful to call Bowers home to brief him on the entire situation.[20]

The Secretary of State, while accepting Bowers' description of the possible Latin American consequences of a Franco victory, just as clearly rejected his proposed solution of aiding the Loyalists. Reasons for this lay outside the Western hemisphere as well as within it. Latin America aside, the State Department had other reasons for maintaining its Spanish policy: the desire not to complicate matters for the French and the British, the complexities arising out of British appeasement, the fear of spreading the Spanish conflict, the strength of the isolationists, and the prospect of causing a "holy war" in the United States, all argued against American aid to the Spanish government.

Within the hemisphere, there were other reasons for not aiding the Loyalists. The Spanish issue was highly controversial. It threatened hemispheric solidarity. In addition to the split between nations, there were too many pro-Franco regimes opposed internally by liberals and radicals who favored the Loyalists. A pro-Loyalist policy in the United States would not only worsen the ideological rift between Washington and more than a dozen Latin American governments, but it would also give strength to disruptive forces within those countries. Neither of these results could do anything but damage the Good Neighbor policy. Washington did not want to upset the trend toward stability in the American nations, whether led by the left or the right.

The internal stability of American nations was as much a strategic necessity to Washington at that time as was hemispheric solidarity. Some Latin American leaders had to be convinced that their regimes did not hang upon the successes of Hitler and Mussolini in Europe. In order to accomplish this, the State Department first had to convince them that their regimes were not threatened by the opposition of the United States—a situation that would be seized upon by liberals and radicals all over Latin America. If these leaders with pro-Fascist inclinations were left unconvinced by the United States, they might, during a world war, feel compelled to aid Germany and Italy. The State Department further sought to urge the wisdom of American nations sticking together for their mutual survival; and more, of strategic importance, Washington campaigned for Latin American trade. In addition to these practical considerations, there was the idealism of Secretary Hull, and many others in the State Department, who entertained the hope of having international peace and order sustained by nations who could cooperate on essential matters despite antagonistic political ideologies. The Secretary always intended the Good Neighbor policy to be a model for international cooperation.

In the State Department, it was clearly understood that this line of reasoning, which tied up the Good Neighbor policy with a policy of noninvolvement in Spain, was not altogether compelling. In fact, the Department was plainly concerned that a Franco victory could drive a wedge into Latin America which the Germans and Italians might well use to their advantage. The issue was put clearly in a major memorandum: whether or not the Fascist states hope to achieve a "permanent foothold" in the Western hemisphere, it is most probably at least their aim "to acquire sufficient sympathy to ensure in the case of a

European war the benevolent neutrality of these Republics, and a consequent restriction in exports of essential raw materials to the probable enemies of the totalitarian states." It was also feared that if European-style Fascism took hold in one Latin American country, it might spread to others "like a disease" and "might easily break up Pan American unity."[21] The Department obviously appreciated Bowers' point of view on this whole issue. But the idea of pursuing a policy predicated upon these tragic possibilities was rejected. Quite predictably, Hull instead determined to continue his discreet, unsensational approach to inter-American affairs. Perhaps this was because he, and others like Welles, already had so much invested in the Good Neighbor policy and, too, because their achievements had come about through methods Hull now chose to continue. But it is likely that Hull simply refused to gamble it all by choosing a course of action certain to cause a crisis in hemispheric relations.

Secretary Hull consistently drew different conclusions from the evidence Bowers presented. On the evidence itself there was substantial agreement, although they did disagree on the extent to which the Spanish Loyalists stood for democracy. On this matter Bowers was plainly too sanguine. The common opinion that Bowers was naive partly explains the lack of respect with which his dispatches were treated—even by Sumner Welles, who during World War II stated his belief that the Spanish policy had been a mistake.[22] As for the prevailing opinion in the State Department that a pro-Loyalist policy could split the Pan American organization wide open, in none of Bowers' reports was there any hint that he appreciated this danger (or some of the others with which the State Department was so familiar). It would not be unjust to call Bowers' position unrealistic. At the same time, the State Department was at fault in its failure to explain its policies adequately to him. It was ironic that the American ambassador to Spain was one of the most ill-informed officials on these matters which were so vital to American policy toward the Spanish strife. It indicated then, and afterward, how much misunderstanding and ill will can result from the failure to inform and to trust an official who is responsible for carrying out policy decisions. An equally fundamental consideration is that if Bowers had been better informed he might have been led to seek out additional kinds of information of interest to the policy-makers.

The Good Neighbor policy, the success of which hung in the balance during the Spanish civil war, became a strategic necessity. While it did not play a decisive role in the continuation of the nonintervention policy, it was a major factor. If Ambassador Bowers failed to appreciate the delicacy of the inter-American problem, this was largely the fault of the State Department.

8

AMERICAN ARMS, AMERICAN MEN

Iᴛ ʜᴀs ʙᴇᴇɴ ᴏʙsᴇʀᴠᴇᴅ that among all the nationalities represented in the International Brigades, the Americans were the
most "innocent." And if one were to characterize in a word
those Americans who attempted by illegal means to sell and to
ship arms to Spain, a fitting choice would be "persistent."
Volunteers and profiteers created a few similar problems for the
State Department, simply by virtue of involving the United
States, to some extent, in the Spanish war. While the Department acknowledged the differences more than the similarities, it
handled the legal problems presented by both groups with
matchless propriety. Efforts to prevent violations were more
scrupulous with respect to those involved in the arms trade
than with those who were volunteering their military services.
But the movement of men was far more difficult to control than
the movement of goods. Prosecutions of both arms dealers and
volunteers were hardly attempted. But in the first instance
proof of guilt was exceedingly difficult to obtain, and in the
second instance it seemed, at the very least, politically expedient to forget about legal charges. A further distinction became clear: arms dealers were not likely candidates for humanitarian sympathy; but upon the disbanding of the International
Brigades, the volunteers were. While American officials behaved

judiciously, there is no question that they concerned themselves with the welfare of those Americans who survived the war.

There is a practical difficulty, of course, in documenting the failures of the State Department in regard to preventing sales and shipments of arms to Spain. But from the evidence available, it would seem that the Office of Arms and Munitions Control was extremely successful in its efforts to frustrate illegal transactions. It encountered some very persistent people with some rather bizarre schemes.

I

The State Department, from time to time, received reports that American arms and planes had reached the Spanish Loyalists. The Italian press was particularly voluble when, for example, Martins and Boeings were shot down by Rebel forces. The same was true with regard to the capture of such items as Lewis machine guns. But the quantity of "American" arms and planes captured by the Rebels was deceptive. In the first place, the United States government had never disposed of some of the arms, such as antitank guns, which purportedly had been in Loyalist hands. Second, many of the arms, particularly rifles and machine guns, were old, obsolete products from World War I—some of which had probably never been removed from the European continent. Others had been disposed of by the government during the 1920's. And third, manufacturing rights for certain types of Martins, Curtisses, Northrops, and Boeings had been sold to the Soviet Union earlier in the decade, when there was a brief flourishing of American business with Russia. Unconfirmed rumors, errors in identification, exaggeration for the purpose of propaganda, and the appearance of weapons which had left the shores of the United States years before, all tended to make the quantity of illegally exported American war materials appear larger than it really was.[1] The State Department in such cases could do little more than explain the circumstances. It was otherwise occupied detecting real attempts at violating the embargo.

The problem of illegal shipments through Mexico persisted after the enactment of the January 1937 embargo. The Ameri-

can government was compelled to rely on the "personal assurances of the Mexican President that transshipment to Spain
would not be permitted." But, even while the Mexican government generally appeared desirous of cooperating with Washington's wishes, the will and the means to prevent transshipment were not always present. President Roosevelt himself once
pointed out to the Mexican ambassador that the reshipment of
American arms and planes to Spain created a difficult situation
for the United States, in view of its policy of strict nonintervention. The Mexicans consistently expressed their desire to
cooperate and just as consistently pointed out their own difficult situation with respect to "public pressures" and the problem of "legal authority."[2]

During February 1937 three American planes reached Mexico and were ultimately shipped to Spain on the S.S. *Ibai*. The
same number also reached Mexico later that same month, but
the State Department apparently lost track of them. The exportation of the latter three planes was initiated with the
request for an export license by the American Armament Corporation. It later withdrew its application, and the planes were
exported by another party. It was perhaps at that time feared
that the association of the American Armament Corporation
with this proposed transaction would automatically arouse the
suspicions of the State Department. Two of its owners, Alfred
and Ignacio Miranda, had in May 1936 been sent to prison for
having shipped war materials through Chile to Bolivia during
the Chaco War in 1935—in violation of the Chaco Embargo
Act. But in November 1937, with the Miranda brothers now out
of prison, the American Armament Corporation again became
involved in schemes to sell and ship arms to Spain. Its operations were by this time "the subject of careful scrutiny." (The
Miranda brothers provide one of the best examples of that kind
of persistence which characterized so many arms dealers attempting illegal transactions.) The Mirandas desired to export
twenty-four .37mm guns and 120,000 rounds of ammunition for
these guns, the ultimate purchaser being the government of
Latvia. The immediate purchaser, as indicated in their application, was an agency in Warsaw. When the American legation in
Riga checked with the Latvian Ministry of War, it was found
that the Latvian government had ordered no such supplies. The
Miranda brothers were refused a license. In January 1938,

Alfred Miranda appeared at the State Department with an application to export the same items to Aero Marine Engines, Limited, in France, where the guns were purportedly to be mounted on torpedo boats for the Chinese government. When the Chinese failed to confirm this order, the license was again refused. In February 1938, the American legation in Riga received a certificate apparently signed by an official in the Latvian Ministry of War, ordering the same twenty-four guns "for the needs of the Latvian Army." It was found that neither the Foreign Ministry nor the Minister of War had anything to do with the presentation of the certificate. The Miranda brothers, although once more frustrated, were undaunted.

In June 1938, the American Armament Corporation unsuccessfully requested a license to export the guns to a party in Gyndia, Poland—the ultimate destination again purportedly Latvia. A last attempt occurred in November that year, when the secretary of the Latvian legation in Washington called upon the Office of Arms and Munitions Control with regard to the granting of export licenses for "24 .37mm guns manufactured by the American Armament Corporation," the licenses to be issued on this occasion to a "Mr. Saks" and a "Mr. Abramowicz." The Latvian official was informed by the State Department that his government had definitely said that it had not purchased the guns.[3] The Mirandas either gave up their efforts at this point or had too little time before the war ended to devise a new scheme.

During 1937 the State Department frustrated attempts to transship at least four planes to Spain through Mexico. But during the spring and summer of that year the Department received some pressure to authorize the release of American-built planes already being detained in Mexico by Mexican authorities. In April the Mexican Foreign Office made such a request, and the State Department reiterated its objection. About the same time James Watson, a former senator from Indiana, endeavored to persuade the Department to authorize release of the planes. In August a similar plea was made by a Washington attorney, who said that the planes would be exported from Mexico to one Chiko Coulas in Athens, Greece. The attorney claimed that Coulas "had purchased the planes." The State Department refused to budge. Meanwhile, the Mexican government complained of increased pressure, and added that while it would not sanction the shipment to Spain of American planes already in Mexico, it would take no responsibility concerning planes which arrived in Mexico at a later date. This placed the responsibility where it legally belonged—with the State Department, which was forced to agree with the Mexican request that the American government be solely responsible for ascertaining the ultimate destination of exported arms and planes.[4] It must be supposed that some American war materials thereafter reached Spain through Mexico. To prevent this traffic altogether was impossible.

The State Department was all the while successfully blocking other attempts to ship war materials to Spain, and it continued to receive the cooperation of most of the larger aircraft and arms manufacturers. Curtiss-Wright, for one, reported that it refused to sell 117 aircraft engines because the transaction would not have been legal. Still, there were others; for example, Fairchild Aviation attempted to export aircraft engines and propellers first to Greece, then to Austria, and finally for use "in a German revolt in Lithuania"—in each case failing to furnish evidence that these were the ultimate destinations.[5]

The most difficult embargo problem which the State Department encountered during the course of the war arose out of an attempt by Bellanca Aircraft Corporation to export twenty-two low-wing monoplanes valued at $1,047,000. It began in December 1937, when the Bellanca Corporation first applied for licenses to export these planes to Greece for use in "a civil reservist school." This claim, as it turned out, was false; it seems the school was a hope for the future. In June 1938, Bellanca presented a telegram from the American commercial attaché in Athens, indicating that he had been shown an official document of the Greek Air Ministry authorizing the importation of the planes for use in training schools. The document also specified that the reexport of the planes from Greece would be prohibited. It was then found that the documents allegedly authorizing the importation of the planes were "either forgeries or issued illegally." It was also later reported that the director of civil aviation in Greece "had been found guilty of irregular action and dismissed from office." Following this attempt, Bellanca tried to export the planes to the Société Française des Transports Aeriens, in France. Knowing that the latter organization was an agent of the Spanish government, the Office of Arms Control again refused to issue licenses to Bellanca.[6]

A few months later the State Department encountered the same twenty-two Bellanca planes. This time General R. C. Marshall, who had appeared with the now deceased Rudolf Wolf almost two years before, called on Counselor Moore. Marshall requested licenses for the Bellanca planes, but was "very vague as to the details of the transaction." When the foreign purchaser was given as Société Française des Transports Aeriens, Moore recounted the situation in great detail. By this time, it was a matter of tiresome explanation, but Moore now concluded with implied warnings of prosecution and conviction. Marshall confessed complete ignorance of the results of the earlier Wolf transaction (and Departmental records indicate the possibility that he was simply being used as a "formal applicant"). The General "stated flatly" that he would not associate himself with any further transactions unless the State Department informed him that they were not in violation of the law. That seems to have been the end of his association with the twenty-two Bellancas, but the planes were still involved in another scheme.[7]

Early in January 1939, Miles Sherover, American purchasing agent for the Spanish government, wanted to export the Bellancas to the Soviet Union.[8] He planned to conclude a contract with the Soviet Amtorg Trading Corporation, "on behalf of another company." When the State Department probed the Soviet embassy in Washington for the necessary assurances against transshipment, a Soviet official implied that the request was an insult to the Soviet government. But the Russians were by this late date more interested in the appearance of solidarity with the Spanish government than with its reality, and the matter was apparently dropped.[9]

Some embargo violators were resourceful enough to devise complicated schemes which, at least for a while, escaped detection by government officials. The most notable of these was uncovered by accident. By March 1938, over a five-month period, Grumman Aircraft Engineering Corporation and Brewster Aeronautical Corporation had obtained licenses to export to the Canadian Car and Foundry Company some 51 fuselages, 70 wing panels, and 66 tail units. The State Department issued these licenses "without question" because it was felt that reliance could be placed in the Canadian government's methods of export control, and because the Canadian government adhered to Chamberlain's European policies. These transactions would not, under ordinary circumstances, have aroused suspicion. But it happened that the American commercial attaché at the embassy in Istanbul was vacationing in New York City, where he heard a rumor that fifty Grumman planes were being assembled by the Canadian Car and Foundry Company for shipment to Turkey. Upon his return to the Turkish capital, he found that no such order had been placed. By the time the necessary investigations were made, and the Royal Canadian Mounted Police and the Federal Bureau of Investigation were brought into the case, at least two shipments of planes had reached France—bound for Spain. While the State Department was checking with the Turkish government, the Brewster Corporation applied for additional licenses. In order to expedite the issuance of these licenses, the Washington representative of the Canadian Car and Foundry Company presented four "official" documents to the State Department, documents which appeared to confirm the Turkish order. The Turkish Foreign Office categorically denied the order, and later found that the documents were forgeries. In the meantime, the State Department refused the additional licenses to the Brewster Corporation. It is not known how many planes reached Spain through Canada. But on July 1, 1938, an estimated forty Grumman planes were held by the Spanish air force. As with each of the other attempted violations, successful or unsuccessful, there was not enough evidence to warrant an attempt at prosecution. This was the judgment of the Department of Justice, which was, of course, faced with professions of good faith from the parties involved. There was nothing in the facts, apparently, to prove that any of the companies involved necessarily knew the real destination of the unassembled planes.[10] Yet it is impossible to escape the impression that government officials also believed it would be bad politics to attempt prosecution. It might create "unnecessary" public debate—and the government was, after all, diligent in its efforts to prevent illegal shipments. Even this, however, should not obscure two facts revealed about the law-enforcing power provided the government by the neutrality legislation. The State Department could be, and was, very effective in preventing illegal transactions. Successful shipments, like the one allegedly intended for Turkey, stand out only because they were known exceptions. But, when there were violations, it is clear that the government was generally (and perhaps, always) handcuffed. In order to prosecute, the Department of Justice needed evidence to show that the violators knew where the exported arms and planes were ultimately destined. This kind of evidence was not easily obtainable.

An important question concerning the State Department's handling of the embargo problem was its relationship to the Department's general policy toward Spain. In this connection, there were the pro-Loyalist sentiments of the President and some of the policy-makers and other executive advisers. If there was one way by which these sentiments could have been translated into an unofficial pro-Loyalist policy, it would have been by paying less scrupulous attention to arms exports. Occasional clandestine shipments of American arms and planes to Spain would not probably have seriously worsened the European situation. There were rumors, particularly in the later stages of the war, to the effect that the Roosevelt administration sought indirect means to aid the Loyalists. In light of the existence of pro-Loyalist sentiments in government circles, the question was not unnatural: Why was the State Department so scrupulous in its investigation of applications for export licenses? A reasonable, but unlikely, answer is that the legal branches of the Department were in the hands of conservatives such as Green, Hackworth, and Moore. This answer suggests that if the more adventurous people in the Department had been in control, then investigations would have been less thorough. The credibility of this speculation is largely destroyed by two facts: first, that most of the "activists" agreed with the Spanish policy; and, second, that those who did not look with special favor upon the policy carried out their assignments dutifully. The answer would rather seem to concern even more practical considerations: Would small quantities of war materials from the United States have made any difference to the Loyalist war effort? And what would have happened if the administration's political opposition had found good reason to suspect a lack of diligence in the State Department?

Not all trading, or attempted trading, with Spain was in arms and airplanes. Other important items were oil and automotive products. The case of greatest notoriety was that of the Texas Oil Company, which continued to trade with the Spanish Nationalists even after being fined by the American government for violating a "no credit" provision of the neutrality law. While the Texas Company was reported to have received cash in these transactions, it also provided long-term credit, which was so badly needed by the Burgos government. Texaco's representative for France, Spain, and Portugal was openly pro-Franco and made frequent trips both to Italy and to Spain during the course of the war. He was reported as stating in March 1939 that Texaco "had already received twenty million dollars in cash" from the Nationalists. At one point, this representative attempted to persuade the Guaranty Trust Company to handle some of General Franco's accounts but was refused because of the risk of lawsuits and "other difficulties." The Texas Company sold Franco some 1,400,000 tons of oil during the civil war, a development which did not sit very well with Secretary Hull. But not everyone shared his concern for the size of this trade; Phillips, for example, was a "bit shocked" when told that "Mr. Hull had sent for the representative of the Texas Company and remonstrated with him for doing business on such a scale with Franco."[11]

General Motors likewise did substantial trading with Nationalist Spain, and some with the Loyalists as well. According to a high official of General Motors, the company sold for cash about 3,500 trucks to the Spanish government alone. It also sold a sizable portion of the 12,000 or more trucks the Nationalists purchased from American companies. (Germany and Italy only sold about 3,000 trucks to Franco; "Axis prices were too high.") These transactions were perfectly in accordance with the neutrality laws, so long as credit was not involved. In September 1938, the Office of Arms Control was told by an official of the General Motors Export Corporation that the authorized agent who had concluded a ninety-day credit contract with the Nationalists had been dismissed from his job. The State Department was told that a revision of the contract would be sought so that it might conform to the law. Apparently this was done, for two months later the Department learned from American officials in Portugal that Franco paid General Motors with pesetas. These pesetas could not be exported; but they could be used to purchase goods which could be sold by General Motors for dollars in London. Transactions of this sort were apparently handled by the German trading company in Spain, HISMA, which controlled the exports of the General Motors subsidiary there. While never tested in the courts, these roundabout arrangements were possibly within the letter of the law. Some large "credits" reportedly accumulated, and these too could not leave Spain; they could, however, be reinvested in Spain. It might well have been the opinion of the State Department that such credits were legal; for, while it warned General Motors officials about the ninety-day credit arrangement, nothing was said about these later contracts. On the other hand, at least through the early months of 1938, the State Department was lax in applying the "no credit" provision. There is no evidence indicating how long the Department looked the other way concerning credit transactions, or why, if this was its general policy, the Department sometimes objected to such dealings. At any rate some credit arrangements with the Loyalists were also overlooked.[12]

Other automotive companies were trading, at least indirectly, with Spain. The Loyalists had many Studebaker, Dodge, Ford, and International trucks, in addition to General Motors products. One example indicates how profitable this trade could be. From a "reliable source" an American foreign service officer learned that Chrysler Export Company sold a large number of Dodge trucks (chassis without body) of a type which sold in the United States for between $450 and $500. For each of these trucks, the Spanish government paid $1,300. The Export Company probably received about $800 or $900 per truck. The trucks were delivered in Antwerp, where an agent received about $100 per unit. The "balance was split among other parties to the transaction." The money for the Export Corporation was placed in a New York bank and could be drawn upon as fast as the shipments were made. Risk to the Export Company was therefore eliminated, while profits per unit soared. Early in the war, for the purchase of such products, the Spanish government had to pay "fancy prices" in cash out of the Spanish gold reserve. But the reserve (part of it being frozen in France and most of it being carted away by the Russians) was rather rapidly depleted, and attempts to acquire credit generally failed—particularly by comparison with Franco's successes. Even in 1938, however, American trade with the

Loyalists was still substantial. Miles Sherover, through the Hanover Sales Corporation, was able to ship sizable cargoes through France to the Spanish government on more than thirty separate occasions during March and April alone.[13] Significantly, these shipments occurred at about the same time that Grumman planes were reaching the Loyalists after being transshipped through Canada and France—also at a time immediately prior to the Nye resolution. These events were further evidence of division and indecision within the French government; for while it opened its frontier, enabling the passage of American products to Spain, it still failed to encourage the Roosevelt administration to repeal the embargo or even to inform Washington of any conditions under which the frontier might be kept open.

Despite the extent of American trade with the Loyalists during 1938, business was shifting noticeably in the direction of Franco Spain. When cash (other than pesetas) was unavailable from the Spanish government, American businessmen generally preferred to deal with Franco. In transactions with the Nationalists, they did not reject peseta contracts or contracts involving complicated credit arrangements. It would have been surprising if American businessmen had provided extensive credit to the Spanish government, in view of its radically socialist orientation and its continual failure to redress injuries to American interests. Businessmen involved in the Spanish trade simply pursued the course of greater profit and increased security. If there was one possibility that concerned them about Franco, it was that Italy and especially Germany might gain the upper hand in the Spanish economy. Franco's economic policy with regard to Texaco and General Motors also suggested the undesirable possibility that under his rule Spain might follow Germany's example and forbid foreign investors to take their profits out of the country. But by February 1939, at least foreign Fascist domination of Spanish economic policies appeared less likely: Firestone was producing tires and magnetos "with half Spanish capital"; Texaco was "in an excellent position" for the reorganization of the Spanish oil industry; and Juan March, one of the world's wealthiest men, had put up the money for "a half interest with General Motors in an automotive manufacturing company." Finally, it is impossible to avoid the conclusion that Franco's economic advisers understood the temper of the international business community—largely because they were one with it; and that even those Loyalists who did understand it were disadvantaged by the ideologies of their friends. Ideology was for the Nationalists only a weapon to be used when needed; for the Loyalists it became a burden which could not be convincingly disavowed. Franco often tantalized businessmen; the Loyalists, by comparison, frightened them.[14]

Neville Chamberlain hoped that Franco would find it to his best interests at the end of the war to turn to the capital available in the democratic states. This was one of the cornerstones of his Spanish policy. The French Foreign Office, with less enthusiasm, placed high priority on the same consideration. And while Washington did less than either London or Paris to encourage this development, it still clearly recognized that, in the event of a Rebel victory, it would be necessary to help woo Franco away from the Fascist states with dollars. While American businessmen were hardly alone, they did help to provide during the last half of the war what the Germans and Italians could not so readily provide. In the pursuit of profits, American businessmen sought to attract the Nationalists away from Axis economic interests. Even when in competition with British commercial and financial interests, American capital shored up the Spanish policy of the British Foreign Office. And the State Department, within the framework of its general policy of noninvolvement, did little to obstruct their activities.

II

When credit arrangements (of one sort or another) were involved, some American businessmen became financially committed to the victory of one side in the Spanish strife. When Americans volunteered for service in the International Brigades, there was more at stake. Of the nearly 3,000 Americans who served the Loyalist cause, some 900 were killed. Starting in January 1937, there was a steady stream of Americans arriving in Spain—until the setting in of disillusionment, when the purity of their various causes became corrupted. Democracy, the working class, Communism, the Spanish peasantry, the promise of a millennium—these were some of the reasons (rarely so plain and simple) why Americans went to Spain. But the rigors and the horrors of war, the cynicism of some of their fellow Brigade members, the intraclass strife, the purging of Trotskyists by the Soviet-dominated secret police, and the revelations of Stalin's great purges in Russia, all struck severe blows to the causes which had brought so many American volunteers to Spain. By late fall 1937, it became difficult to recruit Americans to fight in the Brigades. Among those who survived the ordeal best were those who joined because there was "nothing better to do." But there were others who survived the burdens and pains of the war equally well. Many American Jews, and Negroes too, although far fewer in number, went to Spain on a crusade for legal and moral equality. Fascism represented the worst in racism; the Loyalist government stood for equality. For the Jew and the Negro, Spain may well have appeared a fit battleground.[15]

The origin of the Brigades was due primarily to the desire of Communist leaders to seize upon a propaganda weapon. While undoubtedly a few of them had more grandiose visions of founding an international army, they knew that the fundamental utility of the Brigades lay in their propaganda value. The Comintern was thus given the job in the fall of 1936 of recruiting foreigners for military service in Spain. In the United States the Communist party was particularly active in labor unions and in colleges and universities. The success which the Communists had on docksides and campuses was not due so much to a condition they created as to a situation they exploited. In most European countries the Comintern had even greater success among the working class, which felt the impact of the depression more than its American counterpart. In Europe the Communists drew most of their volunteers from men who were not only materially distraught but who possessed class antagonisms deeply rooted in their history. The largest single bloc of American volunteers was driven by longings for panaceas which would right the world's wrongs. To many of these men, it seemed that the foundations of the Western world were crumbling under the impact of World War I and the Great Depression. The future was now open, and it would be of their construction. This is not to say that the same motives were not at work in the European working class, but compared to the hardened character of the European participants the

Americans appeared most innocent. Many Americans went to Spain on a glorious errand, tragic as it was both in its causes and in its consequences.

There appears not to have been more than a handful of Americans fighting with the Spanish government before 1937. It was not until after the arrival of sixty Americans in Barcelona early in January that the State Department felt it necessary to formulate a policy concerning volunteers. A provision of the United States Code helped to prevent open recruiting within the country. In addition, legislation passed in 1907 prohibited Americans from taking an oath of allegiance to a foreign government under penalty of loss of citizenship. Early in the civil war, the State Department additionally required that all individuals traveling abroad should sign an affidavit that they did not intend to travel in Spain (if their intentions later changed, their passports would have to be amended by an American consular officer). While undoubtedly some illegal recruiting was done in the United States, it was quite easy to circumvent the government's restrictions. For example, Americans traveled to France, and were formally recruited on foreign soil. And there was no evidence to show that the Spanish government required a formal oath of allegiance. Perhaps the recruiters hoped to accomplish "allegiance" by other means; for instance, the passports of Americans were surrendered to recruiting authorities in France. This made it extremely difficult for the American, on his own, to return to his homeland (or even to travel in Europe)—especially without the suspicion that he had participated in the Spanish strife.[16]

At the same time, representatives of the Spanish government were doing another type of recruiting in the United States. The Loyalists were badly in need of experienced pilots. While not plentiful, they were available in the United States. For the most part, these men were anything but volunteers for an ideology. They were well-paid mercenaries. While the first offers were generally higher, these men were reportedly paid $1,500 per month and $1,000 for every Insurgent plane brought down. Making offers of this kind, recruiters were able to attract officers in the United States Air Corps Reserve and a number of well-known fliers such as Harold Dahl, Bert Acosta, and Gordon Berry. Those whose flying ability was less well recognized were ordinarily examined at an airfield in New York. This was reportedly done after interested pilots first made an appearance before the Spanish consul in New York City. As with the volunteers, the fliers' actual recruitment probably took place outside the confines of the United States. Harold Dahl, for one, was recruited in Mexico, where both he and his wife were given Spanish passports and Spanish pseudonyms.[17]

President Roosevelt reflected rather early in the civil war a disposition to "go easy" on violators, suggesting in February 1937 that the government ought not "to go over strong" in prosecuting these aviators, "as this happened before anyone realized what the Spanish thing meant." In the end, American volunteers and the few mercenaries who fought in Spain, like those who sold arms and planes to the Loyalists and those who sold other goods "on credit" to Franco, were not prosecuted by the government.[18]

American volunteers became part of the XVth International Brigade, also composed of English and Canadian forces. The Americans were formed in the Abraham Lincoln Battalion. Later a Washington Battalion was created, but with the depletion of forces the two were subsequently joined. The Americans, after intense and disciplined training, were first thrown into battle at Jarama in February 1937. Four hundred and fifty strong, the Battalion lost 120 men with another 175 wounded in its first engagement. This was an indication not only of the inexperience of the American volunteers, but also of the fact that the Brigades were generally thrown into the thick of the fight. Losses were particularly heavy during an encounter with Rebel forces at Brunete in July 1937. It was after this battle that the combined Lincoln-Washington Battalion came into existence. The XVth Brigade, of which the Americans were still a part, also played a major role on the Saragossa front during August and September; this occurred during the period when Americans largely commanded the XVth. Losses again were terrifyingly heavy and became still another source of disillusionment. The abundance of martyrs quite probably aided the pro-Loyalist cause in America, but just as probably dampened enthusiasm for volunteering. Neither did stories of the brutal "Stalinist tactics" of some Brigade leaders help. And while such instances of cynical duplicity were not as numerous as some sources charged, it is true that some Americans who did not intend to fight in the Brigades were compelled to do so. Inspired in part by the stories of Americans serving in ambulance corps during World War I (and inexperienced even in the art of street fighting with Fascists), volunteers occasionally sought service in the medical corps. Communist recruiters took advantage of these sentiments, and when these men arrived in Spain they were handed not first-aid kits but rifles. This rather quickly led to desertions, and deserters found their lives in grave danger.[19] Occasionally they sought out American consulates, and this, from a practical as well as from an official point of view, created some complicated problems.

After the winter of 1938, the International Brigades played a decreasingly vital role in the Loyalist war effort. By November 1938, when the Brigades were finally disbanded, 75 per cent of the Lincoln-Washington Battalion was composed of Spaniards.

The British and French governments made continuing efforts, most intensively after July 1937, to effect the withdrawal of foreign troops from Spain. Had a *general* settlement been attainable, the Spanish government could not have refused this ; for the number of Germans, Italians, and Moors in the service of General Franco was at least some five or six times greater than the number of non-Spaniards fighting with the Loyalists. But the plans, usually of British origin, continually failed. Each plan was either not comprehensive enough (and the Loyalists would refuse it) or it was too comprehensive (and the Rebels would refuse it). In the spring of 1938, however, the Non-Intervention Committee was at work on its fifth draft of the British plan of July 1937 ; when 10,000 foreign troops departed from the side with the least number, a proportionately higher number would be withdrawn from the forces of the other. The cost of this arrangement to the Spanish government, even if fully carried out, would be dear. The plans also included the granting of belligerent rights to both sides, and as the legitimate government the Loyalists already had some of those rights ; with the democratic states at least, Franco, as yet, had no legal belligerent rights. After the NIC unanimously agreed to this plan, a commission arrived in Spain to put it into effect. Juan Negrín, the Loyalist Premier, later informed the Assembly of the League of Nations that the Committee was not capable of acting in the matter. Then at the height of the Munich crisis, the Spanish government itself announced the beginning of the withdrawal of the Brigades, under the supervision of a League Commission. Shortly afterward, in early October, 10,000 Italians were withdrawn from Spain—hardly the proportionate withdrawal recently hoped for by the NIC commission.[20]

The International Brigades had their farewell parade in Barcelona on November 15, 1938, but the problems created by Americans desiring to return to the United States began several months before. Funds were needed to repatriate them and to provide care for the wounded. Arrangements also had to be made for the release of Americans who had been captured by the Rebels. The most basic problem was that of raising money to house, feed, and clothe the men (and furnish hospital care for a good number), and then to transport them home. The State Department did not have the funds for all these needs, nor was it politically expedient to dig into government coffers for that purpose. The State Department at first seemed to hope, and not without reason, that the organizations responsible for getting the men to Spain would assume the responsibility for transporting them home again. Before the number of repatriates requiring aid reached into the hundreds, it did appear as though such organizations as the Friends of the Abraham Lincoln Brigade and the North American Committee to Aid Spanish Democracy would pay the costs and make the necessary arrangements. But that hope was short-lived; American officials in Spain and France were soon being called upon and asked what the American government could do in the situation. It was then that the State Department began to work in cooperation with organizations and individuals interested in repatriation. The State Department could provide the advice, the much needed contacts, and the network of communications —it was up to the organizations to raise the necessary funds and to deal with the practical problems of organizing large-scale repatriation. The Department acted with as much propriety in this matter as it did in other problems relating to the Spanish strife. If at times this gave the appearance of a half-hearted humanitarianism, it also proved that proper means could be found if they were sought. The regularity with which

American officials corresponded and met with David McKelvy
White, David Amariglio, Earl Browder, Herman Reissig, Ernest Hemingway, Louis Fischer, Edgar Mowrer, John Whit-
taker, and others who had interested themselves in the problem
indicated that the State Department was anything but uninterested in the fate of American volunteers. On one occasion, when
Bernard Baruch donated $10,000 to the Friends of the Abra-
ham Lincoln Brigade in order "to get those boys back home,"
the State Department permitted the American embassy in Paris
to handle $2,000 of the donation for transmission to the Ameri-
can Aid Society in Paris; this was for the repatriation of
Americans who had deserted the Brigades and whom the
Friends of the Abraham Lincoln Brigade apparently refused to
assist.[21] The State Department and the Foreign Service went to
the limits of their authority and capability in an attempt to
ease the problems of repatriation.

Another problem of greater delicacy involved those Americans captured by the Rebel forces. The difficulties raised by the
capture of American volunteers did not become severe until
1938. In March of that year, the usually amiable Rebel general,
Quiepo de Llano, told an American official that a "considerable
number of Americans" had been captured during the Turuel
offensive, and he added, somewhat cryptically, that these men
"would be required to build up Spain after the war." Informed
of this, Secretary Hull instructed the American consul at Seville, Charles Bay, to approach Rebel officials: ". . . it would be
helpful if Franco authorities would confirm our assumption
that rules of war respecting treatment of prisoners are being
respected." Two weeks later, after obtaining such assurances
from Quiepo de Llano, Hull was still dissatisfied and desired a
"definite statement" from the "appropriate authorities of General Franco." This was received by the State Department about
a month later; with it was an invitation to visit the concentra-
tion camps at San Pedro de Cardenas, an ancient convent near
Burgos. Accordingly, Bay visited the camps in the company of
the Rebel officer in charge. With "complete freedom," he interviewed twenty Americans there. Apparently their most serious
complaint concerned infrequent permission to write letters for
the purpose of obtaining money "for their personal desires." In
all, there were reportedly seventy-seven American prisoners, all
of whom were located at San Pedro de Cardenas. When Bay

raised questions about particular Americans thought to have
been captured but not present at the camp, the prison inspector
candidly offered the speculation that they had been put to trial
and shot. (Neither did the Americans at San Pedro know the
whereabouts of these men.) Bay's negative comments in his
report to the Department concerned the small prison yard, the
"small but sufficient" sleeping quarters, the lack of recreational
facilities and reading material, and insufficient latrine and
washing facilities. The latter, he added, were being taken care
of by new construction. After this report, the State Department seems to have decided not to press the issue further.
Perhaps it was felt that representations might be required at
the end of the war to bring about the release of these prisoners,
and as their conditions were not apparently intolerable there
was little sense in creating ill will among Nationalist authorities.[22]

One of the achievements of which Ambassador Bowers was
most proud was his success in helping to effect an exchange of
prisoners—including fourteen Americans. The negotiations
took some three months, during which time Bowers described his
role as that of a "post office." The Nationalists initiated the
move. They desired to approach the Loyalists through Bowers,
and obviously included the Americans in the proposal in the
hope that Bowers might be more inclined to work for the success of the exchange. The cooperation which Bowers received
from the Marquis de Rialp of the Nationalists and Alvarez del
Vayo of the Loyalists was a tribute to the trust which they
placed in the American ambassador—and partly the result of
the "neutral" stance of the United States. (The British, for
example, tried for six months before they succeeded in bringing
about an exchange.) Following Bowers' success there occurred
an extended angry correspondence between the ambassador and
Secretary Hull concerning Bowers' desire to initiate further
exchanges. But the disagreement was apparently resolved by
the passage of time, the clarification of intentions, and the
International Red Cross's intervention into the exchange and
release problem.[23]

It is worth noting, even while figures are unavailable, that
probably not more than a bare handful of Americans joined the
Rebel forces. (An Irish contingent, for example, fought with
the insurgents.) The records of the State Department are al-

most utterly lacking in references to Americans fighting with the insurgents. In 1936 the Loyalists captured an American pilot, Vincent J. Patriarca, and the State Department sought assurances that he would not be executed. Guarantees of good treatment were quickly received from the Spanish government. Another incident involved the son of Arthur Krock of the *New York Times*, T. A. Ashby-Poley-Krock, who for an unknown reason was purportedly awarded the title of "general" (which he proceeded to use) by the insurgent authorities. Those Americans, particularly Roman Catholics, who interpreted the war as a struggle between religion and Communist atheism were apparently not driven by a great impulse to fight the battle themselves. The Rebels had no need, and no disposition, to recruit volunteers in the United States.[24]

As diplomatic problems both the actions of American profiteers and the experiences of American volunteers lose their drama. For the State Department these were awkward, and sometimes thorny, problems requiring diligent attention. The success with which the State Department handled these difficulties can be fairly gauged only by the effect they had upon Secretary Hull's general aim with regard to the Spanish war. In this respect the State Department contained the problems well enough so that they did not dangerously intrude upon its policy of nonintervention.

9

DOMESTIC QUARRELS, 1937–1938

Domestic controversies aroused by the Spanish civil war increased as the months passed. Pro-Loyalist and pro-Franco groups which began to form during the first year of the war achieved greater organization and reached more people as the war progressed. The opening days of 1939 would find them locked in battle in the last of the embargo controversies, and Capitol Hill and the Senate and House office buildings would be for the first time really besieged by partisans of both sides. The earlier embargo quarrels—even the one during the spring of 1938—did not involve such a degree of organization, particularly among supporters of General Franco. But disputes over the Spanish issue did not only concern the embargo. They seriously affected plans for civilian and refugee relief. It was in the struggles over these issues that partisan organizations developed their effectiveness as political pressure groups. The practical experience gained in these battles found its fullest expression in the first months of 1939, the last months of the Spanish war. It was very largely from the arguments arising from these "side issues" that the policy-makers were able to estimate the nature and depth of the public controversy. Further, these issues in themselves created diplomatic and political problems for the Department of State and the White House.

I

The nature of the controversy in the United States was complex. It was religious; it was socioeconomic; and insofar as it was ideological it seemed to be both a reflection of religious and class prejudices and a residue left from intellectual hand-me-downs. There is no doubt that the intelligentsia was ideologically committed in the Spanish civil war, but in the public controversy in the United States, ideology was very much filtered down. The Spanish strife occurred during what was, for many Americans, a period of passionate, even if oftentimes brief, conviction. With all its ramifications, the civil war quite naturally touched upon those issues which divided men everywhere. It came, in fact, to embody all that was tragic in the twentieth century. It was, and still is for some, the great tragic symbol in an era which has now seen the world convulsed by two great wars and countless revolutions.

Most of the quarrels involved the Catholic Church in one way or another. Yet an attempt to isolate the religious factor would be useless. As a single example, for years a liberal political disposition had been extending ever more widely through the Protestant clergy, ultimately affecting the views of many clergymen toward the Spanish war. It was partly an atonement for encouraging the war effort against Germany almost twenty years before, and undoubtedly it was fired by the failure of traditional methods to deal with the disruptive forces of the depression. The former cause encouraged pacifism, the latter encouraged the acceptance of class conflict as a basic historical force and made more attractive new ideas for social change and control, including Marxism. These two lines of development were running a collision course, and the Spanish civil war effectively divided the liberal Protestant clergy into two ideological camps—pacifists on one side and ardent supporters of the Loyalist military cause on the other. Protestant antipathy toward the Spanish Rebels cannot simply be explained by a traditional anti-Catholicism (although the latter certainly had an effect), for the Spanish war was viewed largely as a class conflict—reactionary generals, landholders, financiers, and churchmen standing as barriers to the social progress of the exploited lower classes. Of some, though not great, importance to American Protestants was the fact that the few Spanish Protestants in Rebel-held territory were being persecuted and killed for no other reason than that of being non-Catholics. Although it was in larger measure a matter of race, a similar motivation lay behind the partisan feelings of a good many Jewish religious leaders, who were clearly antagonized by Franco's Nazi supporters and Nazi aid.[1]

Influential members of both these religious groups acted as sponsors and officers in the most powerful pro-Loyalist organizations. Among the Protestants were Herman Reissig, a Congregational minister; Francis J. McConnell, a Methodist bishop; Robert L. Paddock, an Episcopal bishop; Harry F. Ward, of the Union Theological Seminary; and other such distinguished men as Bishops Benjamin Brewster, Edward L. Parsons, and G. Bromley Oxnam. Prominent rabbis, among them Edward L. Israel and Abba Hillel Silver, were also active in pro-Loyalist organizations. Among the most important facts about the participation of these men in such organizations as the North American Committee to Aid Spanish Democracy were the different ways in which they interpreted the Spanish struggle and in particular the role of Communism. Ward was exceptional in that he had in the past shown no aversion to working alongside known Communists and undoubtedly had a fuller appreciation than most of the degree of Communist influence which developed in the Loyalist government. Paddock was willing to work with all who opposed Franco's victory including Communists (although he certainly had no attraction to Communism himself). McConnell and Reissig were somewhat in the same category, even while attempting to keep the Communist party from controlling pro-Loyalist groups in the United States. Brewster, Parsons, Oxnam, Israel, and Silver all seemed to view Spanish Loyalists as democrats and were perhaps less appreciative of the problems raised by the Communist party's power both in Spain and in the organizations which they supported. It would be just as foolish to say that a large body of Protestant and Jewish religious leaders were Communist dupes as it would be to say that none of them were attracted by what they believed to be the messianic vision of Marx and a sometimes sanguine interpretation of the Soviet example. In short there is no easy classification of pro-Loyalist sympathies among the men in the churches and synagogues, except to say that they had a concern for social justice, which they felt could best be achieved in Spain by a Loyalist victory. With a few exceptions, Communist inroads among religious leaders were obliterated by such events as the news of Stalin's purges in 1937. But the fact that this did little to dampen the ardor of many clergymen for the Loyalist cause suggests that some did not appreciate the extent of Soviet involvement in Spain and that many feared Fascism more than Communism. These clergymen were hardly convinced by cries from their Catholic counterparts that the Spanish government was controlled by Bolsheviks.[2]

It is certain that Communist enthusiasm for the Loyalists made some Catholics firm in their belief that the Russians completely dominated the Spanish government. Anyone need only have picked up a Communist party pamphlet—and these were readily available—to get a similar impression. Indeed, the enthusiasm of the Communists, and their widely publicized claims of being deeply involved in the Spanish strife, not only confirmed the views of large numbers of Catholics but undoubtedly kept a good many Protestants and Jews away from pro-Loyalist organizations. The Communist party did have considerable power in the Spanish government at different times during the war, even after Stalin became reluctant to make available additional large quantities of war materials. But the Communists themselves were encountering internecine difficulties in both Spain and the United States. Stalinists and Trotskyists (along with other dissident Communists) were at each other's throats during the entire war—and quite literally so in Spain. In addition, the radical movement in the United States, involving many who were advocates of some variety of Communism, was splintered time and again during the same period. Not even all Communists and socialists favored a Loyalist victory. Some of the more radical ones preferred a Rebel victory, for they felt it would later facilitate the task of provoking a thorough-going Communist revolution in Spain. The extent of antagonism within the radical left was little appreciated by those outside it. Some Americans who fought in Spain and others who visited there (for example, during the International Writers Congress at Valencia in July 1937) were driven away from the Communist party by knowledge of Stalinist liquidation of Spanish anarchists in Barcelona. The question of what effect such facts would ultimately have had upon the Spanish people and upon the nature of the Spanish government, had the Loyalists won, results in mere speculation. But they certainly made little difference to some Americans who adamantly held that a Loyalist victory would obviously result in Stalinist control of Spain.[3]

The position of the Catholic clergy as reflected in the Catholic press underwent a change shortly after the outbreak of the war. In the earliest days of the strife, many Catholic leaders were not reluctant to point to the Spanish Church as an example of backwardness, particularly because of its failure to respond to the needs of the lower classes. (This was sometimes joined with a general criticism of the Church's failure to act on the social teachings in papal encyclicals.) But with the persecution of priests and nuns by anarchist mobs who fought on the side of the government, the increasing involvement of Communists, and some bitter attacks by the Protestant press against the Spanish hierarchy, the American Catholic press generally began to treat the conflict as a Communist war against religion. If the vast majority of pro-Loyalist Protestants and Jews underestimated the extent of Communist influence in Spain, pro-Franco Catholics generally very much overestimated it. As a result, there developed in the press and on the speaker's platform a kind of "holy war." Many religious leaders now resorted on both sides to the most polemical techniques and rejected unfavorable facts just as readily as they accepted favorable distortions and fabrications.[4]

Indirectly, this presented a problem for the State Department. It was not only the known facts of the Spanish situation with which American policy-makers had to deal. What was believed by different segments of the American public proved to be as real as the facts themselves. Accurate information on Spain was difficult enough for the State Department to obtain. Those who read Bowers' and Thurston's evaluations of the role of the Communist party in the Spanish war, for example, must have felt as though they were being informed about two separate developments.[5] Among the American people, the problem was immeasurably magnified.

It is not at all easy to second-guess the evaluations of the men in the State Department and in Congress concerning the breadth and depth of Catholic sentiment for Franco or, at least, against the Spanish government. But it would seem that there was too great a tendency in official circles to view Catholic opinion as "spontaneously monolithic," rather than as being naturally diverse and requiring sustained propaganda to reach a uniform majority. Actually, the Catholic hierarchy and the Catholic press were a long time in arousing pro-Franco, or even firmly anti-Loyalist, sympathies among the laity. This was partly because many Catholics were big-city laborers largely influenced by liberal politicians and labor leaders, as well as by an international working-class sentiment which was anything but uncommon in the 1930's. Furthermore, during the later stages of the war, the Communist party extended to Catholics its strategy of trying to appeal to religious groups. A more speculative explanation is that the Catholic laity, with increasingly substantial non-Catholic contacts, was just becoming comfortable in a pluralistic society and was reluctant to risk the gains it had made toward acceptance in Protestant America by aligning its views with those of the hierarchy on controversial political issues. Among those Catholics who were not indifferent to public affairs, perhaps as many as a majority viewed the Spanish war as a phenomenon which placed them in an awkward, embarrassing position. This goes far to explain the widespread determination among American Catholic commentators (lay and clerical) to find some evidence of liberal democracy in Franco Spain, a determination which led to some curious contrivances: Franco became George Washington, the insurgents resembled the rebels of Valley Forge, and their cause was made equivalent to the American revolt against the British. But the dilemma faced by many Catholics could not always be resolved so easily, as was evident in the case of the *Commonweal*, the liberal Catholic weekly controlled by laymen. In 1938, after almost two years of disagreement, the editors of *Commonweal* adopted a neutral stand on the Spanish issue—to the extent that they began to neglect discussion of it.[6]

Neither lower nor middle-class Catholics were out of touch with liberal views (particularly in urban areas), nor were Catholics out of touch with political radicalism. Some discarded the Catholic Church and made a religion of Marxism; others seemed able to live with both. Still others, for example some politicians and labor leaders, exploited their Catholic religious ties to bring Marxist ideas into political assemblies and labor unions. Out of all this there developed a large bloc of Catholics who, being hit by propaganda from both sides, were little more than neutral toward the Spanish civil war. To conclude from this that the majority of American Catholics might have been induced to support a repeal of the Spanish embargo, however, would be very wrong. Secretary Hull's nonintervention policy, while it did not help to end this embarrassing war, probably could not have coincided better with the views of uncommitted Catholics. Neither can it necessarily be concluded that they would have opposed the lifting of the embargo (at least before the spring of 1938) so much so as to cause a domestic political crisis. When there has been a conflict of opinion, the American Catholic has often found it easier to stand in quiet opposition to the political views of the hierarchy than to oppose the prevalent views on Capitol Hill and in the White House. In many cases, one must suppose that this has been another form of acquiescence.

It was not the flexible political opinions of the Catholic laity in general to which the Roosevelt administration and congressional leaders reacted. They were rather influenced by the power of some Catholic politicians like John McCormack of Massachusetts, Catholic organs such as *America* (the Jesuit weekly magazine), the "opinion makers" at the Catholic University of America, and the leaders of the National Catholic Welfare Conference. Additionally powerful, particularly in the late stages of the civil war, were some members of the hierarchy whose influence was local. In the course of time the pro-Franco (or anti-Loyalist) views of many prominent Catholic leaders undoubtedly gained wider and wider appreciation by the laity. By the spring of 1938, the muscle on the many institutional arms of the Church had been well developed; and it is not unlikely that a shift to a pro-Loyalist policy would then have caused widespread Catholic resentment. By that time there had been several months during which pro-Franco views had funneled out of the national Catholic press to diocesan newspapers, from the headquarters of the national organizations to their local affiliates, from Catholic universities into elementary and secondary schools, and so on into the homes of Catholic families. As a matter of fact, the vibrant radio voice of Father

Charles Coughlin reached into thousands of non-Catholic homes as well. This filtering-down process took a little time, but the filtering-in process consumed even more.

During the last year of the war the pro-Franco element among Catholics—strengthened by isolationist and anti-Loyalist elements—became sufficiently powerful to play a primary role in blocking plans for humanitarian relief for the civilian victims of the war. The issue was significantly different from the embargo controversy. In the American political system, it is far easier for a minority to obstruct government policies and legislative proposals than to create them; and with respect to the embargo, pro-Franco groups had the easiest task of all—obstructing a *change* in an established policy. On the issue of humanitarian aid, successes gained by the Catholic minority must be attributed to other factors.

The civil war, debated as it was throughout American society, divided men at all levels. One of the most revealing dialogues took place between two patricians—Henry Stimson and his friend, an old progressive, Frederic R. Coudert.[7] The exchange between these two men uncovers much that led thoughtful Americans to dispute the meaning of the Spanish crisis.

On January 11, 1937, Coudert and Stimson discussed the Spanish problem "over lunch," a situation probably reenacted all over the country since the President had put his signature to the Spanish Embargo Act only three days before. Coudert believed that their disagreement on this occasion merited an exchange of letters, and that same evening he explained his position in a lengthy message to the former Secretary of State. Coudert, who opposed the Loyalists, was much impressed by the "hideous excesses" committed by "the Spanish Government," and by the generally admitted fact that the government was "largely influenced, if not dominated, by Russian representatives." He mentioned that the conduct of the Rebels "has been little better," and that Arabs, Germans, and Italians were fighting for Franco. Coudert interpreted the Spanish war as a battle of French and Russian Communists against Arabs allied with German and Italian Fascists. After expressing a dislike for both totalitarian systems, he went on to differentiate them. "Fascism," he wrote, "does not attack the family, property or religion, (whether Christian or otherwise)." Communism attacks all three and makes "their negation into a religion." German Fascism, according to Coudert, was "little more than an exaggerated Prussian militarism, dangerous as such, but not a mystical, subversive, doctrine [like Communism] applicable everywhere and eventuating in a general and powerful propaganda." German Fascism was "hyper-nationalism and militarism, with racialism added." Communism aimed at the destruction of fundamental institutions "in order to create a classless society based upon wholly materialist principles" and when preached as a religion was a danger "in every land." Reducing the Spanish struggle to a choice between German Fascism and worldwide Communism, Coudert thus made clear which side he felt presented the greatest danger.

Stimson, in response, confessed that he and Coudert were "pretty far apart" on the basic question of the "relative *immediate* danger to the world in general and in particular to our country of the Communistic versus the Fascist dictatorships." Stimson wrote that all of his "apprehensions are concentrated against what is now being done in Spain" by the Fascists and in the "hopes that their attempts will not be successful." He felt the "old" peril in Russia was dying down, but that "Hitler is powerful and restless, probably being drawn fairly promptly to desperate action by the economic pressure behind him and with a new very powerful army at his hand and some immediate objectives in eastern Europe which will lead to great trouble." Stimson expressed his concern over the immediate danger that a rearmed Germany posed when backed by Italy and Japan. He believed that "any further Fascist excesses in Spain are very likely to be very disastrous."

Coudert shortly afterward ended the exchange for the time being by reemphasizing the disruptive force of Communism and his personal belief that this was a new and dangerous phenomenon in history. The militaristic spirit, such as found in Germany, he wrote, "has been ever present and is no novelty." Ten months later, Coudert again returned to this theme, this time stressing that the Fascist nations were economically "have-not" nations whose people "represent a civilization far higher than that of the Russians" and closer to that of the Western democracies. It is up to England, France, and America, he argued, to "consider the economic necessities" of the Fascist nations "and afford them fair treatment." A clear expression of the idea of appeasement, these words could hardly have been more antagonistic to Stimson's line of reasoning.

It was not merely the difference in practical diplomatic experience which led these two old friends to such opposite conclusions. Stimson saw two dangers, one immediate, one relatively removed. Coudert stressed the latter, Communism, since it was a threat to all he thought good and right. The former, German Fascism, bothered him less, for "Prussia, by reason of historic conditions, was always Fascist. . . ." What obscured Coudert's vision of the unique and revolutionary character of the National Socialists in Germany, was a kind of thinking common among upper social and economic classes in the United States, and found to varying degrees among men in the State Department and in the Foreign Service. It was, ironically enough, a kind of economic determinism. The Fascist nations were have-not nations; solve their economic difficulties, relieve the economic pressures upon them, and peace could be secured. As with other kinds of economic interpretation this one contained the dangerous assumption that men can be expected to act reasonably, to follow the course which is in their best interests—if only those "best interests" are made achievable. Some individuals, partly because of their emphasis on economic aspects, were led to depreciate Nazi methods of terror and Nazi attempts to wreck fundamental institutions.

Behind this manner of discussing the Spanish issue was another questionable simplification. How correct was it to reduce the Spanish strife to an argument over German Fascism and Russian Communism? Even while some American officials, such as Moore, Kennedy, and Phillips, were slow to discard this simplification, the State Department as a whole put it aside very early in the war. Still among the American people the Spanish strife was commonly debated in those terms. The approach was certainly not much better than the liberal simplification of democracy versus Fascism, or the catch-phrases found in Catholic journals, such as the "moral order" versus "godless Communism."

In some of their decisions, American policy-makers were compelled to compromise the facts of the Spanish situation with the various interpretations of the Spanish war prevalent among the American people. In most of its decisions, the State Department appeared to be guided by its policy of nonintervention.

But there were nonpolitical issues, not so directly related to the principle of nonintervention, in which the policy-makers were compelled to decide on other bases between the appeasement of pro-Rebel and pro-Loyalist groups.

II

The task of civilian and refugee relief during the Spanish strife was of grand proportions. The International Committee of the Red Cross very early applied itself to the problem of impartial humanitarian aid, and throughout the war it was plagued by insufficient funds to combat an ever increasing problem. In September 1936, the State Department was informed by the American National Red Cross that a contribution of $10,000 had been forwarded to the International Committee for use in Spain. This was in response to a plea by the International Committee that medical assistance and supplies were greatly needed. Ernest J. Swift of the American Red Cross "advised the International Committee that it would not be opportune at this time to launch an appeal in the United States nor would it be advisable to send personnel." The people of the United States, wrote Swift, are interested in Spain, "but it is an interest rather of curiosity than one which brings out the great sympathies of the public and even if a campaign were launched no one could be sure of the results." When asked if the American Red Cross might make additional contributions, Swift replied that "this is not the time to expect our people to be sympathetic towards Europe's difficulties. The whole sentiment of the country is for keeping out of Europe and in official and private circles the feeling is that we should not expose ourselves in any way that might involve us." Part of the reason for Swift's opposition was probably due to a desire of the State Department to avoid the encouragement of organizations which were intent upon raising money to assist one side only. The State Department had already been informed that an organization called Labor's Red Cross, with David Dubinsky as treasurer, was collecting money "to assist trade unionists and laborites in Spain . . . against the onslaughts of Fascism and reaction." Opposition to sending American Red Cross personnel could have been due to a similar fear that individuals might be encouraged to request passports to do partisan relief work. The American Red Cross gave as the reason for its decision a desire to conform to the government's policy of "scrupulous non-intervention." This position was particularly useful to the State Department, for when it received inquiries from partisan organizations asking for permission to send medical personnel to Spain, the Department simply referred to the Red Cross example and implicitly refused the requests. Otherwise, until May 1937, there were no laws or regulations restricting in any way the export of medical supplies and clothing; so the State Department did not attempt to dissuade organizations from sending such goods (as long as the goods were intended for the relief of the civilian population). The federal government, according to an opinion in April 1937 by the Attorney General's office, also lacked the legal authority to prevent "the encouragement of or financial assistance to prospective combatants." The government did not give this decision publicity—it simply acted in legal accordance with it when required to do so—probably because the State Department once again feared that it might stir a public quarrel.[8]

There was no unanimity in the State Department concerning any of these decisions about medical aid, medical personnel, or aid to prospective combatants. The Passport Division, for example, suggested that if passports were refused to pro-Loyalist individuals desiring to engage in partisan humanitarian work "undesirable publicity" could be brought upon the State Department. But the prevailing opinion in the Department rejected this suggestion for the time being. During February 1937, the State Department and the White House were besieged with mail labeling the administration's policy a "departure from humanitarian tradition." At the same time Ambassador Bowers wrote to Secretary Hull that the United States was missing an opportunity to foster good will by providing humanitarian services through American agencies. Suggesting that such relief be impartial, he added: "We have done nothing in that line to merit the appreciation of the Spanish people in the future."[9] In mid-March 1937, the State Department revised its policy concerning relief personnel, but this apparently had nothing to do with a desire to create good will in Spain. Rather it was the result of domestic pressures upon the State Department and, more important, upon the President. The Department would not have succumbed to this pressure had a badly badgered President not been insistent.

On March 2, the Medical Bureau of the American Friends of Spanish Democracy informed the State Department that it was going to appeal to the President in order to challenge a decision by Moore which prevented partisan relief workers from acquiring passports. The following day the State Department issued a press release reiterating its position, and several days afterward it requested that the Red Cross send a letter to the Department outlining its policy with regard to nonpartisan relief work in Spain and the manner in which the International Committee was carrying out relief projects. The letter from the Red Cross was then given to the press on March 11 by the State Department. Along with this letter, the Department indicated its willingness to issue passports to personnel who volunteered their services to the International Red Cross should that organization "express a need for such persons." The President, then resting at Warm Springs, was late in an attempt to prevent this last press release. He desired that passports be given to individuals if the American Red Cross—without the responsibility of guarantee—could recommend that they were responsible people. Shortly after the release was given out, James Roosevelt telephoned Moore and forwarded a message indicating his father's suggestion. Moore then called Admiral Cary Grayson, president of the American Red Cross. Grayson approved of the existing policy and added that during a recent meeting of the International League of Red Cross Societies national representatives expressed a view essentially the same as that expressed by the State Department. (Also, it was apparently the position of the International League at this time that, while medical supplies were needed in Spain, medical personnel was not.) With this information, Moore returned a telephone call to James Roosevelt and suggested that he talk with Admiral Grayson before speaking with the President. Despite the doubts of Moore and Grayson, and presumably Secretary Hull as well, the President held firm. On March 13, the State Department gave out a "supplemental" release indicating the government's willingness to issue passports to medical personnel who restricted their activities to humanitarian aid.[10] Pro-Loyalist organizations thus achieved one of their few successes.

The Neutrality Act of May 1, 1937 contained provisions relating to the sending of food, clothing, and other supplies to nations involved in international or in civil war. Organizations collecting funds or goods for the purpose of humanitarian relief in war-torn areas were required to file a financial statement each month and a description of the disposition of funds and goods. The Department was thus empowered to regulate, within rather specific limits, the forwarding of such funds and goods to Spain by all organizations whether partisan or otherwise.

The Friends of the Abraham Lincoln Brigade soon successfully circumvented the legal restrictions, on the surface at least because the State Department chose to follow the letter of the law and to neglect thorough investigation. The Department reversed a decision prohibiting the organization from sending funds to Spain. The first application was refused because the indicated recipient was the General Staff of the Abraham Lincoln Battalion, Albacete, Spain. The second was accepted because the listed recipient was "a private individual in Spain."[11] While it appears that the administration once again showed that it was not thoroughly unresponsive to pro-Loyalist groups, it should also be remembered that the difficulties of checking upon the disposition of funds were incredible. If the Department had refused the second application, it would undoubtedly have received a third one which for all practical purposes would have been fool-proof. The government simply could not trace the course taken by money as easily as it could follow that of a dismantled airplane.

As soon as the Neutrality Act was signed by the President, Secretary Hull made an effort to determine the urgency of the need of relief assistance in Spain, the extent of the need, and the nature of the most outstanding wants. From the embassy in Valencia it was learned that the needs were general and urgent, particularly among the civilian population of the larger cities. It was reported that most of the organizations involved in relief work were partisan. Politically important was the fact that the need for supplies and other assistance was greater in Loyalist than in Rebel territory. Therefore aid given on the basis of need would provoke charges of intervention from Rebel and pro-Rebel quarters. The American embassy pointed out that while aid through independent American agencies would enhance

American prestige, any such assistance would have to be given with the utmost caution. From the American consulate in Barcelona it was learned that some American ambulance units in Spain were not there for the purpose of humanitarian aid but rather for assisting the Loyalist military effort. It was claimed that the activities of these units gave credence to the idea that the nonintervention policy of the United States was "a sham." The consul indicated his own acquaintance with Bishop Paddock, one of the sponsors of the organizations sending medical units to Spain, and maintained that the bishop must have been misinformed and misguided in his belief that the Loyalists represented democratic government. The consul then added that the bishop and other distinguished individuals were unwittingly giving their support to a government which had continually shown itself incapable of preventing the gravest crimes of destruction and brutality. Expressing his own belief that one side represented "chaos" and the other "tyranny," the consul urged the State Department to be scrupulous in granting passports only to those who would perform relief work impartially.[12] But the State Department, under much pressure, must have decided not to be too rigorous in its effort to guarantee that only "responsible" medical personnel went to Spain, for such aid continued to be sent through such agencies as the American Friends of Spanish Democracy.

Pro-Franco organizations were at the same time active in the collection of funds for relief in Rebel areas. But these organizations were neither numerous nor powerful. They had difficulty generating enthusiasm, partly because the need for civilian relief in Rebel-held territory was small compared to the desperate situation the Loyalists confronted (particularly during 1938 and 1939). The most important of the pro-Franco groups, the American Committee for Spanish Relief, was a complete failure. It expended some $30,000 dollars in a fundraising campaign, and collected less than $29,000. This failure was even worse when contrasted to the financial dealings of pro-Loyalist organizations. The Medical Bureau and North American Committee to Aid Spanish Democracy raised over $800,000—$573,000 of which was expended on relief activities. The Spanish Societies Confederated to Aid Spain collected almost $375,000; some $290,000 reached Spain. Altogether, pro-Loyalist organizations received contributions amounting to over $1,800,000—a modest estimate. Pro-Rebel groups seem to have collected not more than $150,000 to $200,000, and most of this probably was spent on publicity and other expenses. The most active and most successful of the impartial organizations, aside from the Red Cross, was the American Friends Service Committee, whose contribution (particularly in the last months of the war) cannot be even nearly rendered by a statement of figures.[13]

The greatest task faced by pro-Franco organizations was to present the insurgent movement in a favorable light. This assignment was primarily assumed by some individuals in the National Catholic Welfare Conference (N.C.W.C.), particularly by its capable legal secretary, William F. Montavon. Whatever were Montavon's early prejudices—and after a visit to Spain during the first year of the Republic he returned with rather dispassionate views of both the Church and the state— he became the chief American press agent for the Spanish Nationalists. Part of Montavon's job was to maintain contact with insurgent and Catholic information agencies abroad, for the purpose of disseminating news items to the press in general and to the Catholic press in particular. Dedicated as Montavon was to the task of improving the dismal press image of the Rebel cause, the information agencies in Rebel Spain exasperated him. He pleaded for concrete evidence of atrocities which had been charged to Loyalists, for reliable statistical information, and for copies of governmental decrees and laws. Instead he received, in his own words, "inadequate evidence." At one point he wrote to the Rebel press agency in Salamanca that "the American public demands evidence, not comments. . . ." In March 1937, Juan Francisco de Cardenas, agent of the Rebel government, paid a visit to Montavon and proved evasive when questioned about his credentials, his activities in the United States, and General Franco's plans for the reconstruction of Spain. Montavon advised against cooperation with de Cardenas, unless the N.C.W.C. were approached by the Spanish hierarchy or the Holy See through the Apostolic Delegation in Washington. Montavon's apprehensions proceeded largely from de Cardenas' desire to collect funds in the United States to aid the Rebel cause (a plan for which legal, if devious, means might have been available).[14]

The National Catholic Welfare Conference also acted as a

watch-dog over the activities of pro-Loyalist organizations. In this respect, it received the cooperation of such Catholic congressional leaders as Senator Walsh and Representative McCormack. The N.C.W.C. was not only informed by congressmen about what pro-Loyalist groups were doing on Capitol Hill, but it in turn furnished to congressmen information on pro-Loyalist activities elsewhere. In October 1938, McCormack took straight to President Roosevelt a complaint by the N.C.W.C. that a pro-Loyalist circular was being distributed throughout more than a half dozen federal government agencies. The circular included a plea for contributions. But the President, who was then developing a stiffening attitude toward Fascist aggression in Spain, appeared ill disposed toward stopping this activity. A return letter to McCormack, drafted by Welles and Davis, evaded the specifics of the complaint.[15]

The Roosevelt administration, while it appeared respectful of the pressures from pro-Franco organizations, was not inclined to respond to their demands on minor issues when it was perfectly legal to avoid doing so. On explosive issues the administration acted differently. One of the worst of these controversies grew out of a plan to bring Basque refugee children to the United States, an idea which seemed well enough in accordance with the American image of humanitarianism. Yet, as these were children of Basque Catholics who were fighting for the Spanish government, there arose some angry Catholic opposition in the United States. The notion of aiding Basque refugees had a simple beginning. In April 1937, Alvarez del Vayo asked William Bullitt if the American Red Cross could help relieve the suffering of 100,000 women and children who would shortly have to be evacuated from Bilbao. Premier Blum had already informed del Vayo that evacuees could be brought across the French border. About a month later, a group of Americans formed a committee, the Board of Guardians for Basque Refugee Children, for the purpose of financing the transportation of 500 Basque children to the United States. There appeared to be no lack of people, particularly Basque-Americans, who were willing to assume the responsibility of taking these children. The Board of Guardians was headed by Gardner Jackson, Chairman of the American Friends of Spanish Democracy, Caroline O'Day, a New York congresswoman, President Mary Emma Woolley of Mount Holyoke College, Professor James T.

Shotwell of Columbia University, and Dr. Franck Bohn, who was made secretary of the organization. It received the support of Eleanor Roosevelt, and Ambassador Bowers was named as chairman of a committee to help bring the group's plans to fruition.[16]

While jurisdiction over the admission of refugees was in the hands of the Secretary of Labor, the State Department quickly issued instructions to American officials in Spain. It clearly anticipated that the plan would be carried out. The State Department had hardly instructed its consular officials concerning applications for visas when there was an uproar from Catholics opposing the plan. The most powerful opposition came again from McCormack, who claimed that the scheme was intended for use as Communist propaganda. He put pressure upon the President and upon the Department of State as well. He claimed that some Basque refugee children who already had been sent to England were not always placed in Catholic homes; further, since it was a matter of obtaining visas for a temporary visit, the children might well be taken care of elsewhere at less expense. Probably the strongest argument advanced by Catholic opponents of the plan concerned the leadership of the Board of Guardians; for prominent Catholics, regardless of their views toward the Spanish strife, were not included. The committee was made up largely of individuals who had in one way or another been active pro-Loyalists. The Board of Guardians might well have anticipated opposition from Catholic quarters and prepared for it by seeking a balanced set of sponsors. Charges that the group had a purpose beyond caring for helpless refugees were consequently not easy to refute. The plan collapsed more rapidly than it had begun. The Department of Labor acted upon the advice of Under Secretary Welles that the "children should not be brought to the United States but should be permitted to live in France or some other country nearer their own parents." If organizations in the United States wished to contribute to their support, Welles added, money could be sent abroad for this purpose and disbursed "under the auspices of some appropriate organization over there."[17] The plan was not impartially conceived, nor did it suffer an impartial death. At the beginning there might have been room for compromise if the pro-Loyalist leadership had wanted to initiate it. Likewise, Catholic leaders might also have

offered a compromise solution. Perhaps a common effort was
not possible; but more likely it was considered mutually intolerable. Consequently, there was a political battle over the
welfare of homeless and often starving children. But this was
not the last time that quarrels in the United States would affect
efforts to relieve the suffering of noncombatant victims of the
Spanish war.

III

Aside from the embargo controversy, which was, until
1939, not violent but continuous, the most heated domestic
quarrel over the Spanish strife concerned a plan for massive
"impartial" relief. In addition to the participation of the federal government, it involved three impartial organizations: the
American Red Cross, the American Friends Service Committee,
and a special body formed by the President in December 1938
and known as the Committee for Impartial Civilian Relief in
Spain. Since 1936 both the Red Cross and the Friends had been
actively aiding relief efforts in Spain. The Red Cross particularly welcomed the participation of the Friends since its general
fund was already heavily committed to the task of relieving
disastrous conditions in China. The work of these two organizations caused a minimum of public controversy until late 1938.
Up to that time the greatest danger to their chances of successful work in Spain was caused by some public impatience over
the activities of partisan groups. The Red Cross was apparently very sensitive to the possible effects of partisan activities.
It was, for example, considered a bad omen when the interna-
tionally-oriented editors of the *San Francisco Chronicle* expressed their skepticism about the use of funds contributed to
partisan groups for foreign relief. Public skepticism might
become indiscriminate and hurt the fund drives of the Red
Cross. The Red Cross (along with the President and the State
Department) had already been hurt by a public dispute over its
relief efforts in China. On the whole, however, the funds and
services provided and administered in Spain by the Red Cross
and the American Friends Service Committee went almost un-
criticized for about two years.[18]
Early in the summer of 1938, the State Department ap-

proached Norman Davis, whom Roosevelt had recently appointed President of the Red Cross. Davis was asked if the Red Cross might be able to contribute "any considerable financial assistance to Spain." Davis, at the time struggling with the fund drive for Chinese relief, felt that a large appropriation from the society's general fund would be unwise. Subsequently, however, a number of meetings were directed to this issue, involving at various times Moffat and Welles from the State Department, Ernest Swift of the Red Cross, and Secretary of Agriculture Henry Wallace. The Spanish ambassador was kept informed of general developments and continually pressed for a solution. The group hit upon the idea of making available government-held surplus commodities. Working with the Federal Surplus Commodities Corporation, they unsnarled innumerable legal, financial, and political entanglements. Finally, upon being informed that the plan was possible, Davis gave Swift—along with de los Ríos—the task of working out details. The ambassador was able to provide estimates based upon the memorable relief operations carried on in Belgium in 1918 and 1919. The Red Cross subsequently received from the Federal Surplus Commodities Corporation 250,000 barrels of flour, which could be processed and transported to ports on the east coast for about one dollar per barrel. The United States Maritime Commission offered to transport the flour to Bordeaux or Le Havre at no expense, if the Red Cross would reimburse the commission for loading and unloading costs—about an additional 20 cents per barrel. The Friends offered to receive the wheat in France and to distribute the food as representatives of the American Red Cross. The total cost to the Red Cross, even though the Friends would assume the costs once the flour reached France, still amounted to a minimum of $300,000. Faced with this figure, the Red Cross lowered its aim and appropriated $75,000, which enabled it to send 60,000 barrels of flour to Spain during November and December. In addition to this, the Maritime Commission also shipped gifts contributed by interested groups both in the United States and in Latin America. These contributions included evaporated and powdered milk, soap, chocolate, coffee, and sugar. The State Department was largely responsible for winning the cooperation of the Brazilian government in this scheme.[19]

The Red Cross had expended all that it could then afford.

Yet Davis found from his correspondence with Clarence Pickett of the Friends that 60,000 barrels of flour would not be nearly enough "to prevent starvation and grave malnutrition during the rest of the winter and spring." As a temporary solution, the Red Cross advanced funds to the Friends on condition that it be reimbursed as soon as possible. The Friends thus took on an additional burden, but the problem of starvation was yet to be combated. Under these circumstances, on December 21, 1938, the State Department stepped forward with a statement of distress over reports of misery in Spain. It made clear the Surplus Commodities Corporation's ability to provide 100,000 barrels of flour each month for six months; and it also made clear the government's inability to make a gift of the flour and the Red Cross's inability to purchase it.[20]

At the same time, the Department's press release was intended to weaken the efforts of Ernst Toller, who, apparently on his own initiative, was attempting to organize an international food commission for impartial civilian relief in Spain. A German playwright, then in exile, Toller was well known for his radical sympathies. He was now seeking arrangements for cooperative governmental action, presumably under the leadership of an American. He came to Washington in November 1938, with the aim of seeing President Roosevelt, and brought with him numerous letters of commendation from such diverse sources as the Archbishop of Canterbury and the Crown Prince of Sweden. He even had instructions from Catholic clergymen in Loyalist Spain, directing him to the "President's friend—Cardinal Mundelein," and letters of introduction to about half of the members of Roosevelt's cabinet. He was encouraged by Eleanor Roosevelt and, for a time at least, by Clarence Pickett. But the President, rather than seeing Toller himself, directed him to the State Department. In the meantime, the liberal press, including the *Commonweal*, gave Toller's ambitious plan additional encouragement. But at the State Department, Toller's manifold references gained him nothing but polite discouragement. There were reasons for this treatment. Most simply, Toller's plan was unrealistic, particularly since a large-scale relief effort was needed very quickly. The chances were nil of putting a massive international program into effect within a short time (if at all). But there were other kinds of obstacles. As Moffat recorded in his Diary: "I think Toller is a humanitarian at heart but he wants the commission for political purposes. Sumner Welles and the rest of us are particularly anxious that the humanitarian and the political aspects of feeding are kept entirely separate." John F. Reich of the Friends and Norman Davis were worried about the same problem. Toller was early convinced that right-wing Catholics, "rich Jews," and other conservatives were blocking his efforts because of his reputation as a radical. But Toller also admitted to being hampered by the reluctance of the Spanish government to cooperate with him fully. Apparently believing that his plan would end in failure, Loyalist officials were hesitant to provide him with important information on relief needs. Such information had military importance. Not until the middle of December did he receive any real encouragement from that quarter, and even then Toller was not given vital data. By that time, furthermore, President Roosevelt was completing arrangements for his own program.[21]

The State Department's press release of December 21 was the first indication that the Roosevelt administration was going to step right into the middle of the crisis. Two days earlier the President had completed the first stage of his own plan. It had been known for some time that the Red Cross would not be able to carry out its plan for lack of funds. This prompted various schemes from various sources, none of them satisfactory from an impartial point of view. The most common proposal was that organizations make funds available to the Red Cross for the purchase of the wheat from the Surplus Commodities Corporation, and then these organizations would distribute the wheat themselves. The dangers of this kind of scheme were too obvious to be given serious consideration, and the Red Cross flatly rejected the idea. Then President Roosevelt, with the aid of the State Department and the Red Cross, devised a method of raising funds which appeared to be acceptable. By all appearances the President was trying to learn a lesson from the failure of the child refugee relief plan in which his wife had earlier taken part; he made an obvious attempt to appease pro-Franco Catholics. The outline of the plan was designed in the State Department; and, while it bore almost no resemblance to Toller's project, it was undoubtedly given some impetus by the German playwright's activities. The President decided to create a committee of prominent citizens for the purpose of putting on a large-scale fund-raising campaign. Approximately

$120,000 per month would be needed if the committee were to help the Red Cross purchase and ship the wheat that was available. On December 19, the President wrote to George Mac-Donald, a prominent Catholic layman in New York City, confirming his appointment as head of this special committee. Letters were addressed to eleven other men and women noted for both wealth and position to serve with him. It was thought that a group made up of notable individuals, and cooperating with the Red Cross and the Friends, would be able to procure large sums of money "through the solicitation of a few hundred prominent Americans." Within a matter of days the Committee for Impartial Relief in Spain established its headquarters in New York City. Just as rapidly, Catholics stormed in protest.[22]

In choosing MacDonald to head this commission, the President found that he had not learned the full lesson. At the very least, he had chosen the wrong Catholic, for MacDonald proved unable to resist the attacks made upon the Commission by the Catholic press. A more resilient person than he, however, would not have been able to deal with the basic problem. Catholic resentment in some areas grew so rapidly and to such extremes that even Catholic schools were reportedly neglecting to renew membership in the Junior Red Cross. Bitter editorials in the Catholic press were commonplace. The editors of *America* asked if it was "planned to force this flour on Nationalist Spain so that the term 'non-partisan' might be used in the United States to cover all shipments to Loyalist Spain." It was also suggested that the plan bore a relationship to current movements calling for repeal of the Spanish embargo. The most common complaint was that more flour was going to Loyalist than to Rebel Spain (this charge being made despite the fact that the Insurgents had a wheat surplus in 1938).[23] During February, Davis attempted to offset this criticism by redirecting a shipment from the Loyalists to the Nationalists. This brought a cry from American liberals, who were already very upset over charges that General Franco was using the wheat to purchase German munitions. These were problems MacDonald could not have been expected to avoid nor, in any real way, to solve; but since he accepted the position it would seem to have been his duty to perform his tasks as best he could or resign. He did neither.[24]

In a letter to the President, Davis described the situation

candidly: "Apparently pressure from radical Catholics has about driven MacDonald crazy, and he, in turn, is about to make the Friends crazy." MacDonald claimed that the committee was not his responsibility. He "seldom" went to his office, and those working with the Commission "had to wait for days even to get to speak to him." Other members of the Commission expressed impatience with MacDonald when he personally failed to make a contribution to the fund; without something from the head of the Commission, it was difficult to obtain contributions from outsiders. MacDonald also vented some bitterness over Harold Ickes' participation in the North American Committee to Aid Spanish Democracy, feeling that the Secretary's actions gave official recognition to a partisan organization. In February, MacDonald walked off the job and refused to sanction a replacement. Others tried to salvage what they could, but in the end they raised only $50,000.[25] It was a sad experience for the President, let alone for the Spanish people. Roosevelt's plan was certainly not helped along by Drew Pearson and Robert Allen, who maintained that the President conceived the scheme in order "to keep the Loyalists alive and fighting during the winter." The story had an odor of credibility which no amount of refutation could eradicate. It was clear that aid to refugees would ease the general food problem in Loyalist Spain and thereby indirectly help the Loyalist war effort. Consequently some congressmen were convinced of the truth of the Pearson-Allen story, and this was made clear both to the State Department and to George MacDonald very early in January.[26]

The whole dispute, angry from beginning to end, whipped up partisan organizations to fever heat. When Congress opened its session in January 1939, Capitol Hill was swarming with pressure groups. The embargo controversy once more arose, and it was the "best organized controversy" of the war. Pro-Loyalist groups were inclined to believe that every important effort they had made to bring American policy in line with their sentiments had failed because of Catholic opposition. There was truth to this charge, to varying degrees, on many of the Spanish issues since the spring of 1937. Catholic antagonism alone, however, cannot account for the failure of pro-Loyalist groups to achieve most of their aims. Communist involvement in Spain and in American organizations supporting the cause of the Spanish government, for example, did much to create a widespread attitude of indifference toward Fascist aggression on the Iberian peninsula. Perhaps more important to partisans of both sides was the half-way success each of them achieved in their attempts to influence public opinion. They long failed to create large bodies of pro-Loyalist and pro-Rebel sympathizers. But, with all their confusing cross-fire, they did help bring about anti-Rebel and anti-Loyalist sentiments and thus together encouraged attitudes of indifference and antagonism toward both Spanish parties. Not until the last months of the war did this situation change in any significant way.

10

THE LAST MONTHS OF THE WAR

Eᴀʀʟʏ ɪɴ February 1939, a pro-Loyalist lobbyist remarked that Congress was like a "sponge." "It yields," he said,
"but after you let go what have you got?"[1] Much the same
might have been said about the President concerning pro-Loyalist pressure to repeal the embargo. Neither he nor Congress
had precisely the same reasons as the State Department for
retaining the embargo, for both Congress and the President—
almost of necessity—were more appreciative of domestic pressures than of the delicate complexities of international developments. This in part accounts for the changed character of the
last embargo controversy. As the President assumed an increasingly active role in policy-making, the embargo became less an
international question and more a domestic one. This in turn
meant that the State Department sometimes found itself more
involved with the political than with the diplomatic issues. One
finds in State Department records, for the last three months of
the war, far less debate over what the British might do if the
United States shipped arms to Spain; there is even very little
regarding what form German and Italian reactions might take,
or what effects repeal might have upon the Good Neighbor
policy. The question some congressmen raised in May 1938
took on greater importance. How powerful was the pro-Franco
element of the Catholic Church? Developments in Spain posed
another question. Could the Loyalists win if American arms

reached Spain? Or would the time of misery simply be extended? If congressional leaders, and the President as well, responded like sponges to pro-Loyalist pressure in 1939, the reason lay primarily in the unwillingness of each to assume the political risks of initiating a move for repeal. That a desire to lift the embargo was growing—in Congress and in the White House, and in the State Department, too—there is no doubt. There was desire, but there was no resolution.

Pro-Franco Catholics, a minority within a minority, were primarily responsible for the failure of the government to reverse its Spanish policy in 1939. But this is not the complete explanation. In addition to other factors, such as the questionable results which would accrue from American aid to the Spanish government, there were practical political and strategic considerations as well. Among the most important of these was the administration's armament program, the success of which depended on the administration's ability to convince the public and many congressmen that the program was for defense alone. An "aggressive" policy toward the Spanish conflict could upset the growing support for a larger armament budget. Even here, however, particularly influential Catholics were a factor. One of the staunchest supporters of the administration's defense program was Senator Walsh, as ardent in his belief that the Spanish embargo should be kept as he was diligent in his campaign for an impenetrable naval defense. The prospect of losing his support, as well as that of other isolationist, anti-Loyalist, or pro-Franco congressmen, was not a happy one. There was additionally the matter of legislation to combat the serious economic situation, and in this area the President had faced continual defeat over the past two years. In January 1939, the President confronted the prospect of still another setback, as Congress engaged in a bitter debate over the Works Progress Administration. From the point of view of Roosevelt, and of those loyal to him on Capitol Hill, an attempt to remove the Spanish embargo could bring disastrous results at home without the slightest guarantee that the Spanish government would be victorious. The power of pro-Franco Catholics was very dependent upon these other circumstances. The Roosevelt administration was vulnerable in too many important ways. Finally, there is no way of estimating what role international considerations would have played during these months had the

Spanish embargo not become so terribly explosive as a political issue. The same international complications still existed, and they could possibly have been decisive in blocking the repeal of the embargo had there been no serious domestic controversy.

I

Where the American public stood on the Spanish issue in 1939 can be estimated from opinion polls, of which there were enough to indicate a discernible pattern. A half-dozen polls were taken by the American Institute of Public Opinion between December 16, 1938 and February 2, 1939. They are important if only because pro-Loyalist lobbyists spent much time studying these polls and in some cases planning their strategy accordingly. Three important conclusions could be drawn from them. First, there was a large discrepancy between pro-Loyalist sympathies and the desire to act upon them (a combination of attitudes very like that which then prevailed in the State Department); second, approximately two out of every five Americans apparently had not been following the Spanish conflict; and, third, a good many people within that large "uninformed" group apparently opposed the repeal of the embargo. The peak number of Americans expressing pro-Loyalist sympathies was 51 per cent; and the peak number desiring repeal of the embargo was only 25 per cent. Furthermore, opposition to repeal was always greater than support for it. Those figures found in later polls, when techniques had been refined, indicated that the percentage opposed to repeal dropped dramatically when only those who claimed to have been following the war were questioned about the embargo. Two other conclusions were drawn by leaders of pro-Loyalist pressure groups—one encouraging to them, one distressing. Something less than a third of the Catholics who were polled favored Franco. On the other hand, groups favoring the embargo were making effective use of "war fear." One prorepeal lobbyist complained that fear of war was the "biggest obstacle." If this was true, then the Roosevelt administration had even more reason to be concerned about the relationships among the Spanish policy, the armament program, and public apprehensions about the possibilities of a general conflict.[2]

The extent to which pro-Loyalist pressure groups turned to opinion polls indicated their conviction that the President and Congress could be moved only if convinced that the public would approve of a change of policy—or at least not create a violent controversy. The widespread distribution of misleading poll results was one of the tactics of a newly created organization called the Coordinating Committee to Lift the Embargo. This committee, under the direction of Herman Reissig, brought together the half-dozen most influential pro-Loyalist organizations: the Medical Bureau and North American Committee to Aid Spanish Democracy, the American Friends of Spanish Democracy, the American League for Peace and Democracy (formerly American League against War and Fascism), the Lawyers Committee on American Relations with Spain, the Confederated Spanish Societies, and the Friends of the Abraham Lincoln Brigade. The Coordinating Committee furnished the administration and congressmen with results of polls which lacked the large percentage of "indifferent" and "no opinion" answers to questions concerning sympathies toward one side or the other. In the Committee's propaganda, it appeared that 76 per cent of the Americans questioned favored the Loyalists; in reality it was only 51 per cent. And the question of sympathy was not really the basic issue: rather it was whether or not the public favored repeal of the embargo. Late in January, the Coordinating Committee apparently succeeded in stopping a Gallup press release which would have revealed that only 21 per cent of those polled favored lifting the embargo. An additional 30 per cent favored the Loyalists while opposing repeal of the embargo.[3] But the damage was probably already done to the pro-Loyalist cause, for Gallup polls published before this purported incident (and again after it) indicated only a slightly higher number favoring repeal. All the emphasis the Coordinating Committee placed upon opinion polls would seem to have been self-defeating. Yet it is possible that the Committee decided to counteract the real results with misleading ones for the purpose of creating, at the least, some confusion. These tactics, however, were among the least important activities engaged in by the Coordinating Committee.

Composed as it was of the six most powerful pro-Loyalist groups, the Committee possessed funds substantial enough to finance numerous operations. Much of the latter, however, were still "informally" managed by six field workers who roamed the United States setting up public meetings and rallies, collecting funds, organizing letter-writing campaigns, and encouraging citizens to visit Washington to express their views personally. Just how much of the prorepeal agitation during this time is directly traceable to the Coordinating Committee is impossible to estimate. Sometimes field workers helped set up local committees and then moved on; on other occasions they simply checked to see what existing organizations were doing. One of the field organizers was Fred Keller, a Roman Catholic and a veteran of the Abraham Lincoln Battalion—two desirable affiliations for someone working at this difficult task. Keller and the other organizers encountered two particularly troublesome experiences—first local fears of the strength of the Catholic Church (for example, fear of Catholic boycotts of businesses whose owners expressed public support for the Loyalists); and, second, a defeatist attitude toward the chances of repealing the embargo. Defeatism was reported as having hit even members of the Communist party.[4]

With the opening of Congress in January, the Coordinating Committee began to compile lists of senators and representatives favorable to, and against, repeal—apparently on the theory that the Roosevelt administration would continue its previous refusal to attempt repeal by a simple executive proclamation. It was therefore believed necessary to obtain repeal through congressional action. Lobbyists were set to the task of interviewing congressmen, as much to obtain an idea of their positions on the embargo issue as to provide them with prorepeal arguments. The Coordinating Committee was quick to find out from these interviews that no one wanted to take the initiative on such an explosive issue. One pro-Loyalist contingent complained to the President about a typical rat-in-a-maze experience. Sumner Welles had directed them to Senator Pittman and to Sol Bloom (the new chairman of the House Foreign Affairs Committee), saying "that the State Department could not initiate any action whatever." Then they were told that Pittman could not see them, and Bloom turned them away claiming that it was the State Department's "business to initiate action."

Experiencing the same kind of difficulties, the Coordinating Committee decided that the prospect of repeal by presidential proclamation was better than by congressional action, and it adopted the strategy of getting influential congressmen to assure the President that they would back him (or at least not attack him) if he acted on the embargo himself. This plan seems to have been adopted on January 30, upon the suggestion of Drew Pearson during a meeting in Washington of the Lawyers Committee on American Relations with Spain. It was probably prompted by the fact that the Coordinating Committee's lobbyists had encountered great difficulty acquiring prorepeal commitments from a sufficient number of Northern Democrats. The latter were especially sensitive to their Catholic constituents in large cities. (There, proembargo Catholic leaders had a substantial, even if more liberal, Catholic audience.) Additionally frustrating to the Coordinating Committee was the administration's unwillingness to make a move for support on Capitol Hill. For this reason the lobbyists often found Democrats to be more evasive on the issue than some Republicans like Senators Charles McNary of Oregon and Henry Cabot Lodge of Massachusetts—both of whom plainly stated their prorepeal sentiments. McNary even maintained that he had seen Secretary Hull to express his views. Democratic Senators such as Lister Hill of Alabama, Elbert Thomas of Utah, and Warren Barbour of New Jersey vacillated or contradicted themselves. Several senators, among them Sheridan Downey of California, Claude Pepper of Florida, and James Davis of Pennsylvania, made their positions on repeal contingent upon mail continually coming in from constituents or upon the positions to be taken by the President and the State Department. As for the House, the Coordinating Committee had a problem similar to that which it met in the Senate—the difficulty of obtaining an affirmative commitment seemed to rise in proportion to the stature of the congressman; so that, while the Committee was able to compile lengthy lists of "supporters," the lists were notoriously devoid of influential names.

It would seem reasonable to question the methods used by the Coordinating Committee in its attempt to win support in Congress. Although it is possible that no better methods were available, there seems to have been too little appreciation of the power of party discipline. The Committee wasted much time on congressmen who, when the chips were finally down, would not act independently of their more powerful colleagues. This indeed is why Joel Berrall found Congress to be like a sponge. Verbal commitments and words of encouragement meant nothing as soon as Berrall, or one of his fellow lobbyists, left the presence of prorepeal congressmen. What the committee needed was the aid of a man of Key Pittman's stature; and he habitually dodged explosive issues, postponed them, or seriously compromised them. (The senator, moreover, had a particular aversion to "radicals" and "intellectuals.") But without someone like Pittman, or even Bloom, that "jovial Tammany man," the Committee had little chance of success. It also needed the aid of the White House, at least behind the scenes. But, as it failed to make serious inroads into the House Foreign Affairs and the Senate Foreign Relations Committees, so it failed to penetrate the White House. One of the accomplishments most prized by the Coordinating Committee was Herbert Hoover's purported statement, confidentially made, that he would not attack the President if he lifted the embargo by proclamation. The Committee seemed to place great weight upon the former President's statement, even though Hoover added that he would neither ask Roosevelt to lift it nor give Roosevelt assurances that he would not attack him if he did repeal it. On Capitol Hill, Senator Gerald P. Nye stood almost alone among the prominent senators with his outspoken prorepeal views. He was joined by George Norris, but Norris, like so many others, was unwilling to do anything significant to help the cause. Nye, meanwhile, was busily attacking the administration on other matters. The Coordinating Committee had a measure of success with officials in various executive departments of the government, but these individuals (for example, Ickes) were really without effective power over the Spanish policy. By the accident of circumstances, as well as by design, the continued and extensive efforts of prorepeal groups met continual failure. Even on those occasions when it appeared that some progress had been made, it proved to be elusive.[5]

One of the obstacles which, with good reason, most troubled the Coordinating Committee was the pro-Franco element of the Catholic Church. Early in 1939, the Medical Bureau and North American Committee to Aid Spanish Democracy published a pamphlet entitled "Catholic Evidence on Spain." Reportedly compiled by Catholic laymen who supported the organization, it contained statements by prominent Catholics—among them

George Schuster and Luis Sarasola, a Spanish priest. Copies were sent to the White House, to the State Department, and to congressmen. Richard Hogue, a director of a legislative information agency, and at the time working with Berrall for the Coordinating Committee, believed that the pamphlet was of some value. It did indicate that not all prominent Catholics were necessarily anti-Loyalist; but of perhaps greater importance it stressed the role of the Basque Catholics in the Loyalist military effort and the Pope's charitable attitude toward the Basques. The Coordinating Committee did not entertain the hopeless notion at this late date of changing Catholic anti-Loyalist opinion; it was rather hoping to provide government officials with a crutch upon which to lean should they desire to lift the embargo. The Coordinating Committee fully expected a "threat of united action on the part of the Catholic Church" if the President adopted a pro-Loyalist policy. While there is no record of what Reissig and others on the Committee actually planned to do, they were considering ways in which to mitigate such a threat. They knew that the President feared what effects Catholic and isolationist antagonism might have upon the rest of Roosevelt's legislative program.[6]

During this same period, proembargo groups became increasingly active. Most important was a recently formed organization called the Keep the Spanish Embargo Committee. Composed of pro-Nationalists, anti-Loyalists, and some "ordinary" isolationists, it was sponsored by the National Council of Catholic Men. Like the Coordinating Committee to Lift the Embargo, this organization also provoked a letter-writing campaign. By the end of January, more than a million signatures attached to proembargo petitions had been sent to Congress. This was accomplished with the aid of an appeal by Father Coughlin. A more ominous fact for the President, and for those congressmen who also respected the potential political power of the Catholic Church, was that the "grass-roots" proembargo response was due largely to direct appeals by members of the Catholic hierarchy. In the archdiocese of Philadelphia, Dennis Cardinal Dougherty "directed" Catholics to sign petitions immediately and "to forward them to Congress protesting against the removal of the embargo on munitions." Michael Francis Doyle, a Catholic lawyer from Philadelphia, and a friend of the President, informed the White House of this in mid-January. He told Roosevelt that similar appeals were being made by other bishops throughout the country. Having promised to keep Roosevelt informed about such developments, he forwarded a copy of a circular published by the Keep the Embargo Committee. It had been distributed in the archdiocese on January 15. Some of the points in this circular (and some of its language) were by this time standard; for example, it described the actions of some groups fighting with the Loyalists as "brutish vandalism" and "savagery." But one position was developed which had been surprisingly neglected, and it was believed to be one of the most persuasive proembargo arguments:

Had the United States continued to permit munitions shipments to the government which it recognized in Spain it might have contended, under the principles of international law, that it was not formally taking sides in the Spanish conflict. Such permission would have been the result only of an omission to act on the part of the Government of the United States. But since our Government has formally adopted a law forbidding munitions shipments, and has continued under that law for nearly two years, we can now return to the original position only by a positive act—repeal of the Act of May 1, 1937—and that cannot but be regarded as taking sides. . . .

Parishioners were urged to write, wire, or telephone their representatives and senators, and to sign the petition being passed about with the circular. In less than two weeks some 10,000 telegrams were sent to congressmen from the Philadelphia archdiocese alone.[7]

Proembargo groups were also active on Capitol Hill, using much the same strategy as the Coordinating Committee to Lift the Embargo—but encountering less difficulty. The burden of proof weighed less heavily upon the proembargo groups since they were only arguing for the continuation of an existing policy. Even more to their advantage was the ironic fact that proembargo congressmen, while opposing the current sentiments of the President, were merely advocating a policy initiated by the administration. It was this advantage which William Montavon of the National Catholic Welfare Conference sought to exploit when he met with interested congressmen. Montavon brought with him to some of these meetings Aileen O'Brien, daughter of a former United States ambassador to

Bolivia, recently an organizer for the Irish Red Cross in Spain, and a fairly popular pro-Franco speaker. On January 19, Montavon brought her to a meeting attended by eleven congressmen (plus a member of the Irish parliament). Miss O'Brien was said to have made a "favorable impression" on the group, which included John McCormack. The following morning she and Montavon met with Senator Walsh and after that with another group of congressmen. During the latter meeting, Miss O'Brien's impression was such that one of the congressmen promised to escort her to the State Department. She had first appeared in Washington during a Keep the Spanish Embargo rally at Constitution Hall, an assembly supported by Archbishop Michael J. Curley of Baltimore. On that occasion she spoke on the same program with Irwin Laughlin (who had preceded Bowers as ambassador to Spain), the Right Reverend Fulton J. Sheen, and Martin Conboy, a New York lawyer shortly to be known for his letters to the *New York Times* opposing Henry Stimson's prorepeal views.[8]

President Roosevelt, who was close to Cardinal Mundelein of Chicago, was undoubtedly interested in the Cardinal's interpretation of this Catholic opposition to repeal—as manifested in the activities of the Catholic hierarchy and leaders of dozens of Catholic organizations, as well as in the Catholic press. There was probably no other figure in the hierarchy more sympathetic to Roosevelt's political and international views than Mundelein, and it was natural that some speculation would take place as to what Mundelein might advise the President under the circumstances. Some credence seems to have been placed in a report which first appeared in the *Christian Science Monitor*, claiming that Mundelein telephoned the President and advised against presidential support of efforts aimed at lifting the embargo. Regardless of which man telephoned the other, the substance of the story is very likely true. While Mundelein had even been credited with an attempt to swing Catholic opinion away from Franco, the Cardinal certainly appreciated political realities. The journalist, Jay Allen (once a Catholic himself), believed that Mundelein's real desire was to force mediation in Spain by a threefold policy: send relief to the Spanish Loyalists; maintain the embargo; and cooperate with the Non-Intervention Committee. Presumably this policy would enable the

Loyalists to continue their military effort, keep the United States in an impartial position so as to be able to offer mediation with a chance of success, and sustain the good will of Great Britain, France, and other nations, so that they might cooperate with, or support, efforts at mediation.[9] Obviously, even this moderate position was anathema to most other influential Catholics. And Mundelein was never able to push this view very vigorously.

At the time when pro-Loyalist groups were attempting to minimize the strength of pro-Franco opinion among Catholics, many Catholic leaders set out to prove the contrary. It was finally demonstrated that, in order to maintain the embargo, pro-Franco groups needed only to discourage a radical change in public opinion. Prorepealers were not only fighting pro-Franco organizations but also combating neutral and isolationist sentiment, and plain indifference as well. Because all these attitudes were so well represented in Congress, the prorepealers stood little chance of gaining their ends on Capitol Hill. That was why they turned to the White House. They hoped that should the President act independently the large mass of indifferent Americans would simply acquiesce in an accomplished fact. The Coordinating Committee was informed by some congressional leaders early in February "that a minimum of opposition could be had if the President acted [alone]." Disagreeing with this, Pittman reportedly told Moore that most senators wanted the President to make a recommendation—then they could snipe at it.[10]

II

In the last months of 1938, in preparation for the coming session of Congress, much thought was given to neutrality legislation in both the White House and the State Department. On October 18, a long meeting attended by eleven Departmental officers was held in Counselor Moore's office. The prevailing view at this meeting with regard to civil wars was that the President ought to be given greater discretion in the application of an embargo as well as in making any limitations and exceptions he might desire. It appears that the majority preferred to do away with arms embargo provisions altogether but believed that this was not politically feasible. One month later, there was another meeting in Secretary Hull's office to discuss the possibility of an announcement by the President that he would ask Congress to lift the Spanish embargo. According to Moffat, the President was "clearly anxious to do so." Adolph Berle is the only one known to have supported the President's position at this meeting, although Moffat favored cash-and-carry sales of arms and opposed a public statement. Moore and Hackworth "were opposed to the President's idea, with Dunn inclining to favor them." This same group, and Moore especially, had been consistently opposed to repeal by presidential proclamation and also to direct executive encouragement of repeal by congressional action. Moore had months before prepared a closely reasoned memorandum on the legal question of repeal by proclamation, and he had concluded that the May 1937 legislation did not implicitly amend or repeal the Spanish Embargo Resolution of January 1937. A presidential declaration of repeal would only lift the May 1937 provisions currently in force against Spain. There is no doubt that the Secretary upheld Moore's legal opinion (although immediately following this meeting Hull reportedly confined himself to advising the President to think the matter through "more carefully" before making a public commitment). In fact Hull had given the President this same opinion on May 1, 1937. Roosevelt, however, was not now fully convinced by this legal argument, and sought the interpretation of Attorney General Homer Cummings. The President, in the meantime, took up the question with the State Department once again—this time through Sumner Welles. Roosevelt's actions were prompted in part by a memorandum given to him by Ickes and prepared by the Lawyers Committee on American Relations with Spain; it argued the legality of presidential repeal.[11]

From the State Department and the Attorney General, Roosevelt received conflicting opinions. The question of whether or not the President could legally repeal the embargo by proclamation was never in doubt in the State Department. It consistently held to Hull's original opinion. In fact, the January resolution appeared in *The Laws and Regulations Administered by the Secretary of State Governing International Traffic in Arms*—which was printed in June 1937, and reprinted in April

1938. Further, the Department's view had been made clear in press releases. The opinion of the Attorney General's Office, written by the Assistant Solicitor General, Golden W. Bell, consequently dissented from a well established (but obviously untested) interpretation. Bell reviewed, with sophistication equal to Moore's, the whole problem of two laws dealing with the same subject. He then treated the two central issues: first, repeal by implied intention; and second, repeal by virtue of repugnancy. Bell concluded that, while the State Department's interpretation had considerable legal merit, no one could predict how a court would decide the case should the President act as though the January resolution were no longer in effect and rescind the embargo by proclamation. Yet for all Bell's thoughtful handling of the subject, and he was able to point out a couple of apparent absurdities resulting from the concurrent effectiveness of both laws, there remained a serious flaw in his argument. The bulk of his case rested upon the notion that Congress must have intended the repeal of the January resolution when it passed the May legislation, and that the courts might well see it in that way, too. What Bell failed to point out was that McReynolds had specifically announced to the House that the January resolution would still be in effect. Moreover, the "Statement of the Managers on the Part of the House," which was printed in the Conference Committee's report of April 28, 1937, clearly stated: "All acts heretofore passed as referred to are amended." The January resolution was not "referred to." The State Department's interpretation therefore possessed even more legal merit than Bell accorded it. The President no longer challenged the Department's view, but whether he failed to do so because of the cogency of its legal argument is not known. At any rate, Roosevelt decided that if the embargo was to be repealed it would have to be accomplished by an act of Congress.[12]

During November and December, the administration was primarily concerned with attempts to bring about a mediation proposal at the Lima conference and with the controversy raised at home by the wheat surplus relief plan. The vehemence demonstrated by many influential Catholics against this relief plan undoubtedly contributed to the President's preference for sharing the responsibility of repeal with Congress. It became clear shortly after Congress convened in January that Senator Pittman opposed the presentation of any proposals bearing on neutrality until after there had been lengthy discussions and hearings. According to Pittman, the earlier presentation of a program would prejudice congressional opinion and weaken his position as a compromiser. Pittman, in a memorandum to the President on January 11, clearly implied his unwillingness to tackle the Spanish embargo controversy on the floor of the Senate. Toward the end of February, the State Department learned that Pittman would open the neutrality question upon the conclusion of the Spanish war (which he presumed would come within a matter of days). It was thus the reluctance of the President and pro-Loyalist congressmen to initiate action, and the reluctance of the chairman of the Senate Foreign Relations Committee to consider any neutrality issues until the war was over, that killed the drive to repeal the embargo.[13]

During the repeal controversy, the State Department acted primarily as a clearing house for contending views from a variety of sources. It was true that the Department's legal interpretations had done much to block an attempt at repeal by proclamation, but this had no bearing on the question of whether or not Roosevelt should ask Congress to act on the matter. At any rate, the President and Congress bore most of the weight of prorepeal pressure during this period. Then suddenly the State Department was tossed back into the thick of the political battle.

In a personal letter to Secretary Hull, written January 18, 1939, Henry Stimson attacked the State Department's Spanish policy. While the Department labored over its reply to Stimson, the existence of the letter somehow leaked to members of the press—although, with the exception of columnist Dorothy Thompson, the press apparently lacked the details. On January 23, Stimson again attacked the policy in a letter to the *New York Times*. On the same day, he explained to Hull by telephone that the letter had been sent to the *Times* to relieve the Secretary of any embarrassment which might have resulted from the leakage of the earlier personal letter. The explanation was plausible; but there was an additional confusing fact. Arthur Hays Sulzberger, editor of the *Times*, had, in the time between the personal and the public letter, asked Stimson to write a letter to the *Times* on the subject of the Spanish policy. Sulzberger's letter reached Stimson at least two days before the printing of the *Times* letter and Stimson's telephone conversation with Hull. The Sulzberger-Stimson correspondence can be used either to question or to support Stimson's explanation to Hull that the public letter was meant to relieve Hull of some embarrassment. Perhaps the former Secretary of State seized the opportunity presented by rumors concerning his earlier letter to make his views public, or perhaps he seized upon the opportunity presented by Sulzberger's invitation to send a letter to the *Times* in order to protect Hull. It would seem, however, that Stimson was being honest with Hull, for as he pointed out to the Secretary over the telephone, the letter to the *Times* was "a little more careful and conservative" than the one sent directly to Hull. Whatever the case, an attack on the Spanish policy by a former Secretary of State, and a Republican who had been on other issues a regular supporter of the Roosevelt administration's foreign policy, was bound to be an embarrassment to the State Department.[14]

Stimson's published letter, which caused much debate, argued that the Spanish government had been recognized by the United States as a "friendly government" in terms of international law, and that such a government has the right to purchase arms abroad to protect itself against armed insurrection. It was the traditional policy of the United States to permit the sale of arms to such nations in distress, he argued, and such action is provided for by international law. If the Loyalist government were defeated, the United States, by its refusal to sell the government munitions for its defense, would by implication be party to its defeat. In light of the position assumed by the Keep the Embargo Committee, another point of Stimson's argument was especially telling. He maintained that had the United States from the beginning of the Spanish strife followed its traditional policy there would have been little threat of arousing the resentment of other governments. In light of the effects of the administration's policy, and of the changes in the international situation, Stimson called for a return to traditional practices. Stimson did not call for congressional action, but for action by the President. Since the State Department's response to Stimson would undoubtedly attract great public interest, the Department labored over the content and the tone of its reply during several meetings.[15]

Probably the best indication of Departmental sympathies is found in the papers of Moffat, who was involved in most of the conferences dealing with the Stimson letters. Two facts became clear: a number of officers of the Department were no longer convinced that the embargo should be continued and, even when some of them were, their sympathies apparently lay with the Loyalists. One of the Department's first considerations upon the receipt of the Stimson letter was not the method of answering his argument but rather the merits of the embargo. During the first meeting, Bullitt, on leave from his Paris post, made an appearance. He claimed that if the embargo were lifted, both Britain and France would do the same. Perhaps this surprising remark was a rhetorical device, for Bullitt raised other questions: Would such action save the Loyalists? Would the United States be prepared to follow through should such action provoke "serious trouble or hostilities" between Britain and France on the one hand and Germany and Italy on the other? And, finally, would Congress go along with the administration? It is possible that the State Department was still thinking within the framework of McReynolds' dictum and Moore's legal opinions concerning action by proclamation or by legislation; for when Bullitt suggested that there was no use attempting repeal unless Congress would support it, Hull telephoned Pittman for an assessment of the situation on Capitol Hill. Pittman reportedly answered that individual senators "were on too hot a spot to sit with ease and that the sooner they could get off it by avoiding the issue the happier they would be." The Foreign Relations Committee had "unanimously voted to drop any consideration of the neutrality or Spanish embargo legislation for the present."[16] The Department once more shelved the possibility of repeal and moved on to the delicate problem of dealing with Stimson's letter.

During the next few days several long sessions were devoted to what the men in the State Department believed was a dilemma. Moffat recorded a wide divergence of opinion. Moore and Hackworth wanted a simple statement indicating that the Department was giving careful consideration to Stimson's suggestion. Welles desired an indication of the future revisions of neutrality laws the Department would like to see. Norman Davis, a regular but unofficial adviser, wanted a frontal attack on the whole question of neutrality legislation, while subordinating the Spanish issue. Hull, hoping that he could avoid transferring the bitter debate on the Spanish embargo to the question of general neutrality legislation, apparently leaned toward the views of Moore and Hackworth. But the primary result of these meetings was the recognition that however it answered Stimson the Department could not avoid embarrassment. As Moffat so plainly put it: ". . . if we send a noncommittal reply the press will allege that we are pussyfooting; if we argue with Mr. Stimson and call attention to certain inaccuracies of statement in his letter we shall be offending a man who has supported our foreign policy [in other areas], and we shall, incidentally, not be giving a true picture of our feelings; if, on the other hand, we agree with everything that he says we are admitting that our course during the last two years has been wrong and that the opinions of our Legal Advisors are not valid. . . . anyway you look at it we are in for some trouble."

How many different replies were drafted is not known, but Hull rejected at least one that might have been written by Moore. It referred to the general public's "approval" of the policy and suggested that Congress, should it desire a change, could act in the matter. This kind of response was anything but impartial, since it would actually discourage congressional action. Hull, after mulling over all this advice, finally escaped the dilemma simply and cleverly by writing a personal note to Stimson, thanking him for his views, informing him that they were receiving "deliberate consideration," and adding the hope that this would not discourage him from sending more letters relevant to foreign policy ("with the extremely valuable and wise comment which always characterizes these communications from you"). Hull indirectly made it clear that he was answering Stimson's personal letter, and not the letter to the *Times;* he indicated that he deplored the leak with regard to the personal letter and confessed his inability to account for it. This deterred the publication of Hull's letter. With Stimson obliged not to reveal Hull's response, the issue, so far as the State Department was concerned, was quietly killed. The *New York Times* debate was continued by Martin Conboy of New York, who defended the embargo. Then Charles C. Burlingham, an-

other New York attorney, and Philip C. Jessup, professor of
international law at Columbia University, wrote a third letter
attacking Conboy's position.[17]

III

During February and March, the public continued to
debate the Spanish embargo, but the issue was dead in Congress, in the White House, and in the State Department. During January the State Department had done little but offer
legal advice to the President, while Roosevelt and congressional
leaders were in the center of the controversy. But when both
Roosevelt and congressional leaders refused to take the risk of
calling for repeal, the Spanish problem once more became the
troublesome possession of the policy-makers in the State Department. It was no longer a question of embargo or no embargo, but of recognition of the Franco government. A Rebel
victory had seemed imminent for months, but never more imminent than in February and March 1939. The Department was
thus concerned to follow developments abroad with an eye to
the question of recognition and delicate matters related to it.
Neither the President nor the majority of the men in the State
Department were anxious to recognize the Franco regime. The
prevailing view was that the United States should wait until it
was absolutely necessary to do so. In the meantime they needed
to know the direction which the Rebel government's foreign
policy would take. Would Franco become a Spanish Schwart-
zenburg and prove "ungrateful"? Would he reject German and
Italian demands that Spain line up with the Axis in the event of
a war? Or would the Rebel regime continue its close association
with the Fascist states? Much seemed to depend upon the quickened efforts of the British and the French to win Franco away
from Hitler and Mussolini.

The views of diplomatic observers ran the gamut of possibilities. There were reports that Franco would "dump" the
Fascist leaders and, for economic reasons, line up with the
Western democracies. There were reports that the Germans and
the Italians would maintain military garrisons in Spain and
monopolize the Spanish economy. Rumors were common that
Franco's desires would have little to do with the outcome. He

might want to dissassociate himself from the Fascist states, but Hitler and Mussolini would not let him. He might want to avoid involvement in a world war but the Fascist leaders would force him into it. There were other rumors that Franco would play one bloc off against the other, always attempting to remain neutral for fear of what would happen to Spain should the nation become very actively involved in a general conflict. If the last possibility seems now to have been the most logical, it is probably because history took that course. But in the early months of 1939, almost anything seemed possible.[18] The question of what policy the United States should pursue was left unanswered by any commitments the Burgos government might have made. For this reason the State Department placed greater emphasis on the policies being worked out in London and in Paris, and used these developments as guidelines.

On February 18, the State Department was informed that the British Foreign Office was considering the recognition of the Burgos government; five days later, with more definite information concerning the British move, Hull wirelessed the President, who was then on a cruise. He informed Roosevelt that some sixteen nations had up to that time recognized the Franco regime and that Britain, and then France and the Netherlands, were about to take similar action. On March 1, upon Hull's suggestion, Bowers was called home from Spain for consultation. Only the day before, Ambassador Bullitt was instructed to open conversations with the Burgos representative in Paris, and during these conferences Bullitt was to indicate that the United States was giving careful consideration to the question of recognition. Bullitt was further instructed to obtain "assurances" from the insurgent regime that it would not adopt a policy of reprisal against its opponents, that it would undertake to protect American lives and property, and that it otherwise fulfill the obligations and responsibilities of a sovereign state under international law. A good deal of confusion and ill will resulted from this when Bullitt interpreted his instructions to mean that he should obtain concrete guarantees with respect to the problem of reprisal. The Department quickly informed him that this was not the case. Bullitt was finally presented with a declaration by the Franco authorities which Hull later described as "containing a weasel-worded assurance" concerning the welfare of American interests. The State Department continued to hold off recognition even though the French and British accorded it on February 27. During March a good many Departmental and foreign service officers were advising the Secretary to face up to realities—the Franco government was virtually in control of the Spanish peninsula. It was argued that, if the United States indefinitely postponed its recognition of the Rebels, this would prejudice American interests and minimize the influence the United States might otherwise be able to exert upon the course of Franco's policies. On March 28, Madrid fell to the insurgents. On March 3 Ambassador de los Ríos said farewell to Secretary Hull and closed the Spanish embassy in Washington. Roosevelt approved the decision for recognition, and on the following day the United States acknowledged the Franco regime as the government of Spain.[19]

Claude Bowers later made the incredible suggestion that American recognition had been accorded to the Franco regime without the permission of the President. It was a mere rumor which Bowers chose to perpetuate years after the event.[20] Curiously enough, the State Department, the President, and Key Pittman as well were parties to incidents which encouraged Bowers to believe this rumor and others of the same kind. It was the price they felt they had to pay in order to prevent Bowers from causing immediate difficulties for the administration. The ambassador was the victim of top-level hoaxes. They were thinly disguised, but they worked well enough so that the history of the relations between Bowers and both Roosevelt and Hull has since been distorted.

11

PRESIDENT,
AMBASSADOR, AND SECRETARY

Pʀᴇꜱɪᴅᴇɴᴛ Rᴏᴏꜱᴇᴠᴇʟᴛ, Ambassador Bowers, and Secretary Hull represented the three most common American attitudes in official circles toward the Spanish crisis. The differences in their views were not very important—nor really very great—until the Spanish war approached its third year. Up to the middle of 1938, there seems to have been a fundamental agreement that the United States was pursuing a policy of necessity—despite the fact that both Hull's and Bowers' recollections indicate disagreement. The most tortured soul of the three was probably the President, for he was increasingly possessed of pro-Loyalist sympathies like those of the ambassador and restrained by a caution characteristic of his Secretary of State. But this personal dilemma only reached critical proportions in the last six months of the war.

I

For at least the first two years of the Spanish conflict, Cordell Hull was the key figure behind American policy. William Phillips drafted the first public pronouncement of the moral embargo back in August 1936, and R. Walton Moore was prima-

223

rily responsible for the form of the legal embargo in January 1937. While on both those occasions Hull had been out of Washington, there is no evidence, aside from rumors, to indicate that in either case he strongly disapproved of what had been done. He even gave approval of the way in which Phillips expressed the moral embargo policy. And, while no one can know what different form the embargo might have taken had Hull been in Washington in January 1937, it is safe to conclude that under his direction the embargo would still have been made legally enforceable; for the Secretary was intent upon cooperating with British and French efforts in the Non-Intervention Committee. During this period when the State Department possessed rather firm control over the Spanish policy, the principle of nonintervention was maintained primarily because of international considerations (Moore's isolationist disposition being an important exception). In the spring of 1938 there began a shift in the responsibility for the maintenance of the embargo, and by January 1939 its continuation was primarily the decision of the President along with congressional leaders. By that time, the Spanish embargo issue constituted a full-fledged domestic controversy, and, in consequence, the previously decisive international considerations were no longer given as much attention by the policy-makers.

The extent to which international complications shaped the President's thought in the last months of the war is not easy to estimate. He had been slow to appreciate the complications of the international situation, and the State Department's reasons for the embargo policy were never fully the President's reasons. The exception was that he grasped the vague outlines of what the Department felt was necessary under the circumstances: cooperate with London and Paris, and avoid precipitating a general war. It was not until the summer of 1937, at the earliest, that the President began to give adequate attention to foreign affairs—and then he faced the crisis in the Far East as well as the one on the Iberian peninsula. By that time, too, Neville Chamberlain was Prime Minister. During the whole of the Spanish strife, the President was never free from serious domestic concerns: the election of 1936, the Supreme Court scheme of 1937, a deteriorating economic situation, attempts at military preparedness, the conservative resurgence in the congressional elections of 1938, and the efforts to push through a reluctant Congress new legislative proposals (as well as legislation for existing programs). These problems, along with innumerable others, consumed much of his energy.

Even though the President began to devote more attention to the ominous international developments during 1937, his year of awakening was 1938. It was not only a matter of the Anschluss, or later Munich, or the British "flirtation" with Italy, or even the general lack of resolve shown by both Downing Street and the Quai d'Orsay. It was a matter of figures—of this quantity of planes versus that quantity, of this number of troops versus that number. It was in 1938 that Roosevelt grasped the dimensions of the military problem and its relationship to diplomacy. Roosevelt was basically an uninformed Wilsonian and, despite his love for the navy, not an informed follower of Theodore Roosevelt. He showed little appreciation, at this time, for his distant cousin's dictum: preponderance of force is the only guarantee of peace. As late as January 1939, after reviewing the European military situation, Roosevelt concluded that "he could not understand how Britain and France could have permitted themselves to get in such comparative weak positions."[1] The President had not become interested in this problem until the Rome-Berlin Axis possessed military preponderance over England and France. Exactly how this new appreciation affected his view of the Spanish war is not clear, but it appears that he began to think more in the terms so prevalent in the State Department—that it would be risky business for the democracies to confront Germany.

Beginning in June 1938, the President received progressively disturbing reports about Germany's military build-up, in contrast to the military unpreparedness of France and Great Britain. It was not only a matter of learning about the incredible extent of National Socialist planning in this respect. There was another matter, brought to the President's attention at the end of August 1938 by Hugh Wilson, the American ambassador in Berlin. The German army, Wilson informed him, was in a state of constant mobilization. It was probable, he claimed, that news of German aggression could be had only "some six to eight hours before military action is engaged in." Sometime after the Munich crisis, Roosevelt revealed to his old friend Josephus Daniels the extent of his concern about Fascist military superiority over France and Britain. Daniels expressed his doubts,

but afterward recorded that Roosevelt said he was so convinced of the accuracy of his information "that if he had been
in Chamberlain's place [at Munich] he would have felt con-
strained to have made terms to prevent the war for which
Germany was fully prepared." Doubtless Roosevelt appreciated that, compared to central Europe, the Iberian peninsula
was far removed from Hitler's interests. But this apprehension
over German military power probably played some part in his
failure to carry through his desire to aid the Spanish Loyalists.
Fear of provoking Hitler, and turning him back upon central
Europe, was certainly common in the State Department. When
Roosevelt wrote to "Bertie" Pell in Lisbon that the British
leaders must begin to "fish or cut bait," it betrayed that he
himself was a reluctant accomplice to the failure of appeasement.[2]

While Roosevelt must have reflected on how he became a
partner in Chamberlain's policy, there is no record of those
reflections. Harold Ickes did write that during a cabinet meeting in January 1939 "the President said that the policy we
should have adopted [toward Spain] was to forbid the transportation of munitions in American bottoms."[3] But had this
policy been adopted in August 1936, it would have seriously
endangered the formation of the Non-Intervention Committee,
which was, at the time, genuinely considered to hold some hope.
The President, furthermore, would have been no more empowered to enforce such a policy than he was to enforce the moral
embargo. If there was one remembrance among the American
people about their entrance into the World War in 1917, it was
the prior involvement of the United States in the war because of
attacks upon American shipping (shipping that the American
government had not obtained legal power to prevent).[4] The
second-guess alternative suggested by Roosevelt in 1939 would
very likely have been unacceptable to the American people, who
(during an election year) would have seen a stark contrast
between British and French efforts to maintain general peace
and an American policy which appeared to promote war. The
American government had two alternatives in 1936. The first
was the course actually pursued. The second was simply to take
no action—a decision which could have been explained by the
administration as the result of lacking the legal power to do
anything.

It is possible that the President's statement recorded by Ickes in 1939 was a reference to the mistake of the legal embargo of January 1937. But this is unlikely. The President was compelled at that time to support some kind of legal embargo. It would have been political suicide not to try to prevent shipments of American arms to Spain at that time. His sincerity as a guardian of peace, correctly or incorrectly, would otherwise have been called into question. Who could have missed the irony of the administration asking as the sole limitation on the sale and shipment of arms that their transport in American ships be forbidden—when at that very time Robert Cuse was loading American planes upon a Spanish ship in New York harbor? The President, in 1939, was correct in the sense that one of the most acceptable solutions to some of the political dilemmas presented by the Spanish strife would have been one permitting the sale and shipment of arms to Spain in other than American vessels. But the chance of attaining such a policy was at best very slim. It would only have been attainable if, in January 1937, the President had insisted upon, and had succeeded in acquiring, broad discretionary power over the embargo with respect to Spain. Then later, politics permitting, he might have been able to revise the policy along those lines he came to believe desirable. There is no doubt that in these terms the Embargo Resolution of January 1937 was the most decisive event in the development of the Spanish policy.

There are two other matters very relevant to the policy the President later believed should have been followed. The first is that while the moral embargo was a freely chosen policy, the men in the State Department obviously believed that they were only choosing what they would ultimately be compelled to choose—first because of domestic demands that the United States avoid involvement in European crises, and second because they would otherwise not only appear to be promoting war but also appear to be undermining an Anglo-French effort to maintain general peace. The fact that the policy-makers freely chose the moral embargo before tremendous pressures from domestic and foreign sources were felt might have led the President to believe later that there had been a variety of policy alternatives available early in the war. The second matter relevant to the President's analysis in January 1939 is that he most likely would have found it extremely difficult to change the policy from an outright embargo to one permitting shipment of American arms in foreign vessels. Such a change in policy still would have entailed serious risks concerning his economic legislation, his armament program, the Catholic and isolationist vote, the Latin American policy, and—much more seriously— the peace of Europe. Such a change in policy still would have entailed the risk of further British appeasement to offset American "provocation" of the Fascist states and also the risk that Hitler or Mussolini might immediately seize the opportunity to attempt advances elsewhere than in Spain.

During the first six months of the Spanish strife, a policy of allowing the shipment of American arms in foreign vessels was not a feasible alternative. And from early 1937 until the end of the war, it would have been a very hazardous policy. In these terms there was no particularly decisive event in the development of the policy toward Spain. Rather, the most important fact was American inability to reject British leadership and give strength to the French left. No matter how one approaches the whole question, there is always that confounding void created by French failure to push the issue in Spain— British support or no British support. French reluctance to go it alone made it impossible for the United States to act independently of Great Britain, even if American policy-makers had been eager to aid the Spanish Loyalists. It was long apparent that the sale of American arms to the Spanish government would cause a crisis in Anglo-French relations which could only be averted by French refusal to cooperate with the Americans. By December 1936, large quantities of American arms could only have reached Loyalist Spain across the French frontier. Now open, now closed, now ajar, that frontier was something the French seemed almost apologetic about possessing. The sale of American arms to Spain would have forced a decision in France, probably resulting in another showdown with the British and another capitulation.

II

The Spanish crisis not only became entangled with domestic and other international issues, but the longer the war continued the more complicated these relationships became.

Conversely, the longer the war went on, the more convinced Ambassador Bowers became that something ought to be done by the United States to help counter the Fascists in Spain. In February 1938, he wrote to Hull: "My *personal* feelings are with the Spanish Government. The fight is here a clear-cut combat between democracy and fascism. I would personally like to see us take our stand foursquare. But unless I am misinformed that would not meet with the approval of public opinion in America which appears passionately to insist that we stand aloof from all international conflicts which do not directly affect us."[5] Bowers' capacity for simplifying the issues in Spain increased as he watched Loyalist hopes dwindle during 1938. Reaching the limits of frustration, he finally advised that the United States permit arms shipments to Spain. In June 1938, Bowers wrote to Hull that there was "but one language" the Fascist leaders understood—"the language of force." And he advised that the only way to put an end to Fascist aggression, and Fascist bombing of civilian populations, "is to grant the Spanish Government the right to buy planes and guns necessary for the protection of its people."[6] Bowers' pleas for a reversal of American policy became particularly insistent in December 1938—and again he emphasized the "wholesale slaughter of women and children in towns and villages" having no military objective.[7] In a letter to the President early in December, Bowers queried Roosevelt about neutrality legislation. The letter was forwarded to the State Department for the purpose of drafting a response. The conclusion of Moore and Welles was that "the truth is that at this moment there would seem to be little that could profitably be said to Mr. Bowers on that subject." Welles told the President that in his opinion "it is hardly necessary for you to write further to Mr. Bowers in reference to neutrality legislation."[8] There is no record of specific reasons why the State Department decided not to inform Bowers fully concerning this issue, and he certainly had the right to expect a complete, even if confidential, explanation. Being so treated, it is not surprising that Bowers interpreted the continuation of the policy as a result of anti-Loyalist opinions among well-placed advisers. He did not detect the predicaments in which the State Department and the President found themselves. Bowers' correspondence and his published recollections suggest very strongly that he believed a sincere desire to reverse the policy would have been sufficient to accomplish the change.

During December 1938 and January 1939, under the strain of events, Bowers' analyses of the Spanish crisis were particularly faulty. On one occasion, Moffat and Welles decided not to point out one of Bowers' erroneous observations for the reason that it would have been a useless embarrassment. These were frustrating and disillusioning months for the ambassador, and his evident impatience at America's spectator policy did nothing to improve his reputation among the topsiders of the State Department.[9]

It was apparently Hull's account of the Spanish policy in his *Memoirs* which led Bowers to explain his own position with such vehemence in *My Mission to Spain* and in his memoirs, *My Life*. Yet rather than clarifying the Spanish policy, Bowers' books further distort it. Allowing for a few inconsistencies, it seems to have been true, as Bowers later related, that he had informed Washington for more than two years that American interests ideologically, commercially, and industrially were bound up with those of the Spanish government. But not until mid-1938 did Bowers actually advise Washington to revise its embargo policy. Much of Bowers' self-defense in his recollections is based on argument by implication. This is true of two of the most important events he treated, where Bowers related remarks made to him by both Roosevelt and Pittman following the ambassador's return to the United States in March 1939. The President reportedly said: " 'We made a mistake; you have been right all along.' " Did Bowers at that moment wonder if the President mistakenly believed that he had "all along" advised that the Spanish government be permitted to purchase American arms? The ambassador had repeatedly written Roosevelt of his approval of American policy in unflinching terms.[10] Bowers did not subsequently clarify this issue or even what it was the President intended when he referred to "a mistake." Was it the moral embargo? The legal embargo? His failure to push for repeal on Capitol Hill? Or his failure to lift the embargo by proclamation? The irony is that it probably made little difference at that moment, for Bowers was being deceived. Neither the President, nor the topsiders in the State Department, nor Senator Pittman had any desire to argue with Bowers. More than a week before Bowers reached Washington, "everyone from the President down" was concerned about what to do with him. Moffat recorded in his diary—"they are afraid of Bowers' trenchant pen and are anxious to ease his susceptibilities." The President wanted to call him home and arrange simultaneously for a transfer to another embassy. But Hull said that a transfer could not be accomplished immediately.[11] So they ordered the ambassador home for consultation and braced themselves for his arrival.

Despite the President's reputation for agreeableness in such situations, Bowers never questioned what he was told, or why. Roosevelt, moreover, because he himself by this time wished that the whole Spanish issue could have been handled differently, must not have found it difficult to say that they had made "a mistake," or to buoy Bowers by telling him that he had been right "all along." What difference did details make now? Bowers might blame whomever he wanted for the embargo policy, but he would not blame the President. Neither would he blame Senator Pittman, who afterward told the ambassador: " 'I am afraid we made a mistake in Spain.' " Bowers' recollections of this conversation with Pittman, related in *My Mission to Spain*, reveal a faulty memory. Pittman reportedly told Bowers that in the beginning he thought the embargo good in that it would keep other nations out and localize the war. Bowers agreed with him, but added that "two or three weeks later" it "might well have been lifted." Bowers did not question whether this would have been politically or diplomatically feasible. And even so, the ambassador could not properly have intended this remark to be anything but the product of hindsight—for he himself did not advise a change in American policy until the war was almost two years old. For at least one year Bowers expressed the opinion that the early Anglo-French theory behind the Non-Intervention Agreement was probably correct—that competition between the democracies and the Fascist States in furnishing arms to the rival forces in Spain might lead to a general war. What Bowers regretted, as late as July 1937, was that the Non-Intervention Pact had not been honestly observed nor honestly enforced. What the ambassador really wanted during that summer was a change in French and British policies, because one surrender to the Fascists would lead to another. (But at the same time, he did not believe that a

Franco victory would result in a Fascist Spain.) Consequently there was much that was misleading in his comments to Pittman.

Bowers also remarked to the senator that war material "would have been carried in other than American vessels." He did not indicate why this was to be assumed, let alone how it was to be guaranteed. Such a policy could not have been followed on the basis of a nonlegal understanding that the Spanish government was prepared *"to take the responsibility of . . . delivery on itself"* (as Bowers emphatically put it), for there could be nothing binding about such an understanding with respect to the Spanish government or American shippers. The ambassador did not seem to appreciate such complications. At any rate, Bowers must have misled Roosevelt and Pittman as much as they misled him. And, because of the apparent amiability of both Roosevelt and Pittman, it is little wonder that Bowers believed that a pro-Franco clique in the State Department was primarily responsible for the embargo policy and ultimately for the recognition of Franco "without the permission of the President." Bowers soon afterward might well have become a little suspicious about the game that was being played. He was not, for example, invited to appear at the next hearings held by Pittman's committee, although he finally received an invitation from Sol Bloom to appear before the House Foreign Affairs Committee. Then at a dinner in Bowers' honor, Pittman, as impromptu toastmaster, spent most of the evening calling upon one person after another for speeches ; he did not get around to introducing Bowers until half past eleven. According to Moffat, the ambassador on this occasion was less partisan than expected —though this may have been due to what Bowers "jocularly referred to as 'State Department spies in the company.' "[12]

Nothing is quite so troubling about Bowers' later account of the Spanish policy as his neglect of many of his own letters and dispatches in which he praised American policy. Time and again, Bowers lauded the policy and praised Hull for his statesmanship. "Our position during the entire year," he wrote in July 1937, "has been all that could be desired. We have strictly observed our policy of neutrality. . . . We almost alone at this moment can approach either side on official business with the certainty that they will do all in their power to serve us." Little more than a month later he wrote that since criticisms of the

United States had been mild in Spain, he was persuaded "that the more we remain in the background the better we are served; and that our policy in the long run will make us more friends than the others have made." He added, "I am sure that if we continue our policy without deviation we shall find which ever side wins ardently seeking our friendship the moment the war is over." In February 1938, he expressed his sympathies with the Spanish government. But he also wrote at the same time that American policy had come to be appreciated by both sides. That was the reason, he added, that the United States had encountered less trouble than any other power and the reason, too, why the nation had been treated with more consideration than others by both Burgos and Barcelona. In June 1938, almost three weeks after expressing the view that the Spanish government should be permitted to purchase arms, Bowers praised Hull's policies. He wrote the Secretary that his stature in history would be fixed because, under him, the United States stood solidly for legality and the sanctity of treaties. And, later, in October 1938, he again wrote to Hull in the same vein. Bowers hoped that whatever others did in Spain the United States would continue its course of legality, custom, and decency. America must not be moved by the new madness. He was still certain that both sides in Spain had greater respect for the United States than for any other country in the world.[13]

By reason of the discrepancies in some of his dispatches and between some of his wartime opinions and his later recollections, the ambassador left himself open to charges of hypocrisy or deceit. Yet his behavior does not justify such easy condemnation. His own wartime correspondence suggests that he was a more complicated man than his recollections would indicate. While ambassador, he was aware of the responsibility that must be borne by any diplomatist whose ideas, when put into action, prove disastrous. However early he actually believed that American arms ought to be shipped to Spain, he expressed the notion ambiguously at best. Even when writing Dodd, whose thoughts so resembled his own, Bowers did not commit himself specifically on the vital issue of American arms.[14] He was forthrightly, but still safely, pro-Loyalist. The ambassador was also aware of the "career boys'" lack of enthusiasm for him, and he was not sure just how much influence they would have with the President should there be a showdown. If he had clearly and forcefully expressed his opposition to the embargo much earlier than he did, he would have exposed himself to their attacks. Bowers' affection for Roosevelt, and a desire to see it reciprocated, might simply have discouraged him from risking this relationship. Under the influence of the professionals, the President would likely decide against him and this would mean, quite logically, an official reproof—his removal from the ambassadorship. Bowers' attitude toward Hull was likewise important, for he expressed lofty sentiments about the Secretary and desired Hull's respect in return. But, with Hull even more than with Roosevelt, Bowers had good reason to believe that much value was placed on the experience and judgment of those very career officers who opposed him. The ambassador was not loath to point out to Hull how hard he himself worked, or how scrupulously he maintained the posture of "neutrality," or even how beneficial the existing policy was to the United States. Bowers was plainly proud of his diplomatic accomplishments. This desire for Roosevelt's and Hull's approval, the fear of the professional crowd's antagonism and influence, the awareness of grave responsibilities that go along with initiating new departures, and the pride he took in his work—all these attitudes appear in his correspondence and probably discouraged him from speaking out clearly before the spring of 1938. By that time it was obvious that the President's sympathies were in line with his, that Hull did not really appreciate either his work or the tragedy of his personal-professional conflict, and that he need no longer stand alone in opposing the embargo openly. By that time, too, Loyalist hopes were rapidly disintegrating, with no greater prospect for the adoption of resolute policies by France. American arms were needed, now, if the Loyalists were to have any opportunity of recovery.[15]

The question remains why the ambassador himself did not subsequently clarify the discrepancies. It is possible that he relied too heavily upon his memory when writing his later accounts. And no one publicly called his attention to these discrepancies. With the passage of time, the complex may have appeared a good deal more simple to him. Finally, there exists a third possibility, for regardless of how Bowers might approach the issue it would not be easy for him to deal with two compelling questions. If he did not stand up in opposition to the embargo at a time when personal risks were involved, whom could he hold accountable? And if he did not calculate in necessary detail all the ponderable consequences of aiding the Loyalists, and present them to Roosevelt and Hull, whom could he blame for thinking him an overzealous amateur? Bowers' published recollections contributed to his unwarranted reputation as a steadfast advocate of selling American arms to the Loyalists. They portray him in far too simple terms.

III

Secretary Hull was never really convinced one way or the other concerning the desirability of a Loyalist victory. Cordell Hull, R. Walton Moore, Sumner Welles, and William Phillips never approached the Spanish issue with the idea that they must do all within their limited powers to help bring about a Loyalist victory. The Secretary never really looked at the Spanish war; he always looked beyond it. He viewed it in a larger context; and later he never claimed, as some did, that if the Fascists had lost in Spain there might never have been a second world war. Although he was not the appeaser that, for example, Phillips was during this period, Hull resembled British policy-makers in holding the opinion that, not only would a Fascist defeat in Spain not prevent a world war, but a struggle with the Fascist states on Spanish soil might result in a world conflict.[16] Hull was furthermore not of the opinion, as Bowers was, that the Spanish strife could be reduced to a struggle between democracy and Fascism. Hull did not see much merit in either the Loyalist or the insurgent cause.

With respect to oversimplifications concerning the Spanish policy, Hull's *Memoirs* are not entirely faultless. He wrote that "it would have been unthinkable for the United States to take a contrary course." This was not exactly true. He could have claimed a legal inability to prevent arms shipments in 1936. Second, Hull implied that shipments of American arms would have served to prolong the Spanish war, with the likelihood that other nations would have become involved. The worth of this argument varied during the course of the war and is most questionable if applied to the opening months of the conflict. Hull further argued that American relations with Britain and France were "bettered" by the embargo policy.

The best that can actually be said is that those relations would have been made more difficult if the United States had not adopted the embargo. One of his most surprising comments was this one: "The President and I were in complete agreement on our policy of nonintervention in Spain throughout the war. At no time did any difference of opinion arise between us." Here was a bold claim; yet all that can be said is that whatever the President's inclinations he always returned to Hull's point of view on actual policy.[17]

Looking back to that policy, as it developed, Hull seems to have had three legitimate general reasons for it. First, it was quite reasonable to expect the State Department to support the NIC in its early days, for it then appeared to offer the best hope for the maintenance of general peace. Second, the embargo quickly involved so many international and political complications that it became extremely risky to reverse the policy. And third, Great Britain, France, and the United States were neither "militarily nor psychologically prepared to abandon their efforts toward maintaining peace and embark on a general preventive war." Hitler and Mussolini had reached a point where failure was unacceptable. A loss in Spain would have to be countered by victory elsewhere. The leaders of the Western democracies, not all of them Chamberlains, feared the possibility of an explosion, and they were not prepared to deal with a general war if it came. That the Western democracies were caught in a predicament is certain. Success for the Fascist leaders encouraged them to push further. Setbacks for the Fascist leaders encouraged attempts at compensation. The area for creative statesmanship was limited everywhere, but possibly nowhere more than in Washington. In the United States, there was no force to back up demands and no will to use force had it been available. Further, policy-making took place not only in the State Department and in the White House, but in Congress as well.[18]

If Congress, which played such a vital role in the development of the Spanish policy, lacked confidence in the State Department, the blame is not all to be placed on Capitol Hill. The State Department projected weakness. If American officials possessed great talent for the day-to-day execution of an established policy, they did not demonstrate a capacity for intelligent planning. It is little wonder that congressmen believed they could do as well—and little wonder, too, that during the 1930's the State Department became an executive branch of Congress. Inseparable from this problem was the isolationist or continentalist disposition of the American people.[19]

During the latter months of the war, there was an additional ailment in the State Department, the effects of which cannot really be estimated. Stimson saw it in February 1939, and Messersmith and Moffat both acknowledged it. It was, simply, exhaustion. After a visit to the State Department, Stimson wrote: "I was made sad and rather apprehensive at the very evident condition of physical fatigue and consequent mental pessimism which I found among my best friends in the Department. . . . I think it is nothing more than overwork and fatigue but it is nonetheless serious both for the victims and for the government which they represent."[20] What effect this condition had upon American policies all over the world is of course incalculable. But it might be surmised that exhausted men, confronted every day with problems of great complexity, are quite likely to avoid decisions involving incalculable risks. It was an enormous task attempting to implement existing cautious policies. This is not to say that the policy-makers were unaware that their caution also ultimately entailed grave risks. Indeed it helps to explain the pessimism Stimson recognized in them.

If the idealistic language in which American policy was couched from the beginning of the civil war sounded hollow, it was not because it was essentially hypocritical. It was rather because an "exemplary," "sane," "safe," "decent," and "honest" policy was thought to be more a product of realism than of idealism. The prevailing attitude in the State Department was that the United States did not have the available materials, the will, or the experience to disconnect its European policy from that of the British Foreign Office. There could not be a policy toward Spain alone—all Europe was involved. This explains, in the most general terms, the adoption of the moral embargo and the rejection of Hornbeck's dissenting memorandum of August 1936. Hornbeck's memorandum dealt not with Europe, but with American policies toward civil wars.

The adoption of a legal embargo as an executive proposal passed by Congress was a logical consequence. Either the Roosevelt administration revised its European policy radically or it found means to enforce the embargo. The provisions of that Spanish Embargo Act of January 1937 are another matter. Moore, and Roosevelt as well, clearly gave too little consideration to the possibility that it might some day be thought desirable to change existing policies. The mandatory legal embargo represented the worst in policy-making. It violated one of the most basic principles of good statesmanship—the maintenance of flexibility. There is no conclusive evidence that the administration was compelled by Congress to accept a mandatory embargo act. The President should have been left free to choose from the alternatives of embargo (with discretion as to items covered), cash-and-carry sales, and outright cancellation. Roosevelt permitted himself to be legally immobilized.

What was required, at the least, was a definition of objectives and comprehensive planning—the President devoted himself to neither of these tasks, and he did not require them of the State Department. If he was unable to revise the policy when he became convinced revision was desirable, it was because he had helped create the circumstances inhibiting his freedom of action. At the very least, the President therefore lacked a bargaining tool. He could not ask of the British that they "fish or cut bait"—for he was not free himself to reverse the Spanish policy. His fault, and the fault of the State Department, was the failure beginning in January 1937 to maintain flexibility, to keep other governments sufficiently uncertain of the future course of American policy. It was absolutely necessary to maintain some expectation of change. The President lost one possible means to influence positively the course of events.

Had the policy-makers been given discretion with regard to the Spanish embargo, they would have been compelled to assume continuing responsibility for it. They would have been forced to face up to the decision, every day, of whether or not the existing policy was desirable. Perhaps the possession of unquestionable legal discretion would not have brought about any significant change in policy—but it must have been a troubled conscience late in the war which caused the President to ask for opinions, again and again, as to the legality of revoking the embargo by executive proclamation. It was certainly possible that despite all risks Roosevelt would have lifted the embargo had he been certain of his power to do so. As a matter of fact, the political risks would probably have been less under these circumstances, since the issue would not have been in the hands of Congress. At the same time, it must be assumed that Cordell Hull would have put before the President every argument favoring a continuation of the embargo and would only reluctantly have followed the President in the adoption of a new policy.

Despite the awful complexity of the Spanish conflict, and the tangled events and decisions that shaped American policy toward that civil war, it is still possible to reduce to two the attitudes of American policy-makers which lay behind the formulation and continuation of the embargo policy. First, they could not escape the haunting fear that, while impotent to bring about world peace, they were fully capable of accelerating the drift toward appeasement and toward world war. Had England and France felt themselves prepared to wage general war, this anxiety would not have been so prevalent in Washington. And, second, it was generally believed in the Department of State that the sale of arms to the Spanish Loyalists entailed many risks, at home and abroad, without a single favorable guarantee.

A crisis which for many Americans clarified the great issues of that time and strengthened their opinions, the Spanish civil war only complicated and endangered every policy the State Department believed important—from the Good Neighbor policy to the armament program. The Spanish strife wrought angry ideological and religious antagonism and presented a critical dilemma for a government led by men so practiced in compromise and as yet unpracticed in the skills of diplomatic leadership.

NOTE ON SOURCES

MANUSCRIPTS

The fundamental manuscript sources relevant to the study of American diplomacy and the Spanish civil war are: the Records of the Department of State (DSR), at the National Archives; the Franklin D. Roosevelt Papers, located in the Roosevelt Library, Hyde Park, New York; the Cordell Hull Papers, in the Manuscript Division, Library of Congress; and the R. Walton Moore Papers, at the Roosevelt Library. All four sources have been used extensively.

The Department of State Records are, of course, the most vital and the largest source of information on American policy. For this reason, I have generally followed the rule of citing these official records when there has been duplication in other manuscript sources. Two additional clarifications are necessary: first, some papers relating to official Department business which I did not locate in State Department files were found in the Moore and Hull collections; and, second, a substantial number of documents relating to traffic in American arms and to American volunteers in the International Brigades are currently not open for research. The Department of Justice and the Passport Division of the Department of State operate under a 75 year rule, meaning that documents over which they have authority will not be available for several decades. In each instance where I include a general citation to a DSR "unlawful shipments" file, the reference is only to those documents to which I have had access.

Each of the files of the Roosevelt Manuscripts—the Official File (OF), the President's Personal File (PPF), and the President's Secretary's File (PSF)—contain much material pertinent to the Spanish strife and American policy. Of special note in the Hull Papers is the greater part of an unpublished study by John Morgan, entitled "United States Policy during the Spanish Civil War, July 1936–April 1939." Primarily an investigation of the problems of arms and munitions control, this work was written by Morgan in 1944–45, under the auspices of the Department of State. Known in the Department as the "Green Report" (after Joseph C. Green, head of the Office of Arms and Munitions Control), it is here referred to as the Morgan-Green Report.

Two collections at Houghton Library, Harvard University, are also of special importance. The William Phillips Journals are very helpful on the formulation of the moral embargo, when Phillips was Under Secretary of State. His Journals and Memoranda are less enlightening, in fact they are disappointing on a few crucial issues, after Phillips became ambassador to Italy. The Jay Pierrepont Moffat Papers must be considered a major source on American policy for the last year of the Spanish strife, during which time Moffat was Chief of the European Division. His Diaries contain an invaluable record of the opinions of individual officials and of behind-the-scenes action in the Department of State.

Attempts to obtain permission to use the papers of both William C. Bullitt and Claude Bowers were unsuccessful. The Sumner Welles manuscripts were also not yet available. Clearly, access to their records would be highly desirable, but there is a wealth of correspondence and other materials written by, to, and about all three men in a variety of other manuscript collections.

In the abundant records of congressmen, senators, ambassadors, and other prominent figures, located in the Manuscript Division, Library of Congress, there is surprisingly little pertinent to the Spanish conflict. For example, the papers of Key Pittman, chairman of the Senate Foreign Relations Committee, contain only a very few items in any way helpful to this study. The papers of William E. Borah, Tom Connally, Charles McNary, and George Norris are even less enlightening. Some relevant materials may be found in the Josephus Daniels Manuscripts, although considering the many difficulties raised by the transshipment of American war materials through Mexico, there is less than might be expected. The Norman H. Davis Papers are helpful in the solution of several specific but, on the whole, minor problems. The William E. Dodd Papers add little to the ambassador's observations concerning the Spanish strife which is not already found in the major collections mentioned above and in his published diaries. The records of Laurence A. Steinhardt are entirely lacking in references to the mediation proposals at the Lima conference, even though Steinhardt was at the time ambassador to Peru.

The personal records of some other prominent political and diplomatic figures prove as unrewarding. The George S. Messersmith Papers (University Library, University of Delaware) contain relatively few documents directly pertaining to the Spanish strife, but Messersmith's important official observations can be found elsewhere; for example, in the Department of State files and in the Hull Papers. The Herbert C. Pell Manuscripts (Roosevelt Library) contain very little on the Spanish civil war, despite the fact that he was minister to Portugal for the latter part of the conflict. The Hiram Johnson collection at the Bancroft Library, University of California (Berkeley), contains nothing pertinent to the Spanish policy, but there is some interesting data on the relationships between Anglophobia and opposition to New Deal domestic programs on the one hand and isolationism on the other. The David I. Walsh Papers at College of the Holy Cross, Worcester, Massachusetts, reveal only a few useful items (this small collection being composed almost entirely of press releases and newspaper clippings). Dr. Joseph Huthmacher, presently working on a biography of Robert F. Wagner, has informed me that the Wagner Papers (at Georgetown University) likewise lack material pertinent to the Spanish conflict. For indications of the attitudes and actions of the men on Capitol Hill, one must turn to the Roosevelt, Moore, and Moffat papers, and to some of the manuscript collections mentioned below (in addition to newspaper files, particularly those of the *New York Times* and the *Washington Post*).

In this connection, there are the files of the Senate Committee on Foreign Relations and the House Committee on Foreign Affairs (both located at the National Archives). There are not, however, as many important items here as one might expect. A look at these files alone could easily lead one toward a low estimate of the dimensions of the political controversy. On the other hand, there are some valuable correspondence and memoranda on matters other than the views of individual congressmen and senators.

A large and hitherto untapped manuscript holding is the Spanish Refugee Relief Organization (SRRO) collection, at Butler Library, Columbia University. It includes thousands of documents not only relevant to efforts for refugee relief by American pro-Loyalist organizations but also to other activities of pro-Loyalist pressure groups. In this collection, for example, one finds numerous records of interviews with congressmen, senators, and many figures in the Roosevelt administration.

A small collection, but one valuable for the study of Catholic pro-Franco and proembargo activities, is that of William F. Montavon, located at the Catholic University of America. Montavon was the legal secretary of the National Catholic Welfare Conference, and among his many tasks were those of acquiring news from Rebel and pro-Rebel organizations abroad for dissemination in the United States, engaging in pressure group activities on Capitol Hill, and keeping in touch with such prominent Catholic politicians as John McCormack and David Walsh. On the issues raised by Rebel treatment of Spanish Protestants, there is some relevant material in the papers of the American Board of Commissioners for Foreign Missions (Houghton Library, Harvard University).

Of minor interest in connection with the Spanish war are the Henry L. Stimson Papers, at Yale University. The Stimson Manuscripts contain a revealing exchange of ideas on the Spanish issue between the former Secretary of State and his old friend, Frederic R. Coudert. In connection with the well-known Stimson letter to the *New York Times*, opposing the embargo policy, there is some previously unrevealed correspondence with Arthur Sulzberger of the *Times* which raises a few questions about Stimson's actions. Three other collections located at Yale University Library are also of limited value. The records of Ernst Toller, with respect to his efforts to bring about a cooperative international attempt at humanitarian relief in Spain, are helpful in explaining President Roosevelt's plan for massive relief. The papers of Arthur Bliss Lane, minister at Riga, and of J. Flournoy Montgomery, minister at Budapest, contain a few interesting items on general developments. Unfortunately, there is nothing in the Lane Papers regarding the attempts of some Americans to ship arms to Spain while claiming that they were intended for the Latvian government.

Extremely valuable for the study of some of the domestic controversies raised by humanitarian relief efforts are the abundant records in the Archives of the American National Red Cross, Washington, D.C. Of special note is an unpublished work by Catherine Fennelly, "American Red Cross Disaster Services, 1919–1939" (Vol. XXB of the unpublished series, "The History of the American National Red Cross"). In addition there are files of correspondence, minutes of the Central Committee, and annual reports of the Red Cross.

Manuscripts relevant to the attitudes and actions of leftist parties and organizations, with the exception of the holding mentioned above at Columbia University, are difficult to come by. The next most satisfactory collection is at Tamiment Institute in New York City. Of some value are the manuscript and organizational files of the Socialist party, 1938. Of further interest, although of even more limited use to this particular study, is Tamiment's magnificent pamphlet collection.

PUBLISHED MATERIALS

The following is a select bibliography. More substantial bibliographies on the origins and the course of the civil war itself, on the International Brigades, and on European diplomatic complications may be found elsewhere. For example, see: Juan García Durán, *Bibliography of the Spanish Civil War, 1936–1939* (Montevideo, 1964); Hugh Thomas, *The Spanish Civil War* (New York, 1961); and Gabriel Jackson, *The Spanish Republic and the Civil War, 1931–1939* (Princeton, 1965). Although its bibliography is now somewhat dated, F. Jay Taylor's *The United States and the Spanish Civil War, 1936–1939* (New York, 1956) includes more material on some aspects of the problem than is mentioned here. On American reactions to the Spanish strife, Allen Guttmann provides an excellent bibliography in *The Wound in the Heart: America and the Spanish Civil War* (New York, 1962).

DOCUMENTS

The most essential collection of published documents is *Foreign Relations of the United States* (Department of State Publications, U.S. Government, Washington, D.C.); see the volumes for the years 1936 through 1939. Also see the *Congressional Record* and the Department of State *Press Releases* for the same period. Some helpful material may be found in congressional hearings; for example, Senate Foreign Relations Committee, hearings, "Neutrality," February 13, 1937, and House Foreign Affairs Committee, hearings, "American Neutrality Policy," February 16–23, 1937 (both 75th Congress, 1st Session). Used to a limited extent in this study was the collection: *Documents on German Foreign Policy, 1918–1945,* Series D, Volume III, *Germany and the Spanish Civil War, 1936–1939* (Washington, D.C., 1950). The captured documents of the German Foreign Office contained relatively little on Germany's involvement in the Spanish conflict, probably because so much was handled outside the Foreign Office.

MEMOIRS, RECOLLECTIONS, DIARIES

The most important works in this category are Cordell Hull's *Memoirs* (New York, 2 vols., 1948) and Claude Bowers, *My Mission to Spain: Watching the Dress Rehearsal for World War II* (New York, 1954). Bowers' memoirs, *My Life* (New York, 1962), are much less helpful. Many details relevant to important discussions which took place in the State Department can be found in Nancy Harvison Hooker (ed.), *The Moffat Papers: Selections from the Diplomatic Journals of Jay Pierrepont Moffat, 1919–1943* (Cambridge, Mass., 1956). Although it must be approached with special caution on matters of detail, Harold Ickes' *Secret Diary* (New York, 3 vols., 1953–54) is of some value.

A great number of works in this general category contain little or nothing on the Spanish issue but are helpful in other ways. Some accounts by diplomatic participants which provide revealing material on leading personalities and their relationships are: William Phillips, *Ventures in Diplomacy* (Boston, 1954); Francis Sayre, *Glad Adventure* (New York, 1957); Hugh R. Wilson, *Diplomat between Wars* (New York, 1941); Josephus Daniels, *Shirt-Sleeve Diplomat* (Chapel Hill, 1947); Joseph E. Davies, *Mission to Moscow* (New York, 1941); and Robert D. Murphy, *Diplomat among Warriors* (New York, 1964). Sumner Welles' *The Time for Decision* (New York, 1944) is of minimal assistance, and on the Spanish policy it is marred by important factual errors. Hallett Johnson's *Diplomatic Memoirs, Serious and Frivolous* (New York, 1963) are far more frivolous than serious. William Dodd, Jr., and Martha Dodd (eds.), *Ambassador Dodd's Diary, 1933–1938* (New York, 1941) reveals much about Dodd's personality but should be used with caution. Of some interest, although almost entirely with respect to the domestic scene, are: *The Autobiography of Eleanor Roosevelt* (New York, 1958), *The Autobiography of Sol Bloom* (New York, 1948), *Fighting Liberal: The Autobiography of George Norris* (New York, 1945), and Tom Connally and Alfred Steinberg, *My Name is Tom Connally* (New York, 1954). Connally's recollections are sometimes notably faulty on details. Marquis Childs' *I Write from Washington* (New York, 1942) contains some perceptive observations on prominent figures, both diplomatic and political. Raymond Moley's *After Seven Years* (New York, 1939) is also of interest for background.

In this same memoir category are some British works of very uneven value. The most important and most recent is *The Memoirs of Anthony Eden, Earl of Avon: Facing the Dictators* (Cambridge, Mass., 1962). To the extent that Great Britain's Spanish policy was determined by its general European policy, the following are also useful: Lord Halifax (Edward Frederick Lindley Wood), *Fullness of Days* (New York, 1957); Sir Samuel J. G. Hoare (Viscount Templewood), *Nine Troubled Years* (London, 1954); Neville Henderson, *Failure of a Mission* (New York, 1940); and Duff Cooper, *Old Men Forget* (New York, 1954). Additionally, of course, there are the writings of Sir Winston Churchill; see Volume I of his six-volume work, *The Second World War*. Of further interest are the admittedly chatty, but still poignant, recollections of

A. L. Rowse, in his *Appeasement: A Study in Political Decline, 1933–1939* (New York, 1961). There are several editions of the diaries of Count Galeazzo Ciano. These diaries must be used with extreme care on matters of fact, but they provide an excellent barometer for Italian responses to developments in Spain. For accounts by two leading German diplomats, see Herbert von Dirksen's *Moscow, Tokyo, London: Twenty Years of German Foreign Policy* (Norman, Okla., 1952) and Ernst von Weizsäcker's *Memoirs* (Chicago, 1951). Two works which help to reveal the extent of factionalism among French Popular Front leaders are Paul Reynaud's *In the Thick of the Fight, 1930–1945* (New York, 1955) and Pierre Cot's *Triumph of Treason* (Chicago, 1944).

BIOGRAPHY

There are many helpful biographical studies, but the biographical approach to American diplomacy during this period has been very neglected. By far the best work is Julius Pratt's *Cordell Hull* (New York, 2 vols., 1964), in the "American Secretaries of State" series edited by Samuel Flagg Bemis and Robert H. Ferrell. Other works on Hull include Harold B. Hinton's outdated and uncritical *Cordell Hull, A Biography* (New York, 1942), and Donald Drummond's thoughtful essay in Norman A. Graebner (ed.), *An Uncertain Tradition: American Secretaries of State in the Twentieth Century* (New York, 1961). Studies on Franklin Roosevelt and his administration are too numerous to list here. The notes and bibliographies of the standard studies of the New Deal by James McGregor Burns, William E. Leuchtenburg, Edgar Eugene Robinson, and Arthur M. Schlesinger, Jr., ought to be referred to. Also see the bibliographical essay by Frank Freidel in the *Thirty-First Yearbook of the National Council for the Social Studies* (1961). The standard works above are often useful for observations on State Department personnel and on American ambassadors. The following works are helpful for the same purpose: John M. Blum, *From the Morgenthau Diaries* (Boston, 2 vols., 1959 and 1964); John Franklin Carter ("The Unofficial Observer"), *The New Dealers* (New York, 1934); Katherine Crane, *Mr. Carr of State* (New York, 1960); E. David Cronon, *Josephus Daniels in Mexico* (Madison, 1960); and Herbert Feis, *1933, Characters in Crisis* (New York, 1966). There are several pertinent essays on both European and American diplomatists in Gordon L. Craig and Felix Gilbert (eds.), *The Diplomats, 1919–1939* (Princeton, 1953). For biographies of Chamberlain and Blum, see: Iain MacLeod, *Neville Chamberlain* (London, 1961); Keith Feiling, *The Life of Neville Chamberlain* (London, 1947), Louise Elliott Dalby, *Léon Blum:*

Evolution of a Socialist (New York, 1963), and Joel Colton, *Léon Blum, Humanist in Politics* (New York, 1966). Louis Fischer's *Men and Politics* (New York, 1941) provides some fine observations on international figures.

There are few biographies of prominent congressional figures for the New Deal period, and in these the Spanish issue does not find a very important place. The two most useful studies were Fred L. Israel, *Nevada's Key Pittman* (Lincoln, Neb., 1963) and Wayne S. Cole, *Senator Gerald P. Nye and American Foreign Relations* (Minneapolis, Minn., 1962). Also of some value were Homer Socolofsky, *Arthur Capper: Publisher, Politician and Philanthropist* (Lawrence, Kans., 1962) and Marian McKenna, *Borah* (Ann Arbor, Mich., 1961).

GENERAL WORKS AND MONOGRAPHS

There are numerous works on American policy both preceding and during the Spanish civil war which treat problems relevant to the course pursued toward that conflict. Among the most valuable of these are Robert A. Divine's *The Illusion of Neutrality* (Chicago, 1962) and two studies by Selig Adler, *The Isolationist Impulse: Its Twentieth Century Reaction* (New York, 1957) and *The Uncertain Giant: 1921–1941* (New York, 1966). Divine's study is a particularly thoughtful work on the knotty problem of general neutrality legislation. Two studies used here in helping to explain the connection between the Good Neighbor policy and European developments are Donald Dozer, *Are We Good Neighbors? Three Decades of Inter-American Relations, 1930–1960* (Gainesville, Fla., 1961) and Arthur P. Whitaker, *The Western Hemisphere Idea: Its Rise and Decline* (New York, 1954). A concise treatment of United States relations with Latin America during this period, and a work which provides a useful bibliography of related documents, is Edward O. Guerrant's *Roosevelt's Good Neighbor Policy* (Albuquerque, N.Mex., 1950).

The indirect relationships between the Spanish policy and concurrent Asian policies had their roots as far back as the Manchurian crisis of 1931. American policy and some European reactions may be found in: Robert H. Ferrell, *American Diplomacy and the Great Depression: Hoover-Stimson Foreign Policy, 1929–1933* (New York, 1957); Elting E. Morison, *Turmoil and Tradition: a Study of the Life and Times of Henry L. Stimson* (Boston, 1960); and Armin Rappaport, *Henry L. Stimson and Japan, 1931–1933* (Chicago, 1963). Of special importance for background on Asian policy is Dorothy Borg's *The United States and the Far Eastern Crisis, 1933–1938* (Cambridge, Mass., 1964).

Of the many works covering American foreign policy in general during this period, the most thorough is that of William L. Langer and Everett S. Gleason, *The Challenge to Isolation, 1937–1940* (New York, 1952). In the studies treating American policy in the years immediately prior to World War II, the Spanish strife has been given scant attention. This is particularly the case with the revisionist school. The works of Charles A. Beard and Charles C. Tansill, for example, are all but silent on the issue. More is done to place the Spanish policy in a general context in the annual surveys written for the Council on Foreign Relations; see Whitney H. Shepardson and W. O. Scroggs, *The United States and World Affairs*, for the years 1936 through 1939. For information on the State Department, see: Graham H. Stuart, *The Department of State: A History of Its Organization, Procedure and Personnel* (New York, 1949); Robert Bendiner, *The Riddle of the State Department* (New York, 1942); and Bertram D. Hulen, *Inside the Department of State* (New York, 1939). Two helpful works, of distinctly different types, on German and British policy-making are Paul Seabury's *The Wilhelmstrasse: A Study of German Diplomats under the Nazi Regime* (Berkeley, 1954) and Donald G. Bishop's *The Administration of British Foreign Relations* (Syracuse, 1961).

Among those works treating American responses to the Spanish conflict, the outstanding one is Allen Guttmann, *The Wound in the Heart* (cited above). F. Jay Taylor's *The United States and the Spanish Civil War* (also cited above) provides some good material on domestic controversies. Taylor's book, written before many of the important manuscript sources were available, is weak on the diplomatic side of the problem and overemphasizes the domestic factors behind the embargo policy. The *Communism in American Life* series, edited by Clinton Rossiter, contains a number of works in some measure relevant to the Spanish issue. Two of the most pertinent are Ralph Lord Roy, *Communism and the Churches* (New York, 1960) and Daniel Aaron, *Writers on the Left* (New York, 1962). For a measured analysis of Catholic opinion on the Spanish Civil War, and of its importance with respect to American policy, see J. David Valaik, "Catholics, Neutrality, and the Spanish Embargo, 1937–1939," *Journal of American History*, June 1967. Frank A. Warren's *Liberals and Communism: the Red Decade Revisited* (Bloomington, Ind., 1966) contains an interesting chapter on left-wing reactions to the Spanish war. Manfred Jonas, *Isolationism in America, 1935–1941* (Ithaca, N.Y., 1966) is a commendable intellectual history. For a helpful compilation of opinion polls, see Hadley Cantril and Mildred Strunk (eds.), *Public Opinion, 1935–1946* (Princeton, 1951). Howard E. Kershner's *Quaker Serv-*

ice in Modern War (New York, 1950) treats the relief efforts of the American Friends Service Committee in Spain.

The most recent study of the Abraham Lincoln Battalion is Arthur H. Landis, *The Abraham Lincoln Brigade* (New York, 1967). As revealing and fascinating as substantial portions of this work are, it is seriously marred by the author's still passionate commitment to the Loyalists and to the International Brigades. Many readers will find more freshness in two older works, also written by participants: Alvah Bessie, *Men in Battle* (New York, 1941) and Edwin Rolfe, *The Lincoln Battalion* (New York, 1939). Robert A. Rosenstone is currently doing extensive research on the American volunteers. His article, "The Men of the Abraham Lincoln Battalion," appeared in the *Journal of American History* (Sept. 1967), 327–338.

On the background of the Spanish struggle itself, there are innumerable works. The best is Gerald Brenan, *The Spanish Labyrinth: An Account of the Social and Political Backgrounds of the Spanish Civil War* (London and New York, 2nd ed., 1950). Gabriel Jackson's *The Spanish Republic* and Hugh Thomas' *The Spanish Civil War,* both cited above, contain substantial accounts of the historical background. Jackson's excellent study should also be consulted for military and political events during the war, but Thomas provides somewhat more on general diplomatic developments. Also helpful on historical background is Salvador de Madariaga, *Spain, a Modern History* (New York, 1958 ed.). For two perceptive contemporary analyses, see E. Alison Peers, *The Spanish Tragedy* (London, 1936), and Charles A. Thompson, "Spain: Issues behind the Conflict," *Foreign Policy Reports,* January 1, 1937.

For international problems and the matter of foreign intervention there are likewise many useful studies. On questions of international law, see Norman J. Padelford, *International Law and Diplomacy in the Spanish Civil Strife* (New York, June 1939), and Philip C. Jessup, "The Spanish Rebellion and International Law," *Foreign Affairs,* January 1937. It should be noted that Padelford approved of the American embargo policy and that Jessup came to oppose it. Information on the Texas Oil Company's trade with Franco may be found in Herbert Feis, *The Spanish Story* (New York, 1948). On the activities of the European Non-Intervention Committee, the best balanced study is an unpublished doctoral dissertation by John Bowyer Bell, "The Non-Intervention Committee and the Spanish Civil War, 1936–1939" (Duke University, 1958). Two other works, both with pro-Loyalist bias, are Patricia A. M. van der Esch, *Prelude to War: The International Repercussions of the Spanish Civil War* (The Hague, 1951), and Dante A. Puzzo, *Spain and the*

Great Powers, 1936–1941 (New York, 1962). Vera Micheles Dean wrote a perceptive article early in the war entitled "European Diplomacy and the Spanish Crisis," *Foreign Policy Reports,* December 1, 1936. Also see John R. Hubbard, "How Franco Financed His War," *Journal of Modern History,* December 1953.

Among the many accounts of other European developments to which the Spanish conflict was related, the following ought to be considered: Elizabeth Monroe, *The Mediterranean in Politics* (London, 1939); Arnold Wolfers, *Britain and France between Two Wars* (Hamden, Conn., 1963 printing); Martin Gilbert and Richard Gott, *The Appeasers* (Boston, 1963); John Wheeler Wheeler-Bennett, *Munich: Prologue to Tragedy* (New York, 1948); Peter J. Larmour, *The French Radical Party in the 1930's* (Stanford, Calif., 1964); Eugen Weber, *Action Française: Royalism and Reaction in Twentieth Century France* (Stanford, Calif., 1962); Luigi Villari, *Italian Foreign Policy under Mussolini* (New York, 1956); Charles F. Delzell, *Mussolini's Enemies: The Italian Anti-Fascist Resistance* (Princeton, N.J., 1961); Edward Hallett Carr, *German-Soviet Relations between the World Wars* (Baltimore, 1951); George Kennan, *Russia and the West under Lenin and Stalin* (Boston, 1960); and David C. Cattell, *Communism and the Spanish Civil War* (Berkeley, Calif., 1955) and *Soviet Diplomacy in the Spanish Civil War* (Berkeley, Calif., 1957). While the roles of both the Soviet Union and the Communist party in the Spanish strife have undergone continual historical scrutiny, Cattell's two fine studies are still the most reliable. The Villari book on Italian foreign policy is notable for its defense of Mussolini's course of action in Spain.

NEWSPAPERS AND PERIODICALS

The files of the following newspapers were used in gathering editorial opinion at critical stages in the development of American policy (for example in August 1936 and January 1937): *Boston Evening Transcript, Chicago Tribune, Christian Science Monitor, Denver Post, Los Angeles Times,* New Orleans *Times-Picayune, San Francisco Chronicle,* and, for a Hearst paper, the *San Francisco Examiner.* The *New York Times* and the *Washington Post* were used for straight news and for editorial opinion.

The files of the *Nation, New Republic, Christian Century, Commonweal,* and *America* were also used, again with an emphasis on critical periods. Some helpful articles are also found in a variety of other periodicals and journals. The most extensive bibliography of articles is provided by Guttmann, *Wound in the Heart.*

NOTES

DSR   = Department of State Records
FR   = *Foreign Relations of the United States*
SRRO = Spanish Refugee Relief Organization collection, Columbia
      University

1. SPANISH AND AMERICAN BACKGROUND

1. In this résumé of Spanish conditions since the beginning of the Republic, Bowers concluded that "the political future of the new republic presents a gloomy picture." Bowers (Madrid) to Secretary of State, Dec. 10, 1935, Department of State Records, DSR, 852.00/2122.

2. Bowers (Madrid) to Secretary, Apr. 21 and June 29, 1936, DSR, 852.00/2157 and 852.00 P.R./454. The rapidly changing situation in Spain made it difficult for Bowers to report any consistent trends. For example, on Apr. 1, 1936, he had been "inclined to believe" that at that time there was no "real danger of communism in Spain" (DSR, 852.00/2153). On Apr. 21, he reported that there was such a danger. On May 20, he had indicated his "belief" that "the Government is today in a strong position and is able to enforce its authority in all parts of Spain." While it is a "revolutionary period," and the "public mind" is "excited," the "sporadic disturbances are a flash in the pan." While "unfortunately a few mortalities take place, they are not significant of wide-spread disorder" (DSR, 852.00/2166). On June 29, he wrote of "widespread unrest," with little prospect of a return to "normality" in the near future.

3. *New York Times*, Mar. 26, 1933.

4. *New York Times*, Jan. 5, 1933. Laughlin reportedly inquired

251

about the seating arrangements and then declined the invitation on account of "illness."

5. *My Name Is Tom Connally* (New York, 1954), 111.

6. Quoted in Katherine Crane, *Mr. Carr of State* (New York, 1960), 324-325.

7. "The Unofficial Observer," *The New Dealers* (New York, 1934), 295.

8. Drummond, "Cordell Hull," in Norman Graebner, ed., *An Uncertain Tradition: American Secretaries of State in the Twentieth Century* (New York, 1961), 193.

9. Feis, *1933: Characters in Crisis* (New York, 1966), 98-99.

10. *I Write from Washington* (New York, 1942), 150.

11. *Ventures in Diplomacy* (Boston, 1953), 185-186.

12. See Crane, *Mr. Carr of State*, 327.

13. Robert A. Divine, *The Illusion of Neutrality* (Chicago, 1962), 58 and 101. Moore was certainly correct; drawing such distinctions could be difficult if not sometimes impossible. But the way in which he chose to view the problem was typically isolationist. He ignored the larger issue of whether or not the United States should bind itself beforehand to a denial of assistance to one side when American self-interest called for such aid.

2. PARIS AND LONDON

1. A little later it became common for European statesmen to suggest that only the intervention of President Roosevelt in European affairs could save Europe from war. Since such comments rarely went beyond that point, it is doubtful how much, and what kind of, "intervention" these Europeans would have tolerated and what good might have come from the very limited intervention which the American public would have tolerated. Prevailing opinion among British leaders was utterly opposed to such ideas.

2. American Chargé d'Affaires (Moscow) to Secretary of State, Sept. 12, 1936, DSR, 852.00/3130. Also, Franklin L. Ford and Carl E. Schorske, "The Voice in the Wilderness: Robert Coulondre," in Gordon A. Craig and Felix Gilbert, eds., *The Diplomats, 1919-1939* (Princeton, 1953), 555-578. Coulondre had two premises: first, that Germany must be stopped; second, that the Western powers must strengthen their ties with Russia to accomplish this.

3. Elizabeth R. Cameron has a useful essay on Léger in Craig and Gilbert, *The Diplomats*, 378-405. William W. Kaufmann's essay "Two American Ambassadors: Bullitt and [Joseph P.] Kennedy" (*The Diplomats*, 649-681) is also helpful although its emphasis is on a later period.

4. There were attempts on the part of some of these interests to do business in arms and ammunition with the Spanish Rebels. One instance of this kind, purportedly involving more than two million dollars, was reported to the Department of State early in the war.

Robert Caldwell (American Minister to Lisbon) to Secretary, Sept. 30, 1936, DSR, 852.00/3454.

5. See Patricia A. M. van der Esch, *Prelude to War: The International Repercussions of the Spanish Civil War* (The Hague, 1951), 15–16; and Elizabeth Monroe, *The Mediterranean in Politics* (London, 1939), 222.

6. *Old Men Forget* (New York, 1954), 205. Sir Samuel Hoare later wrote: "During the last two years of his premiership, he never seemed to have any clear-cut idea of what our foreign policy should be." Viscount Templewood (Sir Samuel J. G. Hoare), *Nine Troubled Years* (London, 1954), 290–291.

7. See Hugh Thomas, *The Spanish Civil War* (New York, 1961), 205–206.

8. Straus to Secretary, July 27, *FR 1936*, II, 447–449. There are numerous accounts of this encounter between Blum and Eden. Eden's memoirs are here important because no two accounts agree and because Eden's recollections omit any such discussion. Eden does point out that both he and Corbin did not later recollect any discussion at that time of a plan for a European nonintervention agreement. This is not unlikely, but standing alone the comment is somewhat misleading, for it misses the central point. Did Eden impress Blum with the British point of view on the Spanish crisis? If he did not, then he was derelict in his duty. If he did, then Blum was compelled to choose between acting contrary to British desires or finding some other means to control the Spanish situation. See *The Memoirs of Anthony Eden, Earl of Avon: Facing the Dictators* (Cambridge, Mass., 1962), 450–456.

Also in this context, Elizabeth Cameron's account of Léger's role is of additional importance, for Corbin and Léger were intimates, and the Secretary General had Blum's highest respect: "When war broke out in the peninsula . . . once more Léger's first concern was with the state of opinion in Britain. He saw with alarm that the new socialist government in France, the turmoil of French strikes and workers' agitation, had raised a red scare across the Channel. Accordingly, he persuaded Blum to accompany him to the diplomatic conferences scheduled for London. Léger's *cauchemar* was nothing short of a British alignment with White Spain, Germany, and Italy 'in a new Holy Alliance in the style of Metternich.' And however right or wrong his judgment, he was convinced that British neutrality could not be assumed unless the French government agreed to forego the shipment of arms and volunteers to the legal government of Spain. Therefore, against all Blum's sympathies, he got him to propose non-intervention as the best available insurance against the spread of the conflict." "Léger," in *The Diplomats*, 391.

Léger persisted in this view for some time. A rather similar interpretation of British policy was prevalent in the State Department during the summer of 1937—although it fell significantly short of the idea of Britain actually allying with those powers. See below, Chapter 5.

9. Straus to Secretary, July 31, *FR 1936,* II, 450–452.

10. For example, on October 5, 1936, the American Embassy in London reported to Washington: ". . . it is fair to say that Labor never had serious illusions that the Agreement would be adhered to rigidly by those Powers which were reluctant to join it. In point of fact, neither the leaders nor the supporters of the Labor Party are prepared to advocate or support a policy which would entail a substantial risk of Great Britain's being brought into a European struggle arising out of the Spanish Civil War." DSR, 841.00 P.R./460. This was the dilemma of peace-minded liberals everywhere.

11. See Straus to Secretary, July 31, *FR 1936,* II, 451; and, American Chargé (Paris) to Secretary, Aug. 6, *FR 1936,* II, 467–468.

12. Because of the scarcity of evidence, it would be difficult to say how justified the British were, at this early date, in holding this opinion. In Eden's mind, it seems to have been a well-grounded wish. See *Facing the Dictators,* 455–456.

13. *FR 1936,* II, 474; First Secretary of American Embassy (London) to Secretary, Aug. 24, 1936, DSR, 841.00 P.R./455; and, Eden, *Facing the Dictators,* 453.

14. Welczeck to Foreign Ministry, August 21, 1936, *Documents on German Foreign Policy, 1918–1945,* Ser. D., vol. III, *Germany and the Spanish Civil War, 1936–1939* (Washington, 1950), p. 49. Hereafter referred to as *German Documents,* "D," III.

15. American Chargé (Paris) to Secretary, Aug. 25, DSR, 852.00/2793.

16. See *German Documents,* "D," III, 60.

17. See Gabriel Jackson, *The Spanish Republic and the Civil War, 1931–1939* (Princeton, 1965), 248–249. It would seem that both the Germans and the Italians knew that the uprising was afoot, however.

18. On this matter during September, of enlisting the Vatican in Germany's anti-Communist crusade, what looked like a German success one week appeared to be a failure the next. George Messersmith, then stationed in Vienna, wrote to Secretary Hull, on September 10, that the Vatican was reaching an agreement with Germany by which the Germans would ease up their activity against the Catholic Church in Germany in return for the Vatican's support against Communism. On September 18, Messersmith wrote that the Vatican had seen "the dangers of the bargain which it had so definitely contemplated" (Cordell Hull Papers, cont. 39, folder 92). By January 1937, however, German Catholics were instructed by Church leaders to cooperate with the Nazis' anti-Bolshevist campaigns.

19. American Chargé, Loy Henderson (Moscow) to Secretary, Aug. 4, *FR 1936,* II, 461; and, Henderson to Secretary, Aug. 18, 1936, DSR, 852.00/3051.

20. Thomas, *Spanish Civil War,* 309–310 and 331–332; and Jackson, *Spanish Republic,* 317–318.

21. See *FR 1936,* II, 515–516.

22. See *FR 1936,* II, 485–487, 493–494, and 507–508.

23. John Bowyer Bell, "The Non-Intervention Committee and the Spanish Civil War, 1936–1939" (unpublished doctoral dissertation, Duke University, 1958), 89–90.

24. See *FR 1936,* II, 532–533. The United States was, intentionally or not, mistakenly mentioned in one of the Spanish Government's protests as a member of the Non-Intervention Committee.

25. *FR 1936,* II, 608–610.

26. *FR 1936,* II, 517.

27. While in late September, the German Chargé in Moscow found "it has been impossible to obtain reliable proof of violation of the arms embargo by the Soviet Union," reports of Soviet military intervention in Spain were common at the end of October and early November (*German Documents,* "D," III, 97–100). Also, Bowers to Secretary, Oct. 30, 1936, DSR, 852.00/3739; and American Consul (Valencia) to Secretary, Nov. 9, 1936, DSR, 852.00/3726.

28. Bell, "Non-Intervention Committee," 112.

29. Eric Wendelin, in charge of the American embassy at Madrid, had reported on October 29 that assumptions of an imminent fall of Madrid were premature. Wendelin based his analysis on reports of increased foodstuffs and supplies from Russia and a "new note of optimism in press and public" (*FR 1936,* II, 543–544). The reorganization of the Spanish Government took place only a few days later, under the guidance of Largo Caballero and supported by all the parties of the Popular Front. One of the most influential figures in Madrid during this time was Marcel Rosenberg, the Soviet ambassador.

30. For example, Ambassador Bingham reported from London on November 19 that in the opinion of the British Foreign Office "It looked as though the war would drag on almost indefinitely" (*FR 1936,* II, 560).

31. For American accounts of the rise of Spanish Communism during the war, see *FR 1936,* II, 543–544, 552, 555–557, and 563–569. The rise of Spanish Fascism was treated in: Bowers to Acting Secretary, Nov. 11, 1936, DSR, 852.00/3863; and American Consulate (Seville) to Secretary, received Oct. 2, 1936, DSR 852.00/3330. It appeared to be the conviction of American officials in Spain that Communism and Fascism were attracting followers who did not particularly interest themselves in the ideologies. These "nonbelievers" did, however, adopt the foreign Communist and Fascist parties' organizational structures, symbols, slogans, and, more important, methods of dealing with opposition.

32. For examples of further military aid, arrivals of Russian tanks and planes were reported by Bowers (Oct. 30, 1936, DSR,

852.00/3739) and by the American Consul at Valencia (Nov. 9, 1936, DSR, 852.00/3726). The American Consul in Rebel-held Seville reported the arrival of 7,000 Germans at Cádiz on November 16 (*FR 1936*, II, 558 and 575–576).

33. *FR 1936*, II, 558. On October 8, the Italians had been informed that Hitler preferred to recognize the Nationalists as the *de facto* government of Spain upon the capture of Madrid "if an agreement was reached with Italy on a similar procedure." Mussolini was said to have agreed. But Mussolini later changed his mind and the Germans went along with him (*German Documents* "D," III, 105 and 131).

34. For French and British attitudes toward the possibility of recognizing a state of belligerency, see *FR 1936*, 547–548, 550–551, and 574. Also see Eden, *Facing the Dictators*, 465.

Ambassador Bowers' opinion on the propriety of granting *recognition* to the Franco government can be found in *FR 1936*, II, 555–557 (dispatch dated Nov. 9). Bowers concluded: "We certainly ought not to consider recognition before France and England but act simultaneously with them." Bowers did not think there were yet sufficient grounds for doing so. In this he was hardly alone.

35. French estimates of Soviet intentions were reported by Ambassador Bullitt. *FR 1936*, II, 539 and 574–575; also Bullitt to Secretary, Nov. 1, 1936, DSR, 851.00/1602.

Three weeks earlier, the British Chargé in Moscow had told Loy Henderson that in his opinion the Soviet Union was causing problems in the NIC "in order to strengthen its position with the radical and liberal elements of the world who sympathized with the Spanish Government and in the hope of embarrassing those British circles which had been seeking to find a way for improving British-German relations" (to Secretary, Oct. 11, 1936, DSR, 852.00/3609). Henderson later wrote that it was "highly probable" that Litvinov was persuading the Soviet leaders to pursue an equivocal course in Spain so as not to "alienate" France and Great Britain "entirely" (Oct. 24, *FR 1936*, II, 541–542).

36. Eden feared that without the NIC, France might reverse itself and aid Madrid. "A breakdown of the Committee would have baleful consequences, perhaps even on the Anglo-French alliance, which I regarded as indispensable to our joint survival, and that of freedom in Europe" (*Facing the Dictators*, 459–460).

37. Eden, *Facing the Dictators*, 459–460.

38. To Acting Secretary, Nov. 20, 1936, DSR, 852.00/3823.

39. *Facing the Dictators*, 463. Cordell Hull quoted Eden's December 19 speech in his own *Memoirs* (I, 482).

40. Bullitt to Roosevelt, Nov. 24, 1936. Roosevelt Papers, President's Secretary's Files [PSF]—France.

41. *FR 1936*, II, 574–575.

42. The ambassador successfully conveyed the suggestion of a double meaning by saying that the British would be "very strongly

opposed" to any territorial expansion by Italy in the Mediterranean. Perhaps it was meant that this, combined with Franco's reluctance to grant such concessions, would prevent Italian expansion. But the over-all tone of the conversation as it appears in the memorandum was one of optimism on the part of the British. Memorandum by James Dunn, Chief, Western European Division, Nov. 2, 1936, DSR, 811.71247H/69.

43. For instance, Bowers, writing on December 1, 1936, was convinced that the British favored Franco: "It would be sheer nonsense to insist that the British Government, reflected by Eden, is the least neutral. I have called attention from time to time to its extreme bias. . . . [In] conversations with the British Ambassador here I have observed an intense partisanship from the very beginning of the war. . . . I ascribe the attitude of the British Government to class feeling. . . ." (to Acting Secretary, DSR, 852.00/4063). While it would seem that Bowers was approaching the truth in his assessment of the situation as it stood in early December, the rest of his analysis does not coincide with some of his earlier reports as he would have had the State Department believe. As an illustration, on October 21, 1936, he wrote: "She [Britain] has been nearer neutral throughout than any nation, I think, except the United States" (to Secretary, DSR, 852.00/3644).

Only three days after Bowers' December report, the American embassy in London forwarded a memorandum of a conversation with Sir Robert Vansittart, who confirmed the viewpoint expressed earlier by the British Foreign Office "that the British Government did not consider the Spanish situation likely to lead to an international conflict . . ." (Counselor of Embassy to Acting Secretary, Dec. 4, 1936, DSR, 740.00/79). This concurred with the opinion of Bullitt expressed in his letter of November 24 to the President (Roosevelt Papers, PSF-France). All this of course was predicated upon the continued nonintervention of Britain, France, and the United States.

44. See Eden, *Facing the Dictators,* 462. According to Eden, Corbin, as early as October 23, "had come to the conclusion that the Committee might consider a proposal to supervise its work on the spot." But the exact origin of the idea is still in doubt.

45. Bell, "Non-Intervention Committee," 134–135.

46. To some Western analysts, the precarious condition of the German economy was not a blessing. For instance, Sir Robert Vansittart informed the American embassy in London of his belief that the German situation was the greatest danger to European peace, for the "economic pressure might have political repercussions." Counselor of Embassy (London) to Acting Secretary, Dec. 4, 1936, DSR, 740.00/79.

47. Memorandum by James Dunn, Nov. 2, 1936, DSR, 811.7127H/69.

48. *FR 1936,* II, 574–575 and 614–615.

49. See *German Documents,* "D," III, 170–173. The report also remarked that the Spaniards "have proved to be very unsatisfactory political and military material."

3. MORAL EMBARGO

1. *The Nation,* editorial, Aug. 29, 1936, 228–229. "In warning American shipping lines not to carry arms to Spain, the Administration is making precisely the same error as England and France."

2. *FR 1936,* II, 440–441 and 444. Despite the suggestion of Blake, the Vacuum Oil Company decided that it was advisable to supply a "small quantity" of oil "on demand of Spanish Minister at Tangier." The transaction was to be handled through a third party.

3. *FR 1936,* II, 445–6.

4. *FR 1936,* II, 445 and 446; and J. E. Slater (vice president, Export Steamship Company, New York) to Secretary, July 22, DSR, 852.00/2218.

5. The Committee of Control decided that the presence and refueling of Spanish war vessels violated the Statute of Tangier. This decision was actually made before Hull sent his "conditional" instruction favoring international cooperation to Blake on July 22. Blake's telegram informing the Department of both this decision and the *Exmouth* incident arrived almost two hours before Hull's instructions were telegraphed to Blake. But Hull obviously did not yet know of its existence: first, he referred directly to Blake's telegram of July 21; second, he certainly would not have been compelled to guess what the decision of the Committee of Control would be had he known of Blake's later telegram (see *FR 1936,* II, 444–446).

Even had Hull known of the Committee's decision, he would still have been anticipating international cooperation; the Committee's ruling had yet to be confirmed by the foreign offices of the participating powers. In a dispatch written July 28 (received August 7), Blake reported: ". . . the principally interested political Powers are pursuing a policy of procrastination before taking definite action in the hope that circumstances may prevent them from being compelled to take sides in an issue the results of which are still so indecisive." And whatever were the implications of Blake's remarks, he added his personal feeling that Franco was acting with "considerable restraint and sagacity in the face of much provocation." Blake concluded that conditions were such that "neutrality" must be enforced at Tangier (DSR, 852.00/2467).

6. Memorandum by Secretary, Aug. 4, *FR 1936,* II, 457–458. Also see *FR 1936,* II, 454–455 and 464–466; and Hull, *Memoirs,* I, 476–477.

7. John Morgan, "United States Policy during the Spanish Civil War, July 1936–April 1939" (located in the Hull Papers, and hereafter referred to as the Morgan-Green Report), 31–32. Also, Hull, *Memoirs,* I, 477.

8. The definition of terms is taken from Philip C. Jessup, "The Spanish Rebellion and International Law," *Foreign Affairs,* Jan. 1937, 260–279. The application of the definitions to the Spanish strife is partially Jessup's, partially mine. Also see Norman J. Padelford, *International Law and Diplomacy in the Spanish Civil Strife* (New York, June 1939), 51–52.

9. Padelford, *International Law and Diplomacy in the Spanish Civil Strife,* viii. The fact that no foreign power did grant belligerent rights contributed to Padelford's title. In choosing "civil strife," rather than "civil war," he was forced to choose between the above fact and another—"the formal legislative and executive acts of at least thirteen states . . . contained express use of the words 'civil war in Spain.' " As precedents for the term "civil strife" Padelford referred to the Havana Convention of 1928 and to the neutrality law passed by Congress and then signed by the President on May 1, 1937 (Padelford, viii).

10. Jessup, "Spanish Rebellion," 263.

11. Padelford, *International Law,* 188.

12. "The question of the export of arms to Spain," however, "had not been directly before the Department" at the time of the August 5 meeting (Morgan-Green Report, 35). But this is only to say that no inquiries regarding applications for license to export arms to Spain had yet been received by the Department. The first inquiry was made the following day by the Spanish ambassador.

13. Morgan-Green Report, 32–33.

14. *FR 1936,* II, 471. On the same day, apparently earlier, Phillips was given a copy of the French draft of a declaration of nonintervention, a draft which the French hoped would be signed by the European powers (*FR 1936,* II, 469–470). The French chargé said that the Germans and the Italians had accepted nonintervention in principle. But since the decision to send the telegraphic instruction to American officials had been made two days earlier, there is no necessary connection between the information given Phillips on August 7 and his circular telegram of the same date.

15. William Phillips Papers, Journals, August 11, 1936; and *FR 1936,* II, 478–479. The American embassy at London learned that von Neurath "considers adherence of the United States to the proposed agreement essential to make it effective."

16. *FR 1936,* II, 493–494 and 510–511.

17. Hull, *Memoirs,* I, 478; and Morgan-Green Report, 34. Those words within quotation marks are Morgan's. But Morgan's work, researched and written under the auspices of the State Department, is so circumspect that it is doubtful that he would have used the words "extreme embarrassment" if Phillips had not used them or their equivalents. Hull, who clearly used Morgan's work extensively for his discussion of the Spanish civil war in his *Memoirs,* omitted these words.

18. Phillips Journals, Aug. 3 and 4; and Morgan-Green Report, 35.

19. Phillips Journals, Aug. 10; Morgan-Green Report, 35-36; Hull, *Memoirs*, I, 478-479; and *FR 1936*, II, 474-475.

20. Phillips Journals, Aug. 11; and *FR 1936*, II, 475-476.

21. Phillips, quoted in Morgan-Green Report, 36. Also see Hull, *Memoirs*, I, 478-479. According to Morgan, a deviation from the adopted policy of embargo "would have called for a readjustment of the policies of Great Britain, France, and other nations who were trying to keep arms out of Spain . . ." (p. 38). It must not be assumed, however, that such "readjustments" would have favored the Spanish government. That they might well have resulted in the opposite is a point which is discussed in later chapters.

22. *FR 1936*, II, 506-507. Italics mine.

23. Morgan-Green Report, 38-39.

24. Morgan-Green Report, 37.

25. *San Francisco Examiner*, Aug. 12; *Times-Picayune*, Aug. 13; and *San Francisco Chronicle*, Aug. 12.

26. *Boston Evening Transcript*, Aug. 13; *New York Times*, Aug. 8; and *Christian Science Monitor*, Aug. 15.

27. *New York Times*, July 28; *Boston Evening Transcript*, Aug. 19 and 21; *Chicago Tribune*, Aug. 26; *Times-Picayune*, Aug. 20; *San Francisco Chronicle*, Aug. 20; and, *Los Angeles Times*, Aug. 19.

28. *The Secret Diary of Harold Ickes* (New York, 3 vols., 1953-54), Vol. I, *The First Thousand Days*, 655-658, Aug. 6-10 entries. Also Wayne S. Cole, *Senator Gerald P. Nye and American Foreign Relations* (Minneapolis, 1962), 136-138.

The congressmen who joined Nye and Benson in signing the August 14 telegram to the President were: Fred Biermann, Guy Gillette, Fred Hildebrandt, Herman Kopplemann, Henry Luckey, Byron Scott, and Fred Sisson (Roosevelt Papers, OF 1561 Neutrality). A number of these men were among the first to call for the lifting of the Spanish embargo in later months.

29. This hardly means that Hull was unaware of Catholic opinion. For example, during September he wrote to Josephus Daniels, ambassador to Mexico, concerning the problems arising out of the treatment of the Catholic Church in that country: "The extreme partisan republicans, especially the K. of C. [Knights of Columbus] are watching every pretext to foment the religious situation. The matter, however, has been quiescent for some days, and I am not sure but that an increasing number of the higher and more influential members of the Church are becoming less vocal" (Sept. 18, 1936, Daniels Papers, box 750).

30. Lippmann, quoted in Morgan-Green Report, 39. Also Hull, *Memoirs*, I, 479.

31. Memorandum of telephone conversation between Hull and Eric C. Wendelin (third secretary of embassy, Madrid), July 25, Hull Papers, carton 39; and Wendelin to Secretary, Aug. 1, DSR, 852.00/2349.

32. Hull, *Memoirs*, I, 475. The message to the President is found in *FR 1936*, II, 635-636.

33. *FR 1936,* II, 442 and 506–507.

34. Wendelin to Secretary, received Aug. 25, DSR, 852.00/2817.

35. Bowers to Secretary, Aug. 11, Hull Papers, carton 39.

36. *FR 1936,* II, 459, 679–680, and 723–724; and Bowers to Secretary, Oct. 21, DSR, 852.00/3644, and Oct. 30, DSR, 852.00/3739.

37. Problems created by the participation of American nationals in the war are discussed in Chapter 8. The protection of lives and property during the first six months of the war is heavily documented in *FR 1936,* II, 626–784.

38. One American woman charged that her apartment had been forcibly entered and that she had been raped. The case apparently was dropped following a doctor's examination, although she continued to insist that she had been attacked. In another incident, an American woman was injured when fighting took place at Guadarrama, about 50 kilometers northwest of Madrid. See *FR 1936,* II, 628–632.

A Spanish clerk, who was a trusted employee of the embassy at Madrid for seventeen years, was killed while on duty in an automobile bearing the American flag. See *FR 1936,* II, 636–637, 639, and 641.

39. By mid-January 1937, 1,700 American nationals had been evacuated from Spain. Division of Western European Affairs, reply to inquiry concerning activities of American officials in Spain, Jan. 19, 1937, DSR, 852.00/4419½.

40. Division of Western European Affairs, Jan. 19, 1937, DSR, 852.00/4419½.

41. Bowers to Acting Secretary Moore, Nov. 20, *FR 1936,* II, 563–569. There was a rumor that the shelling occurred because Colonel Behn, president of I.T. & T., had refused to contribute to the Rebel war chest. Bowers discarded that possibility, preferring the interpretation that it was due to the military use of the building by Spanish government forces. During the war International Telephone and Telegraph played an unusual role which Bowers described as perfectly proper: it served both armies.

42. *FR 1936,* II, 653–654. Also see Bowers, *My Mission to Spain: Watching the Rehearsal for World War II* (New York, 1954), 262.

43. See *FR 1936,* II, 657–658, 661–662, and 703. Also *New York Times,* Aug. 5 and 7.

44. *FR 1936,* II, 657–658.

45. *FR 1936,* II, 669, 717–718, and 725; also 728–751 passim.

46. *FR 1936,* II, 669 and 704–705.

47. Bowers to Hull, Oct. 6, Hull Papers, carton 39.

48. *FR 1936,* II, 687–709 passim; Hull *Memoirs,* I, 480; and Secretary to Bay (consul, Seville), Sept. 9, DSR, 852.00/3043.

49. *New York Times,* Dec. 19, 1936, Jan. 22, 1938, and June 20, 1938; and, State Department *Press Releases,* Jan. 22 and Feb. 5 and 12, 1938. Also Padelford, *International Law,*

172–173. The unpublished portions of Jay Pierrepont Moffat's Journals contain several entries on the details of these problems occurring in 1938.

50. *FR 1936,* II, 519. Earlier, after Wendelin had informed Bowers that the withdrawal of certain embassies might take place, Bowers telegraphed Hull: "I agree entirely Wendelin's conclusion that the effect if not the purpose is to embarrass the Government and assist the rebels" (Sept. 22, DSR, 852.00/2753).

51. Wendelin to Secretary, Sept. 7, DSR, 852.00/3023.

52. *FR 1936,* II, 724–725.

53. *FR 1936,* II, 727–728.

54. Taken from Crane, *Mr. Carr of State,* 323–324, 326, and 327. Hull later characterized Moore as "a person of unusual ability and high purpose, a profound student of both domestic and international affairs, and [he] possessed character and patriotism of the highest order." Hull made these observations in his *Memoirs* (pp. 301–302) in the midst of a discussion of American recognition of the Soviet government in 1933. Moore handled some of the negotiations preliminary to recognition.

55. The following impressions of Moore are very largely taken from correspondence in the Moore Papers. There are innumerable pieces of relevant material in the folders of John Cudahy, William Dodd, William Bullitt, and Claude Bowers. Also, from the Roosevelt Papers, Moore to Roosevelt, Nov. 11, 1936, President's Personal Files [PPF] 1043 (Dodd); and, Moore to Roosevelt, Nov. 21, 1936, PSF, R. Walton Moore.

56. *FR 1936,* II, 558–559 and 763–766.

57. *FR 1936,* II, 766–767. The Burgos government had just expressed its intention to prevent all traffic with the port of Barcelona, even if it should be necessary to destroy the port. Moore then contemplated withdrawing the consulate from that city, but was dissuaded by consul general Perkins. See *FR 1936,* II, 559, 764, 765, and 768.

As early as August 31, Moore wrote Dodd: "There is absolutely only one course for us, namely to evacuate Americans from Spain and be prepared to bring our officials [home?] from Madrid and the various consulates when it is no longer safe for them to remain" (Dodd Papers, carton 49).

It is conceivable that Moore's plan was further motivated by the idea that the Rebels were soon to be victorious. On November 11, he asked Dodd for suggestions on "the question of recognizing a new Government in Spain." He expressly expected the problem to arise "in the near future" (Dodd Papers, carton 49).

58. *FR 1936,* II, 769.

59. A copy of the entire conversation is found in the Moore Papers.

60. A copy of the entire conversation of November 23 is contained in the Moore Papers.

61. *FR 1936,* II, 774–775.

62. Frank C. Page to President Roosevelt, Nov. 24, and copy of unsigned letter to Page dated Nov. 23; Roosevelt Papers, Official File (OF) 422, Spain 1933–1938. It is likely that the unsigned copy of the letter to Page is misdated, although considering the time differential between Madrid and Washington it is conceivably correct.

One of Behn's major complaints about the embassy move was that it was ordered without Hull's approval. Behn was apparently difficult to please. He complained about both Bowers and Hallett Johnson and said that Wendelin was lacking in cooperation, deference, and gratitude. Moffat Papers, Diaries, July 26, 1937.

63. Moore to President, Nov. 21 and Nov. 25, Roosevelt Papers, PSF, R. Walton Moore. In the letter of November 25, Moore curiously indicated his conviction that American officials in Barcelona ought to leave that port; yet from all other available evidence that idea had been dropped almost immediately after Moore brought it up on November 20.

64. Memo of telephone conversation between Dunn and Wendelin, Nov. 21, Moore Papers; and Wendelin to Acting Secretary, Nov. 22, *FR 1936,* II, 770–772.

65. Moore to President, Nov. 27, Moore Papers, box 17.

66. Moore to Hull, Nov. 24, Moore Papers, box 8.

67. Moore to President, Nov. 27, Moore Papers, box 17.

68. American consulate (Seville) to Secretary, political report, received Oct. 2, DSR, 852.00/3330. The view that "democracy" was endangered (and that there was no hope for the success of a "liberal republic") was commonly held. It could be found in the *New York Times* before the war was three weeks old (editorials, July 23, and August 6). An editorial in the August 12 issue of *Christian Century* put the matter simply: A Loyalist victory "will still leave it to be determined whether the relatively moderate and orderly liberalism of the republic, having conquered its enemies, can restrain its friends."

69. In October, Bowers indicated that he was "puzzled" by the French and British policies, and believed that they were due to the conviction that the Rebels would win the war. Less than two months later, he was firm in his conviction that the Baldwin Government favored Franco. By the middle of January 1937, he was sure that the British had wanted a quick Rebel victory since the beginning of the war. Bowers to Secretary, Oct. 21, 1936, DSR, 852.00/3644; Dec. 1, 1936, DSR, 852.00/4063; and January 12, 1937, *FR 1937,* I, 223–227.

4. FROM MORAL TO LEGAL EMBARGO

1. DSR, 852.00/2552.

2. Western European Division, memorandum of conversation with First Secretary of British embassy, Aug. 27, 1936; and Office of Arms and Munitions Control, memorandum, Aug. 27, 1936. Both items are located in DSR, 852.24/95.

3. Morgan-Green Report, 65–70.

4. Daniels to President Roosevelt, Sept. 20, 1936, Daniels Papers, box 16. According to Daniels, the conversation had taken place "a few weeks ago." Also memorandum by Chief of Division of Mexican Affairs, Sept. 14, *FR 1936,* II, 530–531.

5. *FR 1937,* I, 564; Morgan-Green Report, 69–70; and *New York Times,* Jan. 8, 1937.

6. The Rudolf Wolf episode is related in the Morgan-Green Report, 62–65; relevant documents are found in DSR, 711.00111 Lic. Wolf, Rudolf. Arms Traffic.

7. See *New York Times,* Dec. 28, 1936.

8. *New York Times,* Dec. 30, 1936; and *Washington Post,* Dec. 30 and 31, 1936.

9. The Cuse incident is related in the Morgan-Green Report, 71–72; relevant documents are found in DSR, 711.00111 Lic. Vimalert Co. Ltd. Arms Traffic.

10. *New York Times,* Dec. 29, 1936.

11. Morgan-Green Report, 72: and, *New York Times,* Dec. 30, 1936.

12. *New York Times,* Dec. 29, 1936.

13. Eden, *Facing the Dictators,* 485–486.

14. *FR 1936,* II, 615–617, 620–621, and 625; and *FR 1937,* I, 216.

15. Dodd to Acting Secretary, Dec. 29, *FR 1936,* II, 617; and Eden, *Facing the Dictators,* 486–490. It was shortly afterward that Bowers recorded his conviction that the British favored a Franco victory (*FR 1937,* I, 223–227).

16. See *New York Times,* Dec. 30, 1936.

17. Bowers to Acting Secretary, Dec. 31, *FR 1936,* II, 624. Bowers had been informed of the German response by the British ambassador. Bowers personally advised, the day before, that a debate on neutrality legislation might precipitate a debate on the merits of the Spanish controversy and "greatly weaken our position of neutrality with both sides." He further suggested impressing upon "Congressional leaders the importance of discouraging such discussion in these critical times" (DSR, 811.04418/199). Bowers gave no other reasons against such legislation at that time.

For the Italian response, Phillips to Acting Secretary, Dec. 30, 1936, DSR, 852.00/4233. For Anglo-French reactions, *New York Times,* Dec. 30, 1936.

An American embargo on arms to both Germany and Spain would have been interpreted by the Italians as "taking sides in the Spanish conflict" (*FR 1937,* I, 215).

18. Roosevelt Papers, PSF—R. Walton Moore. Moore wrote: "I am not troubling you with any elaboration, but I am prepared to do that whenever you desire." Section 7 of the memo dealt entirely with discretionary versus mandatory legislation and the desirability of discussing the matter with Key Pittman, chairman of the Senate Foreign Relations Committee, during December. Moore felt that he

and Hackworth (legal advisor) ought to talk with the President "even before Mr. Hull returns. . . ." Moore mentioned that he himself had talked with Pittman "a short time ago."

19. *New York Times*, Dec. 26, 1936.

20. *New York Times*, Dec. 26, 27, and 28, 1936. There was also talk of a proposal to deprive of their citizenship those Americans taking part in a foreign war in which the United States had no part. This idea was said to have come from "an influential Senatorial quarter" and seems to have been provoked by a report that the Socialist Party of New York was attempting to enlist 500 volunteers to fight for the Spanish Loyalists.

21. *New York Times*, Dec. 29, 1936; and London *Times*, Dec. 30, 1936.

22. *New York Times*, Dec. 30, 1936. If Hull had been in Washington, he certainly would have put an end to Pittman's and Roosevelt's use of the term "civil war"—for it implied the recognition of belligerent rights.

President to Moore, Jan. 4, 1937 (Moore Papers, box 17); the original Pittman memorandum (of December 30) to the President is attached.

23. For example, see *Washington Post*, Jan. 11, 1937. The London *Times* correspondent concurred with this view (Dec. 31, 1936, and again on Jan. 6, 1937). Also in agreement was the *New York Times*, Jan. 3, 1937.

24. *New York Times*, Dec. 30, 1936; and *Washington Post*, Dec. 31, 1936.

25. Barnet Nover's column, *Washington Post*, Dec. 31, 1936.

26. *Washington Post*, Dec. 31, 1936. The press was as yet uncertain, however, whether the amendment would provide that the President "may" or "shall" apply munitions embargoes when he finds a foreign war has reached the "qualifying" proportions. It is difficult to determine just how serious this "may" or "shall" question was, since the President would in either case have the power to decide what constituted a civil conflict of sufficient gravity. The implication of "shall" would seem to be that the President, once having acted, would not be able to lift the embargo while the civil conflict was still in progress. With the "may" provision, he might be able to apply it and lift it at his discretion.

Also: Moore's appointment book, 1936 (with corrected entries), Moore Papers; *New York Times*, Dec. 31, 1936; and Divine, *Illusion of Neutrality*, 170.

27. *Washington Post*, Dec. 31, 1936, and Jan. 1 and 3, 1937; also *New York Times*, Jan. 3, 1937. In some quarters the President was charged with seizing this opportunity to attempt to obtain discretionary powers. For example, see *The Christian Century* (July 13, 1937), 38–39. Also, see the *New Republic* of the same date (p. 311).

28. *New York Times*, Jan. 5, 1937; and *Washington Post*, Jan. 5, 1937. Simultaneously, there was a rumor, probably planted by the

White House in order to counter the pressure being exerted by the promandatory opposition, that the President might apply embargoes on both Spain and Germany by using existing legislation and "simply deeming them in a state of war." The fear was expressed by some outside the administration who favored discretion that a mandatory bill, referring only to Spain, would compel an embargo on Spain but not on Germany (since there was no declared war between the two nations).

29. The Dinely episode is related in the Morgan-Green Report, 73–74. Also relevant is a memo by Joseph Green, Jan. 5, *FR 1937,* I, 565. Important documents are found in DSR, 711.00111 Lic. Dinely, R. L. Arms Traffic.

30. Moore's appointment book, 1937, Moore Papers.

31. Fred L. Israel, *Nevada's Key Pittman* (Lincoln, Neb., 1963), 142.

32. Morgan-Green Report, 75. According to Morgan, the January 4 memorandum, containing Moore's ideas, was "unfiled" and under Carlton Savage's name. Savage was Assistant Historical Advisor.

33. Moore to President, Jan. 5, 1937, Roosevelt Papers, OF 1561 Neutrality.

34. Memorandum for Acting Secretary Moore, apparently sent from the White House, Jan. 5, 1937, Roosevelt Papers, OF 1561 Neutrality.

35. *Washington Post,* Jan. 6, 1937.

36. Moore to President, Jan. 5, 1937, Moore Papers, box 14. It is possible that this was never sent to the President. The original could not be found in the Roosevelt Papers. Moore might anyway have brought these matters up at the White House meeting that afternoon.

37. *New York Times,* Jan. 6, 1937; and *Washington Post,* Jan. 6, 1937.

38. Moore to President, Jan. 5, 1937, Moore Papers, box 14.

39. *Congressional Record,* 75th Cong., 1st Sess., Vol. 81, Pt. 1, 74.

40. *Ibid.,* 75–79.

41. *Ibid.,* 79–80.

42. *Ibid.,* 86–87.

43. *Ibid.,* 92 and 95.

44. Quoted in *Washington Post,* Jan. 6, 1937.

45. Dinely quoted in *Washington Post,* Jan. 8, 1937.

46. There were very few dissenters. *The Nation* labeled the Embargo Act "pro-fascist," while adding that in other cases the magazine favored mandatory neutrality legislation (Jan. 9, 1937, pp. 33–34). The *New Republic* favored cash and carry legislation regarding the Spanish strife, arguing that this would permit American support of democracy in Spain without actually taking sides (Jan. 13, 1937, p. 316).

47. Jan. 7, 1937, Moore Papers, box 6.

48. The remark was attributed to Hull in an article by Paul Y. Anderson (*The Nation,* Apr. 30, 1938, p. 495). Anderson did not indicate his source of information; and in the highly charged political climate at the time the article was written, exaggerations were becoming commonplace.

At Buenos Aires, Hull found that the Spanish civil war was a "hot" issue in Latin America. It was clear that should the United States "take sides" in the Spanish dispute, the Good Neighbor policy would be endangered. This was simply one more reason why he preferred an embargo policy. It does not mean, however, that Hull favored a mandatory embargo. See Chapter 7, below.

5. NETWORK OF APPEASEMENT

1. Cudahy to Moore, Mar. 20, 1937, Moore Papers, box 4; and Bullitt to Moore, Jan. 8, 1937, Moore Papers, box 3.

2. Memorandum, "Brief Estimate of the Present Military Situation in Spain," Feb. 12, 1937, Hull Papers, carton 40; Bowers to Secretary, Apr. 12, *FR 1937,* I, 278–282; and Jackson, *Spanish Republic,* 333–391 passim.

3. Bullitt to Secretary, Feb. 20, *FR 1937,* I, 46–54; and Cattell, *Communism and the Spanish Civil War,* 153–163.

4. See George Kennan, *Russia and the West under Lenin and Stalin* (Boston, 1960), 308–313.

5. Biddle, memorandum, Feb. 19, *FR 1937,* I, 41–46.

6. Concerning Italian aid to Franco: Consul Bay (Seville) to Secretary, Feb. 2, 1937, DSR, 852.00/4569; Consulate (Gibraltar) to Secretary, Feb. 4, 1937, DSR, 852.00/4587; Phillips (Rome) to Secretary, Feb. 9, 1937, DSR, 852.00/4629; and Bowers to Secretary, Feb. 15, 1937, DSR, 852.00/4676.

Concerning "violation" of Anglo-Italian accord: Phillips to Secretary, Apr. 3, 1937, DSR, 741.65/348. Phillips reported the Italian view that "Spanish affairs were never discussed during the [January] negotiations [with the British] and did not enter into the agreements concluded."

Concerning estimates of Italian troops in Spain: Phillips to Secretary, Feb. 9, 1937, DSR, 852.00/4629; Bullitt to Secretary, Feb. 20, *FR 1937,* I, 46–54; and Bullitt to Secretary, April 30, *FR 1937,* I, 291–292.

Concerning Italo-French ill will: Bowers to Secretary, Feb. 15, 1937, DSR, 852.00/4676; Phillips to Secretary, Feb. 19, 1937, DSR, 852.00/4869; Bullitt to Secretary, Feb. 20, *FR 1937,* I, 46–54.

Concerning British Government and public opinion: Bingham to Secretary, Mar. 25, *FR 1937,* I, 64–66.

7. An estimated 8,000+ volunteers arrived in Barcelona during January alone; Atherton (London) to Secretary, Feb. 12, *FR 1937,* I, 239–240. Bullitt to Roosevelt, Apr. 12, 1937, Roosevelt Papers, PPF 1124-Bullitt.

8. Bullitt to Secretary, Jan. 26, 1937, DSR, 852.00/4496 and Apr. 19, 1937, DSR, 852.00/5187.

9. Bullitt to Secretary, Feb. 15, *FR 1937,* I, 241; also Bowers to Secretary, Feb. 2, 1937, DSR, 852.00/4692 and Mar. 3, 1937, DSR, 852.00/4958.

10. Atherton (London) to Secretary, Feb. 12, *FR 1937,* I, 239–240.

11. Bullitt to Secretary, Feb. 20, *FR 1937,* I, 46–54.

12. Bowers to Hull, Feb. 23, 1937, DSR, 852.00/4947; Hull to Bowers, Mar. 9, 1937, DSR, 852.00/4947; and Bowers to Secretary, Mar. 22, 1937, DSR, 852.00/5076. The commercial attaché was actually sent before Bowers forwarded his dispatch of March 22, but with instructions only to observe and evaluate the economic situation.

13. State Department to Bullitt, Jan. 13, 1937, DSR, 121.5551/95.

14. Bowers to Secretary, Jan. 12, *FR 1937,* I, 223–227 (this was, of course, written only four days after the enactment of the embargo resolution). On December 10, 1936, Bowers had written: "We have concentrated entirely on the protection of Americans. We have therefore retained the respect and confidence of the Government, and we have done absolutely nothing to justify the slightest complaint from the rebels. We have done so by attending to our own business" (*FR 1936,* II, 600–605). The same notions are expressed in letters from Bowers to President Roosevelt (Dec. 16, 1936 and Feb. 16, 1937, Roosevelt Papers).

15. President Roosevelt to President Azaña, April 4, 1937, Roosevelt Papers, OF 422, Spain 1933–1938; memorandum by Secretary Hull, Jan. 27, *FR 1937,* I, 233; and Bullitt to Secretary, Jan. 30, *FR 1937,* I, 235–237.

16. At one point during the spring of 1937, there was apparently some thought of replacing the popular Bowers. From the one document available, it would seem that Roosevelt himself squelched the idea. The move would probably have had unfavorable repercussions, since moderate Loyalists felt a certain rapport with Bowers and might have taken his removal as a rebuke. (Roosevelt to Hull, memo, Apr. 5, 1937, Hull Papers, carton 40.) There is no record of other discussions on the matter in either the Hull or Roosevelt collections. In the Jay Pierrepont Moffat Diaries, on March 12, 1937, there is mention of a desire within the Department to order Bowers home for consultation. The President purportedly vetoed the idea because he wanted Bowers to make periodic trips to Barcelona. Roosevelt actually wanted Bowers ordered back into Spain from France. The reason why Bowers was never ordered to return to Spain was never entirely clear, but it may have been due to his wife's illness.

17. Phillips to Secretary, Apr. 23, *FR 1937,* I, 287–289. The conversation, with García Condé, took place April 16, 1937.

18. See Hadley Cantril and Mildred Strunk (eds.), *Public Opin-*

ion 1935–1946 (Princeton, 1951), 807–809. In January 1939, 51 per cent of those polled favored the Loyalists—but only half of that number desired the repeal of the embargo. See chapter 10, below.

19. See below, chapters 9 and 10, for a discussion of divisions in American opinion and the activities of pressure groups.

20. President Roosevelt to Thomas, Dec. [January] 25, 1937, Roosevelt Papers, OF 422-C. It was written in answer to Thomas' letter of Dec. 29, 1936, which objected "to the policy of discouraging the export of arms from this country to Spain for the use of the Spanish Government."

21. Roosevelt to Phillips, Feb. 6, 1937, Roosevelt Papers, PPF 552-Phillips.

22. Davies to Secretary, Mar. 18, 1937, DSR, 852.00/5089; Bingham to Secretary, Jan. 18, 1937, DSR, 852.00/4409; and Neville Chamberlain, Chancellor of the Exchequer, to Morgenthau, about Mar. 30, 1937, *FR 1937*, I, 98–102.

23. See Hull, *Memoirs*, I, 506.

24. United States Congress, Senate Foreign Relations Committee, "Neutrality," Hearings relative to proposed neutrality legislation, 75th Cong., 1st Sess., Feb. 13, 1937, 25 pp.; and House Foreign Affairs Committee, "American Neutrality Policy," Hearings, 75th Cong., 1st Sess., Feb. 16–23, 1937, 177 pp.

Roy E. Burt represented the Socialist Party; James Waterman Wise, American League Against War and Fascism; and Gardner Jackson, American Friends of Spanish Democracy. Herman Reissig, who later became probably the most influential administrator of pro-Loyalist organizations, also testified.

25. Moore to Roosevelt, Jan. 30, 1937, Roosevelt Papers, OF 1561-Neutrality.

26. Moore to Roosevelt, Mar. 4, 1937, Roosevelt Papers, OF 1561-Neutrality. Roosevelt, "Confidential Memorandum for Senator Robinson," Apr. 20, 1937, Roosevelt Papers, PSF Neutrality.

27. Divine, *Illusion of Neutrality,* 193. See chapter 6 of Divine for a discussion of the "cash-and-carry compromise" legislation of May 1, 1937. The Spanish issue was only a small part of the neutrality debate that spring.

28. *Congressional Record,* 75th Cong., 1st Sess., vol. 81, pt. 4, 3975.

29. Hull to Roosevelt, Apr. 30, 1937, Roosevelt Papers, PSF Neutrality. Hull did not refer specifically to McReynolds.

Minutes of the Central Committee of the American National Red Cross, vol. XVI, 3280. Meeting of May 10, 1937. Archives of the American National Red Cross, Washington, D.C.

McReynolds had early inserted a provision which might have excluded humanitarian aid, but this caused so great an uproar from pressure groups that it was quickly removed. House Committee on Foreign Affairs Records (National Archives), American Neutrality Policy, H. J. Res. 242 and S. J. Res. 51, 75A-D13 (7 parts), part 3.

30. Gardner Jackson to Herman Reissig, Jan. 27, 1937 and Feb. 4, 1937; also Reissig to Maverick, Feb. 3, 1937. "Spanish Refugee Relief Organizations" Collection (Butler Library, Columbia University), Misc. File 22, Neutrality legislation folder #1. Collection hereafter referred to as "SRRO."

31. Hull, *Memoirs*, I, 510–511.

32. Secretary to Bingham, Mar. 27, *FR 1937*, I, 268; and Bingham to Secretary, Mar. 31, *FR 1937*, 270–272.

33. Bingham to Secretary, June 1, 1937, DSR, 852.00/5586; and Phillips to Secretary, June 1, 1937, DSR, 852.00/5596.

34. There is little dispute, now, about the German bombing of Guernica. The speculation that the Russians bombed the *Deutschland* is less well known, but the rumor at that time was common in diplomatic circles. For example, see Bingham to Secretary, May 31, *FR 1937*, I, 312–313; and Arthur Bliss Lane (Riga) to Loy Henderson (Moscow), June 3, 1937, Arthur Bliss Lane Papers, Yale University. Henderson, however, found no positive evidence that the Soviets were directly responsible. Henderson to Secretary, June 9, *FR 1937*, I, 326–328. The most that can be said is that the Russians were pleased by the incident. (And they were displeased by the current failure of the Spanish government to charge Germany with intervention before the League of Nations. Charges were brought only against Italy.) See *FR 1937*, I, 303–328 passim.

35. Hull, memorandum, May 31, 1937, DSR, 852.00/5607.

36. Ralph Lord Roy, *Communism and the Churches* (New York, 1960), 135.

O'Connell (along with Representatives Bernard, Scott, and Coffee) exchanged letters with Hull on May 5 and 7, concerning an extension of the arms embargo (*FR 1937*, I, 294–295). On May 11, O'Connell attacked the State Department for agreeing with Senator Pittman's remark over the radio that " 'there is no evidence' that Germany and Italy are participating in the Spanish invasion" (*Cong. Rec.*, 75th Cong., 1st Sess., Appendix, 1131). On June 2, O'Connell and six other representatives again wrote Hull concerning an embargo (DSR, 852.00/5873, enclosed in 852.00/5629). At one point, after four congressmen met with the Secretary of State, Coffee wrote to the organizational secretary of the North American Committee to Aid Spanish Democracy, pointing out that Hull "seemed disinclined to permit us to enter upon a discussion of the topic [of an embargo] . . ." (Coffee to Russell Thayer, June 14, 1937, SRRO, Misc. file 22, Neutrality Legislation folder #2).

37. Thomas to President (copy to Secretary of State), June 9, 1937; Office of Arms and Munitions Control, memorandum, June 18, 1937; and Secretary of State to Norman Thomas, June 28, 1937 (all DSR, 852.00/5701).

38. Quoted in Thurston to Secretary, June 24, 1937, DSR, 852.00/5823.

39. Roosevelt to Hull, June 29, 1937, Hull Papers, carton 41; and Hull, *Memoirs*, I, 511.

40. *FR 1937*, I, 344–347 and 353–355; and Phillips Journals, July 1, 1937. Bingham did not directly respond to Hull's inquiry until July 6, although he did provide some relevant information in a telegram on July 3 (*FR 1937*, I, 349). It is not known exactly when Hull telephoned the President, although his *Memoirs* would seem to indicate that the call was made after Bingham's report of July 6. See Hull, *Memoirs*, 511–513.

41. June 28, 1937, DSR, 852.00/6336.

42. "July 8?" 1937, DSR, 852.00/5957. Internal evidence would indicate that there is only a day or two error, if any, in the dating.

6. EMBARGO: "UNCHANGEABLE" POLICY

1. See Divine, *Illusion of Neutrality*, chapter 7, for a discussion of the Far Eastern crisis and neutrality legislation. Divine also touches upon the Spanish issue in the same chapter.

2. In a Gallup poll taken October 4, 1937, 59 per cent of those interviewed favored China, 40 per cent were for neither country, and only one per cent for Japan. See Cantril and Strunk (eds.), *Public Opinion, 1935–1946,* 1081.

3. Norman Davis to Neville Chamberlain, June 10, 1937; Chamberlain to Davis, July 8, 1937; and President Roosevelt to Chamberlain, July 28, 1937. All located in the Norman H. Davis Papers, carton 8. For possibility of visit to the United States by Léon Blum, see Cordell Hull to Norman Davis, Aug. 9, 1937, Davis Papers, carton 27.

4. See Dorothy Borg, "Notes on Roosevelt's 'Quarantine' Speech," *Political Science Quarterly,* Sept. 1957, 405–433.

5. See Hull, *Memoirs,* I, 546–548. Hull described the plan as "somewhat pyrotechnical." For the documents pertaining to the plan itself, see *FR 1937*, I, 665–670.

6. Chamberlain's account was recorded in his *Diary,* the relevant parts of which are found in Iain MacLeod, *Neville Chamberlain* (London, 1961), 212–213.

7. Lord Halifax [Edward Frederick Lindley Wood], *Fullness of Days* (New York, 1957), 194.

8. The documents, and exchange of notes, relevant to the President's initiative are found in *FR 1938*, I, 115–132.

9. *The Second World War* (Cambridge, Mass., 6 vols., 1948), I, 283.

10. *FR 1938*, I, 164–165.

11. Messersmith to Secretary, Oct. 11, *FR 1937*, I, 140–145, and Feb. 18, *FR 1938*, I, 17–24. Also, Messersmith to Dodd, Nov. 27, 1937, Dodd Papers, carton 51.

12. Messersmith to Montgomery, Apr. 6, 1938, Montgomery Papers; Messersmith to Secretary, Feb. 18, *FR 1938*, I, 17–24.

13. Bullitt to Roosevelt, Jan. 20, 1938, Roosevelt Papers, PSF

France—Bullitt; and Davies to McIntyre, presidential secretary, Apr. 4, 1938, Roosevelt Papers, PPF 1381. For an analysis of Dodd, see Franklin L. Ford, "Three Observers in Berlin: Rumbold, Dodd, and François-Poncet," in Craig and Gilbert (eds.), *The Diplomats,* 437–476. For an account of Bowers' changing views, see below, chapter 11.

14. Moffat Diaries, Jan. 31 and Feb. 10, 1938. Hull was still quite sensitive to isolationist criticism; he did not "like to be accused of veering from what he calls the middle road" (Moffat Diaries, Feb. 1, 1938).

15. See Taylor, *The United States and the Spanish Civil War,* 155–158. Senator Walsh's bitter attack against the telegram is found in his press release of February 2, 1938 (located in the Walsh Papers).

16. *New York Times,* Feb. 16, 1938.

17. For example, in a letter to Bishop Robert L. Paddock, chairman of the American Friends of Spanish Democracy, R. Walton Moore mentioned that "Congress saw fit to adopt" the embargo (Feb. 14, 1938 [DSR], 711.00111 Armament Control/1670). As another example, on April 4, 1938, George Messersmith told a pro-Loyalist delegation that "the Department could not well take the initiative in this matter." The act of January 1937 "had been enacted by Congress on its own initiative" (DSR, 852.24/567). Since Messersmith had not been in Washington in January 1937, and since others' memories later proved to be "weak," it is likely that Messersmith did not realize that his statement was incorrect.

18. *Christian Century,* May 18, 1938, 612–613; Moffat Diaries, April 5, 1938; McReynolds to Congressman W. R. Poage, Feb. 28, 1938, Papers of the House Committee on Foreign Affairs, HR75A-F16.1; Nye quotation taken from Cole, *Senator Gerald P. Nye,* 114; also Daniels to Dodd, Jan. 25, 1938, Dodd Papers, carton 52.

19. *New York Times,* Mar. 27, 1938.

20. *New York Times,* Mar. 23, 1938. Moffat also apparently helped prepare the response to Buell (Moffat Diaries, Mar. 19 and 20, 1938).

21. Moffat Diaries, Mar. 24, 1938; and Richberg to James Roosevelt, Mar. 28, 1938, Roosevelt Papers, OF 422-C. Galley proofs of DeWilde's article are found in the Hull Papers, carton 83A; the article appeared in *Foreign Policy Reports,* April 1, 1938, 281–290. In his conclusion, DeWilde actually said "Spain may remain essentially independent"; but earlier in the article he mentioned that a victorious Franco might have difficulty getting rid of foreign troops.

22. Counselor, American embassy (Barcelona) to Secretary, Apr. 3, and Secretary to Counselor, Apr. 7 (*FR 1938,* I, 171–173 and 175).

23. Moore to Dunn, Apr. 2, 1938, Moore Papers, box 9.

24. Moffat Diaries, Apr. 4, 1938.

25. McIntyre to the President, April 27, 1938, Roosevelt Pa-

pers, OF 422-C. The remark attributed to Vandenberg is found in the Moffat Diaries, May 2, 1938.

26. To the comment "no concern," Moore excepted the preamble to the resolution; but objections to preambles almost constitute standard procedure. Moore's Appointment Book, 1938; and Moore to Hull, May 3, 1938, Moore Papers, box 9.

There is an unsigned, undated memorandum in the Papers of the Senate Committee on Foreign Relations (Papers Accompanying S.J. Res. 288, the Nye Resolution), which is very probably a copy of the inquiry presented to the State Department by Pittman on May 3. It asked: (1) "Is the policy approved?" (2) Would shipments of American arms "interfere with any efforts if they are being made by European countries to bring about a settlement of the war in Spain?" (3) Is it the opinion of the State Department that shipments of American arms would reach the Loyalists? And, (4) Has the administration's purpose in sponsoring the resolution of January 1937 been accomplished?

27. Moffat Diaries, Apr. 12 and 14, 1938; and Lerner, "Behind Hull's Embargo," *The Nation,* May 28, 1938, 607–610.

28. Moffat Diaries, May 2, 1938.

29. Moffat Diaries, May 4, 1938.

30. Moffat Diaries, May 4 and 5, 1938.

31. Moffat Diaries, May 4, 1938. Moore was extremely bitter about this attack by Pearson (Moore to Hull, May 5, 1938, Hull Papers, carton 42).

32. The headline was unusually sensational for the *New York Times:* "ROOSEVELT BACKS LIFTING ARMS EMBARGO ON SPAIN: CONGRESS AGREES IT FAILS." A subhead read, rather boldly, "Policy is Doomed."

There were subsequently rumors that the article had been "planted" in the *Times* for the purpose of creating a political crisis sufficient to prevent the passage of the resolution. Such rumors, even though they lacked specifics, were attractive. But there is no evidence to corroborate them.

There is an undated memorandum written by Moore which denies a detailed report regarding the State Department's "approval" of the Nye resolution. The story, Moore wrote, "is absolutely untrue and misrepresents everyone concerned including Senator Pittman and myself." It was apparently intended to be a press release, for the phrase "not given out" is written on the memo. (Moore Papers, box 11.) As might have been expected, the Department never publicly refuted any of the accounts that it had once decided to support the Nye resolution.

33. Moffat Diaries, May 6, 1938. Hull and Pearson also argued about the legality of American shipments of airplane engines and parts to Germany.

34. *New York Times,* May 6, 7, and 8, 1938. Senator Pittman wrote Ambassador Kennedy on May 2: "The fight over the resolution—if there is a fight—will add another grief to the Democratic

Congressmen who are running this year." Papers of the Senate Committee on Foreign Relations, SEN 75A-F9-1(105C).

35. Phillips to the President, May 13, 1938, Roosevelt Papers, PSF Italy; *New York Times,* May 3, 4 and 5, 1938; American consul (Seville) to Hull, May 4, 1938, DSR, 852.00/7919.

36. *FR 1938,* I, 183–193, for correspondence of Hull, Bullitt, Kennedy, and Bowers.

37. *New York Times,* May 6, 8, and 12, 1938.

38. *New York Times,* May 14, 1938.

39. Moffat Diaries, May 9, 1938.

40. *New York Times,* May 9 and 10, 1938; Moffat Diaries, May 9, 1938; and Pittman to Kennedy, May 2, 1938, Papers of the Senate Committee on Foreign Relations, SEN 75A-F9-1(105C). Nye later reported that Senator Connally had been very important in leading him to urge repeal. If Nye's memory is accurate, this would provide further indication of the political climate; for Connally apparently soon "defected." See Cole, *Senator Gerald P. Nye,* 255.

41. Hull, memorandum for the President, May 11, 1938, Roosevelt Papers, OF 422-C; and *New York Times,* May 14, 1938.

42. See *FR 1938,* I, 194–195.

43. *New York Times,* May 14, 1938; and, Ickes, *Secret Diary,* II, 388–390. There was an unconfirmed rumor that George Cardinal Mundelein interceded with the President at the time of the Nye Resolution (Lerner, "Behind Hull's Embargo," *The Nation,* May 28, 1938, 607–610). If Mundelein did, there was really no need for it.

44. *New York Times,* May 8, 1938.

45. Perhaps Sumner Welles' personal records will reveal more details on this point.

46. Moffat Diaries, May 4, 1938.

47. Chargé d'Affaires, American embassy (Paris) to Secretary, May 3, *FR 1938,* I, 47–49; and Kennedy to Secretary, May 5, *FR 1938,* I, 50–51.

7. THE GOOD NEIGHBOR

1. See Arthur P. Whitaker, *The Western Hemisphere Idea: Its Rise and Decline* (New York, 1954), 139–154.

2. Hull, *Memoirs,* I, 501. Donald M. Dozer has pointed out the threat which the Spanish civil war posed to the doctrine of the two spheres. *Are We Good Neighbors? Three Decades of Inter-American Relations, 1930–1960* (Gainesville, Fla., 1961), 40–45.

3. American Minister (San José) to Secretary, Nov. 1, 1937, DSR, 702.5218/7; and American Embassy (Bogotá) to Secretary, July 21, 1937, DSR, 852.00/6033. In April 1937, the Mexicans presented a brief legal argument of their position to Secretary Hull (Mexican Ambassador to Secretary Hull, Apr. 10, 1937, DSR, 852. 24/355).

4. *FR 1936*, II, 553–576; and American Chargé (Nicaragua) to Secretary, Nov. 27, 1936, DSR, 852.00/3902.

5. Hull, *Memoirs*, I, 501; and, Bullitt to Acting Secretary Moore, Dec. 9, *FR 1936*, II, 599–600. Bullitt reported a conversation between Delbos and the Argentine ambassador to France. For Hull's difficulties with Saavedra Lamas, see Hull, *Memoirs*, I, 497.

6. See *FR 1936*, II, 509, 512, and 519–523.

7. Alexander Weddell to Secretary, Oct. 21, *FR 1936*, II, 745–746.

In 1937, Latin American nations prevented the reelection of Spain to the League Council largely because the Spanish government refused to evacuate the hundreds of anti-Loyalist guests in Latin American embassies. According to Harold Ickes, de Los Ríos had requested of President Roosevelt that the United States put in a good word for the Spanish government with respect "to Venezuela and one or two other Central and South American countries," as the Spanish were anxious to be reelected. But Hull was reluctant to intercede. American embassy (Valencia) to Secretary, Sept. 26, 1937, DSR, 852.00/6548; and Ickes, *Secret Diary*, II, 210–211 (entry for Aug. 19, 1937).

About this time it was rumored that neither Argentina nor Chile would grant belligerent status to Franco, because they feared retaliation upon the people still in asylum in their embassies. Weddell to Secretary, Sept. 10, 1937, Hull Papers, carton 41.

8. See *FR 1936*, II, 489–492, 494–499, and 528. Also see Dozer, *Good Neighbors?*, 41. Three nations accepted the Uruguayan proposal with reservations: Cuba, Chile, and Peru.

Once again the United States and Argentina were at odds over the Spanish issue. Only one day before Saavedra Lamas informed United States officials that Argentina was politely refusing the Uruguayan plan, the State Department had rejected a mediation proposal put forth by the Argentine ambassador to Spain. See *FR 1936*, II, 488, 492, and 497.

9. The Uruguayan proposal led to a disagreement between Hugh Wilson (who believed that the European powers would welcome "outside initiative" to break the "deadlock") and Moffat (who believed that such a move would be "construed as pro-Fascist" by the American people). "I saw no reason," Moffat remarked, "to pull British and French chestnuts out of the fire for them." Moffat Diaries, Aug. 28 and 29, 1937.

10. *FR 1936*, II, 380 and 385–386; American embassy (Caracas) to Secretary, Sept. 3, 1937, DSR, 852.00/6382; Dozer, *Good Neighbors?*, 42; American minister (Montevideo) to Secretary, Sept. 10, 1937, DSR, 852.00/6473; and Pittman, memorandum, Sept. 2, 1937, DSR, 852.00/6416.

Italy's interest in Latin American affairs, in relation to the Spanish strife, was always a subject of concern to the State Department. The American minister to Uruguay reported on September 4, 1936. The American Legation "is informed from . . . sources close to the

Italian Minister in Uruguay that the Italian Legation here is paying the salary of the Spanish Chargé d'Affaires, who resigned several weeks ago. The source of this information adds that it is the policy of the Italian Government to offer Spanish diplomats everywhere to pay their salaries if they resign from their positions under the present Spanish Government" (DSR, 852.00/3116).

11. Wendelin to Secretary, Oct. 13, 1936, *FR 1936,* II, 737–738; Spruille Braden (delegate to Buenos Aires conference) to Secretary General of the Buenos Aires conference, Jan. 4, 1937 and to Secretary of State, Feb. 4, 1937, DSR, 834.248/26; American embassy (Rome), copy of "attaché report," Nov. 24, 1937, 852.00/7032; Acting Secretary of State to American embassy (Havana), Oct. 30, 1937, *FR 1937,* I, 440–441; Dozer, *Good Neighbors?,* 43; *New York Times,* Apr. 12, 1938; and Caffery to Secretary, Apr. 11, 1938, DSR, 724.34119/1289.

12. Secretary Hull to Acting Secretary Moore, Dec. 7, 1937, DSR, 852.00/4015; Moore, memo of conversation with British ambassador, Dec. 7, 1936, DSR, 852.00/4018; Moore to President, Dec. 8, 1936, DSR, 852.00/4033a; and President to Acting Secretary Moore, Dec. 9, 1936, DSR, 852.00/4034. Also see *FR 1936,* II, 578–607 passim.

13. Bowers to Secretary, Apr. 19, 1937, Hull Papers, carton 41; Bullitt to Secretary, July 30, *FR 1937,* I, 367; Bowers to President, Aug. 11, *FR 1937,* I, 372–374; Secretary to Bullitt, Jan. 26, *FR 1938,* I, 153; Moffat, memorandum of conversation with Salvador de Madariaga, Feb. 1, 1938, DSR, 852.00/7326; Moffat Diaries, Feb. 1, 1938; and American Chargé (Paris) to Secretary, May 3, *FR 1938,* I, 48.

Yvon Delbos appeared particularly anxious to have President Roosevelt and Pius XI attempt mediation. But both Hull and Bowers firmly opposed the idea when advising the President. Moffat Diaries, Jan. 26, 1938.

14. See chapter 9.

15. Memorandum by Berle to President Roosevelt, Nov. 19, *FR 1938,* I, 255. The particulars of the plan appear to have grown out of a conversation with the President on November 7, and then matured during subsequent conversations within the State Department. Berle told Roosevelt that "the career people" in the Department "feel there is at least an even chance of its being successful."

The plan, as recorded in the Berle memorandum, resembled one submitted to the State Department more than a year before by Raymond Leslie Buell—at least in its essential notion of holding an olive branch in one hand and a sword in the other. Buell's plan contained a few alternatives, one of which was to have a commission of representatives from three American nations (one of them the United States)—sanctioned by the other American nations—to offer and conduct mediation. If this approach failed, the United States had two diplomatic weapons: it could announce its refusal to make trade agreements with those nations intervening in the Spanish war, or it could invoke the neutrality statutes against intervening nations. By "intervening nations" Buell clearly meant Germany and Italy. Hull distributed the memorandum to Welles, Moore, Moffat, and Hornbeck. No action was taken. Buell memorandum, dated July 13, 1937, DSR, 852.00/6109.

Also Cardinal Mundelein to President Roosevelt, Nov. 10, 1938, Roosevelt Papers, PSF Italy—Phillips. Ambassador Phillips put great care into the American embassy's reception of the Chicago cardinal when he arrived at Rome.

16. Messersmith to D. N. Heineman (Brussels), Dec. 7 and 22, 1938, Messersmith Papers.

17. Acting Secretary Welles to Secretary (Lima), Dec. 10 and Dec. 15, *FR 1938*, I, 260 and 261; and, Hull to Acting Secretary Welles, Dec. 17 and 19, 1938, Hull Papers, carton 43. Also, Messersmith, memorandum of conversation with French Ambassador, Dec. 10, 1938, DSR, 852.00/8704; and Moffat Diaries, Dec. 15, 1938.

18. Dodd to Secretary, Oct. 7, 1936, Hull Papers, carton 39. Also, Dodd to Moore, Aug. 31, 1936; Dodd to President, April 13, 1937; Roosevelt to Dodd, Jan. 9, 1937 (Roosevelt Papers, PSF Germany—Dodd); and Bowers to Roosevelt, Nov. 22, 1938, Roosevelt Papers.

19. Bowers to Hull, May 9, 1938, Hull Papers, carton 42; and, Bowers to Secretary, June 27 and Dec. 6, 1938, DSR, 852.00/8204 and 852.00/8699.

20. For Hull's criticism of Bowers, see *Memoirs,* I, 485. For Bowers' criticism of the Spanish policy in regard to Latin America, see Bowers, *Mission to Spain,* 412–413. Bowers complained that he "never received any comment [on his views] from the [State] department." While Bowers seems to have made the remark to indicate that the Department was not really able to refute his position, the remark more directly reveals the Department's failure to keep him informed.

It was in part Roosevelt's fault that Bowers was not called home for consultation. He rejected, on at least one occasion, the State Department's suggestion to do so. But the President's mistake was really accidental. The Department's recommendation was actually made because it believed that Franco might well end the war in two or three months (and presumably that it would be better if Bowers did not have to deal with that situation). Moffat Diaries, Mar. 12, 1938.

21. The quotations are taken from an important paper prepared in the State Department in March 1938. Entitled, "Memorandum on Italian Fascist and German Nazi Activities in the American Republics," it was some thirty-five pages in length. It is important not only for the details which it provides but also for the ambiguous situations which it acknowledged (with respect both to the impact of Italian and German activities in Latin America and to the impact of

the Spanish civil war there). Putting aside all other considerations than that of inter-American affairs, this memorandum could have been used to justify the adoption of a pro-Loyalist policy just as readily as the continuation of noninvolvement. It must be noted, however, that this was not the issue with which this memorandum was actually concerned. Hence it does not raise all the questions involved with respect to the relationships between the Spanish and inter-American policies of the United States. Papers of the Senate Committee on Foreign Relations, SEN 75A-F9-1 (105C).

22. During December 1938 and January 1939, when Bowers was most insistent that the United States aid the Loyalists, Sumner Welles handled much of the correspondence answering Bowers' plea. Moore and Moffat helped Welles in this task. Records left by all three men indicate that Bowers' views received very little respect. They were sometimes treated with condescension. See Chapter 11.

Welles later wrote: "Of all our blind isolationist policies, the most disastrous was our attitude on the Spanish civil war." This was more easily said in 1944 than it would have been any time during the Spanish strife. Welles' book, in which he made the above remark, was intended to show the wisdom of active participation in international affairs, and he attempted to do this in part by stressing the failure of isolationist policies in the past. His later account of the Spanish policy is marred by important factual errors and misleading comments, particularly concerning the passage of the Spanish Embargo Act of January 1937. See *The Time for Decision* (New York and London, 1944), 57–61.

Robert Bendiner later described Welles' position during the war with considerable accuracy: ". . . despite his reputed inclinations, he sided with the embargo forces in the Spanish war—largely with an eye on the pro-Franco dictators whose friendship he was so earnestly courting as a Good Neighbor." *The Riddle of the State Department* (New York, 1942), 165.

8. AMERICAN ARMS, AMERICAN MEN

1. Phillips to Secretary, Apr. 9, 1937, DSR, 852.00/5206; Phillips to Secretary, May 23, 1937, DSR, 852.00/5493; Bowers to Secretary, June 24, 1937, DSR, 852.00/5821; Office of Arms Control, memorandum, June 26, 1937, DSR, F. W. 852.00/6084; American consulate (Seville) to Secretary, July 27 and 28 (2), 1937, DSR, 852.00/6080, 852.00/6095, and 852.00/6178; R. W. Moore to consulate (Seville), Aug. 17, 1937, DSR, 852.00/6178; European Division to consulate (Vigo), July 29, 1938, DSR, 852.00/8396; Secretary to consulate (Vigo), Aug. 29, *FR 1938*, I, 361; consul (Seville) to Secretary, Oct. 18, 1938, DSR, 852.00/8623; and Charles W. Yost (Office of Arms Control) to consulate (Seville), Dec. 23, 1938, DSR, 852.00/8747.

2. The most complete expression of the Mexican and American positions occurred in a conversation between the Counselor of the

American embassy in Mexico City and the Mexican Under Secretary for Foreign Affairs. Copy of memorandum forwarded to the State Department by Josephus Daniels, Apr. 30, 1937, DSR, 812.52C71/41. Also Morgan-Green Report, 100–104.

3. Morgan-Green Report, 100–102 and 139–141. Relevant documents are found in DSR file, 711.00111 Lic. American Armament Corporation, Arms Traffic.

4. Morgan-Green Report, 100–104.

5. Morgan-Green Report, 106–107.

6. Morgan-Green Report, 141–143. Relevant documents are found in DSR file, 711.00111 Lic. Bellanca Aircraft Corporation, Arms Traffic. Part of the story coincides somewhat with an account by Ickes that "the Spanish Loyalists bribed the Air Minister [sic] of Greece, who placed an order in the United States for war planes to the number of forty [sic]" (Ickes, *Secret Diary*, II, 424–425).

7. Morgan-Green Report, 143–144.

8. Through his brother-in-law, G. Hall Roosevelt, the President once met with Sherover. The only known result of this conversation, which took place on October 15, 1938, was that Sherover promised to try to obtain German and Italian planes and other Fascist war materials. Some captured planes and equipment were purportedly turned over to an official of the American embassy by Spanish authorities. Sherover to President Roosevelt, Apr. 11, 1939; and Le Hand to Sherover, Apr. 21, 1939 (Roosevelt Papers, OF-249).

Because of Mrs. Roosevelt's pro-Loyalist sympathies and her brother's as well, it was rumored in some quarters that the President sometimes found it necessary to "humor the family." And similar speculations have been made about his treatment of pro-Loyalist members of his "other family," for example Ickes and Corcoran. These rumors may have some connection with a claim made by Ickes that Roosevelt once sent assurances (through Corcoran) to Drew Pearson that American arms would be quietly cleared for shipment through France to Spain. Ickes went on to say that when Bullitt heard about this, he queried the State Department. The Department, not having been informed of the President's "interest," squelched the idea (Ickes, *Secret Diary*, II, 424–425). This story may have been false from beginning to end. But it must not be considered impossible; for the President could easily give such "assurances," knowing that he himself would not be the one to obstruct them.

9. Morgan-Green Report, 145–146 and 104–106. Also, Moffat Diaries, Jan. 28 through Feb. 3, 1939. Relevant documents are found in DSR files: 711.00111 Lic. Grumman Aircraft Engineering Corporation, Arms Traffic; and 711.00111 Lic. Brewster Aeronautical Corporation, Arms Traffic.

10. *FR 1938*, I, 345–363 passim; and Morgan-Green Report, 147–152.

11. American embassy (Paris) to Secretary, Sept. 15, 1937,

DSR, 852.00/6562; Bowers to Secretary, Jan. 7, 1939, DSR, 852.00/8816; Thomas, *Spanish Civil War*, 273; and Allen Gutt- mann, *The Wound in the Heart: America and the Spanish Civil War* (New York, 1962), 137–138. Also Herbert Feis, *The Spanish Story* (New York, 1948), 269; and Phillips Journals, Mar. 8, 1939.

"According to the Nationalist petroleum monopoly company, CAMPSA, oil and gasoline were paid for in cash, three-fourths of it purchased from the United States and the remainder from middle- men in British and Belgian ports" (John R. Hubbard, "How Franco Financed His War," *Journal of Modern History*, Dec. 1953, 404). Also *New York Times*, May 14, 1938.

12. Herbert C. Pell (Lisbon) to Secretary, May 26, 1938, DSR, 852.00/8058; Office of Arms and Munitions Control, memo- randum, Sept. 8, 1938, DSR, 852.24/769; Bowers to Secretary, Oct. 22, 1938, DSR, 852.00/8589; State Department to Bowers (with copy of memorandum, 852.24/769), Dec. 6, 1938, 852.00/ 8589; Pell to Secretary, Nov. 10, 1938, DSR, 852.00/8651; Bowers to Secretary, Jan. 7, 1939, DSR, 852.00/8816; and Moffat Diaries, Sept. 16, 18 & 19, and 23, 1937, Jan. 31, 1938, Feb. 1 and 3, 1938, and June 14, 1938. Also Hubbard, "How Franco Financed His War," 404.

13. Attaché's report (Valencia?) to Secretary, Oct. 28, 1937, DSR, 852.00/6992; and L. A. Friedman, Jr., to Miles Sherover, May 2, 1938 (Papers of the Senate Committee on Foreign Rela- tions, Papers Accompanying S. J. Res. 288, the Nye Resolution). The last item includes a schedule of shipments arranged through the Hanover Corporation, showing the name of the steamer, steamship line, date of sailing from American port, and a brief description of the materials shipped. The Hanover shipments, via France, purport- edly included: 949 truck chassis, 315 trucks, 294 automobiles, and 447 unspecified trucks and/or automobiles; 10,000 cases of dyna- mite; one ambulance; an unspecified number of "truck bodies" and machinery tools; three shiploads of scrap iron, pig iron, and tin plate; plus "miscellaneous" items. Most of these cargoes were shipped out of New York and in American bottoms.

14. Pell to Secretary, Feb. 8, 1939, DSR, 852.00/8986. On the shrewdness of Franco's economic advisers, see Hubbard, "How Franco Financed His War," 390–406.

15. See Guttmann, *Wound in the Heart*, 93–115. Research done by Robert A. Rosenstone at the California Institute of Technology suggests that "disillusionment" was not all that decisive a factor; rather, for a variety of reasons, there was not much recruitment after the summer of 1937. Still, the enthusiasm for volunteering seems to have declined.

16. Consul general (Barcelona) to Assistant Secretary, Jan. 8, 1937 (received Jan. 25, but confirmed by consul general in tele- gram Jan. 11, DSR, 852.00/4327), *FR 1937*, I, 469–470; Moore to consul general, Jan. 13, *FR 1937*, I, 471–472; consul general

(Barcelona) to Secretary, Jan. 19, 1937, DSR, 852.00/4604; consul (Valencia) to Secretary, Mar. 15, *FR 1937*, I, 495–497; Morgan-Green Report, 118–119; and Hull, *Memoirs*, I, 505.

The whole recruitment-passport-citizenship problem caused such a variety of disagreements in the State Department that it never did iron out all the details of the comprehensive policy.

The manner in which the consulate at Le Havre dealt with these problems was related in a memorandum by Consul S. H. Wiley (October 4, 1937). Messersmith relayed the information to Sam McReynolds on November 16, 1937 (Papers of the House Committee on Foreign Affairs, HR75A-F16.1). The memorandum indicates, among many things, that the French were genuinely interested, at that time at least, in preventing American volunteers from reaching Spain.

17. Information on the Dahl case comes from: *FR 1937*, I, 528–555 passim; and Moffat Diaries, July 23 and 28, 1937.

18. Memorandum given to the Division of European Affairs, Jan. 7, 1937, DSR, 852.00/4357; *FR 1937*, I, 417, 528–534, 540, 547–548, 552, and 555; and, President, Memorandum for McIntyre, Feb. 26, 1937, Roosevelt Papers, OF 422-C.

19. Thomas, *Spanish Civil War*, does not treat the story of the Brigades in depth, but it has the value of placing the story in the full context of the war. For the origins of the Brigades and American participation in the Brigades, see Thomas, 294–306, 377, 380, 461–473 passim, and 557. Also see Jackson, *The Spanish Republic*, 327–348 passim.

20. See van der Esch, *Prelude to War*, 134–138.

21. See *FR 1938*, I, 275–345 passim. Also, Moffat Diaries, Mar. 31, 1938; and Hull to McReynolds, May 27, 1938 (Papers of the House Committee on Foreign Affairs, HR75A-F16.1, Correspondence). The last item includes a copy of a letter from Hull to David McKelvy White, National Chairman of the Friends of the Abraham Lincoln Brigade.

22. See *FR 1938*, I, 273, 275, 283, 295–298, and 302–304. In January 1939, representatives of the Friends of the Abraham Lincoln Brigade and relatives of American prisoners held by the Rebels told the State Department that their information conflicted with Bay's appraisal of conditions. While Moffat was able to dispel some of their misapprehensions, it remained true that conditions were not always as adequate as Bay described; for example, clothing was sometimes inadequate and the right to correspond with relatives was respected irregularly. Moffat Diaries, Jan. 9, 1939.

23. *FR 1938*, I, 285–342 passim. Bowers once tried to protect his role by advising, angrily, against an attempt by the State Department to have Consul Bay investigate the possibility of a simple release of American prisoners. This was being requested on the ground that the Spanish government was withdrawing foreign troops and the Friends of the Abraham Lincoln Brigade could

guarantee the repatriation of Americans held as prisoners. Bowers indicated that the use of Bay might be interpreted as a reflection upon himself. If Bowers appeared overly sensitive, it was not entirely his fault. The Department, if it believed that Bay's Rebel contacts had greater influence than Bowers', might at least have informed him of its appraisal. Indeed, Hull seemed to place greater trust in men like Wendelin (and then Thurston, who remained close by the Spanish government) and Bay (who spent the entire war as consul in Seville) than he did in Bowers.

24. For Patriarca, see Secretary to Wendelin, Oct. 22, 1936, and Wendelin to Secretary, Oct. 13, 1936, *FR 1936*, II, 735–736. On Ashby-Poley-Krock, the information is found in Senator Pittman's correspondence with him concerning a general letter of introduction to be written by Pittman. The letter was dated June 29, 1937 (Pittman Papers, carton 79).

9. DOMESTIC QUARRELS, 1937–1938

1. See Ralph Lord Roy, *Communism and the Churches* (New York, 1960), ch. III ("The Communists Discover the Churches") and pp. 88–89 and 121. Roy points out that in 1935, Communist party strategy shifted radically by making an attempt to cooperate with liberal clergymen.

A collection of papers left by the American Board of Commissioners for Foreign Missions reveals some of the activities of Protestants in Spain, their views toward the Spanish government, and the persecution which some of them encountered in Rebel-held territory (file ABC 17.9, vols. III and IV). Some mention is also made of persecution of Jews. Since there were few Protestants and Jews in Spain, this particular issue was neither very lively nor utterly neglected.

2. See Roy, *Communism and the Churches*, 71, 80, 82, 90–94, 121–122.

3. A great deal of information on the attitudes of, and the conflicts within, the radical left can be gleaned from the mass of materials available at Tamiment Institute in New York City. In addition to a large collection of pamphlets (most of which are of very limited value to this study), there are the more valuable manuscript and organization files. In the latter, there are a number of relevant letters as well as copies of proceedings of meetings held by various organizations. Particularly relevant are: Manuscript Files, Socialist Party, U.S., 1937; the Organization File for the same; and, the Proceedings of the National Convention of the Socialist party, Apr. 21–23, 1938. Most of the information on the Communist party must be taken from these sources, the general pamphlet collection, and such Communist party publications as the *Party Organizer*.

The responses of some American writers to the Spanish experience can be found in Daniel Aaron's *Writers on the Left* (New

York, 1962). For example, see pages 156–157 and 344–345. Aaron also cites some of the more relevant original sources (p. 440).

4. See Guttmann, *Wound in the Heart,* chapter 3, for a fine treatment of Catholic attitudes.

5. For Bowers' and Thurston's appraisals of Communist influence in Spain, see *FR 1937,* I, 436–439 and 459–462.

6. See Roy, *Communism and the Churches,* 111–113, 118, and 134–139; and Guttmann, *Wound in the Heart,* 41–45. Also, *Commonweal,* June 24, 1938, 229–230.

7. The Stimson-Coudert correspondence is found in the Stimson Papers; Coudert to Stimson, Jan. 11, Jan. 19, and Nov. 8, 1937; and Stimson to Coudert, Jan. 18, 1937.

8. Ernest J. Swift (Vice Chairman in Charge, Insular and Foreign Operations, American National Red Cross) to James Dunn (Western European Division), Sept. 16, 1936, DSR, 852.48/10.

Swift's other correspondence is taken from an unpublished monograph by Catherine Fennelly, "American Red Cross Disaster Service, 1919–1939," pp. 79–80. The Fennelly study is Volume XX-B of "The History of the American National Red Cross" (Red Cross Archives).

The State Department acknowledged receipt of information concerning Labor's Red Cross on Sept. 16, 1936, DSR, 852.00/3093. On legal issues: Western European Division to Walter B. Cannon, a sponsor of the Medical Division of the American Friends of Spanish Democracy, Jan. 9, 1937, DSR, 852.00/4267; and Office of Arms and Munitions Control to General Secretary, Pennsylvania State Christian Association, Jan. 9, 1937, DSR, 852.00/4268. Also Assistant Attorney General to Knights of Columbus (New Haven, Connecticut), Apr. 17, 1937, DSR, 852.00/5188. The Attorney General's office handled this correspondence for the State Department. The decision was based on a legal technicality: while it was illegal to enlist men in the United States for participation in a foreign conflict, it was not illegal to provide assistance for "prospective combatants."

9. Passport Division, memorandum on decision concerning passport requests, Feb. 16, 1937, DSR, 852.00/4673. A few examples of correspondence attacking the Department's policy can be found in DSR, 852.00/4750–4754. Also Bowers to Secretary, Feb. 23, 1937, Secretary to Bowers, Mar. 9, 1937, and Bowers to Secretary, Mar. 22, 1937 (all DSR, 852.00/5076). After Hull responded with a rough explanation of the decision of the American Red Cross, Bowers wrote that if any respectable amount were contributed by the American people for use in Spain then that fact should be publicized.

10. Morgan-Green Report, 109–117; Medical Bureau, American Friends of Spanish Democracy, to Francis Sayre, State Department, Mar. 2, 1937, DSR, 852.00/4867; Moore, memorandum for Secretary of State, Mar. 12, 1937, Moore Papers, box 14; and Ickes, *Secret Diary,* II, 93.

11. Green to Executive Secretary, Friends of the Abraham Lincoln Battalion (New York City), May 19, 1937, DSR, 852.48 Relief (Regis. Friends of Abraham Lincoln Battalion)/5; and Wendelin (European Division), memorandum, May 28, 1938, DSR 852.00/8082.

12. Secretary to embassy (Valencia), May 1, 1938, DSR, 852.48/71A; embassy (Valencia) to Secretary, May 2, 1937, 852.48/72; and George Perkins (Barcelona) to Secretary, Apr. 20, *FR 1937*, I, 284–286.

13. Taylor, *United States and the Spanish Civil War*, 131 and 141; and Morgan-Green Report, 130–138. The figures given in the Morgan-Green Report are for the period May 1, 1937 to April 1, 1939. In some cases the amounts include expenditures for relief made before May 1, 1937. The recorded collections by registered organizations totaled $2,356,214. Of this amount, $1,733,259 was transmitted to Spain. The American Friends Service Committee received $218,612 and expended $141,234.52 on relief.

14. Montavon to Delegación del Estado para Prensa, Salamanca, July 24, 1937; and Montavon to Monsignor Michael J. Ready, memorandum of conversation with Juan de Cardenas, Mar. 11, 1937. Both items found in the William F. Montavon Papers.

Montavon also corresponded with the Centro de Información Católica Internacional in Burgos and with a pro-Rebel information agency in London.

15. Walsh to Eugene Butler (N.C.W.C.), May 3, 1938; and McCormack to Eugene Butler, June 10, 1938. Both items in Montavon Papers.

John W. McCormack to President Roosevelt, Oct. 14, 1938; President to McCormack, undated copy; Welles to Davis, undated. All located in Norman Davis Papers, carton 63. The President's letter to McCormack was simply a restatement of American policy.

16. Bullitt to Secretary, Apr. 30, 1937, DSR, 852.00/5280. Also Taylor, *United States and the Spanish Civil War*, 158; and *Time*, June 7, 1937, 75.

17. *FR 1937*, I, 511–516; Welles (for Secretary Hull) to McIntyre, June 18, 1937, Roosevelt Papers, OF 422-C. Also Taylor, 158–159.

18. Fennelly, 80–81; and collection of press comments, file no. FDR-109.2 Spain Civil War 8/36 Finance and Accounts (both items in American National Red Cross Archives). "Throughout the revolution in Spain the American National Red Cross gave assistance and made available in cash contributions and material relief approximately $200,000." Annual Report of the American National Red Cross for the year ended June 30, 1939, pp. 78–79 (Red Cross Archives).

19. Fennelly, 82–83; American Red Cross, Annual Report for the year ended June 30, 1939; Minutes of the Red Cross Central Committee, vol. XVI, 3349–3353 (meeting of Sept. 7, 1938). All

these items are in Red Cross Archives. Also Moffat Diaries, Aug. 3 through Sept. 16, 1938.

Davis to William Phillips, May 10, 1938, Davis Papers, carton 47. In selecting Davis for this post the President was partially motivated by the desire to have Davis in Washington where he could use him in other advisory capacities. R. Walton Moore had earlier been selected by the President to serve as a member of the Central Committee of the Red Cross (President to Moore, Nov. 8, 1937, Moore Papers, box 17).

20. Fennelly, 83–84.

21. From the Ernst Toller Collection: Toller to Pablo Azcárate y Florez, Oct. 16, 1938; Clarence E. Pickett to Toller, Nov. 10, 1938; Toller to H. N. Brailsford, Stockholm, Nov. 22 and Dec. 19, 1938; Marvin McIntyre to Toller, Dec. 7, 1938; James Dunn to Toller, Dec. 12 and 30, 1938, and Jan. 9, 1939; and Pedro Lecuona (minister-counsellor, Spanish embassy, Washington) to Toller, Dec. 16, 1938. Also Moffat Diaries, Dec. 16 and 21, 1938.

22. Memorandum by Swift, Sept. 21, 1938, FDR 120.92 Spain; memorandum by James K. McClintock, Dec. 1, 1938, FDR 120.92; and Fennelly, 84–85 (all in Red Cross Archives). Moffat Diaries, Dec. 12, 1938.

President Roosevelt to George MacDonald, Dec. 19, 1938, Roosevelt Papers, OF 422-D. Norman Davis had previously spoken to MacDonald about the plan.

23. See *New York Times,* May 1, 1938. Wheat was being exported from Franco Spain to Italy, which had experienced a bad wheat year.

Late in January 1939, Juan de Cardenas informed MacDonald that wheat was needed by the Nationalist government "to attend the needs of women and children" in areas recently occupied by Nationalist troops. Letter of Jan. 25, 1939, FDR 120.91 Spain-China, Distribution of Wheat and Flour (Red Cross Archives).

24. Fennelly, 85–87. Early in 1939, John Reich responded to an inquiry by Francis X. Talbot, S. J., editor of *America,* who felt that the plan could not "preserve impartiality." Reich said that the greatest need for food was in Republican Spain, so that "it is there that we must do the bulk of our work with due regards for the needs of both sides. . . . Our fixed policy has been, and remains, to divide our supplies between both sides *according to need.* Or to put it in a more Quakerly manner, we will endeavor to render aid to the Spanish people wherever they may be in need, *regardless of sides.* This we believe to be true impartiality."

Answering another of *America*'s charges, Reich added: "Insofar as the Society of Friends is concerned, our relief work in Spain is in no way connected with the agitation to lift the American embargo on shipments of munitions. That is entirely outside our field of service as peace-minded Christians." Reich to Talbot, Jan. 7, 1939, FDR 120.91 Spain and China, Distribution of Flour and Wheat (Red Cross Archives). There is little reason to question Reich's sincerity.

At one point, when Franco was demanding that Nationalist authorities administer distribution, Moffat told Reich that shipments of flour to Rebel Spain should be denied under that condition. But Reich was "loath" to stop these shipments (Moffat Diaries, Oct. 19, 1938). Franco eventually dropped his threat.

25. Davis to Roosevelt, Feb. 2, 1939 (with enclosure of memorandum by Reich and Paul Harvey of same date), Roosevelt Papers, OF 422-D; and Fennelly, 87–88.

26. In mid-November, the State Department (and Toller as well) did learn from a representative of the Friends who had spoken with the British Foreign Office that the British "were convinced that Franco could not win unless he were able to starve out the Loyalists." It is possible to speculate on the connection between this information and the "flour plan" of December. But it would seem to miss the central question: would the Roosevelt administration, the Red Cross, and the Friends have desired to relieve the misery of Spanish refugees if such relief lacked even the remotest connection to the Loyalist military cause? It would be difficult to see how the answer could be anything but affirmative. Moreover, the evidence as a whole indicates that, despite the political and military effects of the President's plan, it was chosen because it had fewer political and military complications. Moffat, memo of conversation with representative of the Friends, Nov. 19, 1938, DSR, 852.48/298; Toller to Brailsford, Nov. 22, 1938, Toller Papers; and Congressman William B. Barry to Sumner Welles (copy, and one to MacDonald), Jan. 5, 1939, FDR 120.91 Spain and China, Distribution of Wheat and Flour (Red Cross Archives).

10. THE LAST MONTHS OF THE WAR

1. Joel Berrall to Herman Reissig (executive secretary of the Coordinating Committee to Lift the Spanish Embargo), Feb. 2, 1939. Spanish Refugee Relief Organizations Collection (hereafter, SRRO), Embargo file, Berrall folder.

2. See Cantril and Strunk (eds.), *Public Opinion 1935–1946,* 808. Additional light is thrown on these and other polls included in the Cantril-Strunk book (p. 808), in the following correspondence: Coordinating Committee (to Lift the Spanish Embargo) to the President and to the House Foreign Affairs and Senate Foreign Relations Committees, Jan. 3, 1939, SRRO, Misc. file 21, Administration-Congress-Public Officials folder; Charles Rabbins (Secretary of the Lawyers Committee on American Relations with Spain) to Herman Reissig, Jan. 22, 1939, SRRO, Embargo file, Hogue folder; Joel Berrall to Reissig, Jan. 31, 1939, SRRO, Embargo file, Berrall folder; and Jay Allen to Henry Stimson, Jan. 10, 1939, Stimson Papers.

If one takes these Gallup polls and indulges in a bit of academic solitaire, he can arrive at some interesting speculations. For example, by comparing and contrasting the results of the December and January polls with the more refined ones of February, it is possible to draw the following conclusions: (1) that most Americans who favored the repeal of the embargo felt themselves knowledgeable about the war; and (2) that the majority of Americans opposed to repeal claimed not to have been following the events of the war. Consequently, it is possible to conclude that widespread, self-confessed ignorance contributed to the maintenance of the embargo policy—if one further accepts the proposition that the views of the public at large help to determine policies of this kind.

3. See note 2 above, especially Berrall to Reissig, Jan. 31, 1939. Berrall wrote: "Spent most of today trying to stop Gallup release. Glad to learn you succeeded." This success could not have been very lasting, because two Gallup polls soon appeared, both dated February 2, 1939.

4. SRRO, Embargo file, biographical item, Keller folder; Dorothy Fontaine (a field organizer) to Reissig, Mar. 1, 1939, and Fontaine to Reissig (field reports of February and March), SRRO, Embargo file, Fontaine folder; and "Organized Catholic Opposition to Republican Spain" (title given to items from field reports from January 29 to March 1, 1939), SRRO, Embargo file, Organizers (field) folder.

5. The Coordinating Committee's strategy and its failures during January are documented in the following correspondence found in SRRO collection, Embargo file, folders of: Hogue, Berrall, Keller, and Fontaine. Also Misc. file no. 21: Lawyers Committee folder and Administration-Congress-Public Officials folder. Also Roosevelt Papers, OF 422-C: Rockwell Kent, et al., to the President, Jan. 10, 1939; and Reissig to Mrs. Roosevelt, Feb. 8, 1939.

6. "Catholic Evidence on Spain," Roosevelt Papers, OF 422-C; Lawyers Committee on American Relations with Spain, Minutes of Meeting at Hotel Mayflower, Washington, D.C., Jan. 30, 1939, SRRO, Misc. file no. 21, Lawyers Committee folder; and Hogue to Reissig, Jan. 24, 1939, and Reissig to Hogue, Feb. 2, 1939, SRRO, Embargo file, Hogue folder.

7. Keep the Spanish Embargo Committee to "all Committee members," Jan. 27, 1939, Montavon Papers; and Doyle to McIntyre, Jan. 18, 1939 (with enclosure), Roosevelt Papers, OF 422-C. Herbert Wright, professor of international law at the Catholic University of America, was almost certainly the inspiration for the circular's argument concerning the embargo. He prepared a "Memorandum in Support of the Retention of the Spanish Embargo" for the Keep the Embargo Committee in Washington, D.C. (Montavon Papers). Whatever the strength of the rest of the argument, it certainly could have been enhanced by including the January 1937 resolution with the Act of May 1937.

8. Montavon (memorandum) to Monsignor Michael J. Ready (General Secretary of the N.C.W.C.), Jan. 24, 1939, Montavon Papers. Hull himself "turned down the interview for fear of starting a rash of them." This job was given to lesser officials. Also Allen to Stimson, Jan. 10, 1939, Stimson Papers. Marquis

Childs (*I Write From Washington,* 138) viewed Mundelein in the same sympathetic light.

9. See Taylor, *United States and the Spanish Civil War,* 187; and *Christian Science Monitor,* Jan. 26, 1939. Also Allen to Stimson, Jan. 10, 1939, Stimson Papers.

10. Berrall to Reissig, Feb. 2, 1939, SRRO, Embargo file, Berrall folder; and Moffat Diaries, Jan. 23, 1939. Fred Israel provided the following account, which complements Moffat's report on Pittman: Early in January, "Secretary Hull suggested to Pittman that the State Department prepare a resolution repealing the arms embargo, which the Senator would introduce. Pittman disagreed and emphatically declared that he had to draft any revised neutrality legislation, because an administration measure would be interpreted as the first step toward lifting the Spanish embargo" (*Pittman,* 159).

11. "Proposed Changes in the Neutrality Act of May 1, 1937," memorandum, Oct. 28, 1938, initialed GHH [Hackworth], JCG [Green], and CS [Savage]; and Moore to Hull, Nov. 7, 1938. Both items in Moore Papers, box 15.

Nancy Harvison Hooker (ed.), *The Moffat Papers: Selections from the Diplomatic Journals of Jay Pierrepont Moffat, 1919–1943* (Cambridge, Mass., 1956), 228n–229n. Also Moffat Diaries, Nov. 19 and 20, 1938.

President Roosevelt to Attorney General, memorandum, Nov. 28, 1938; and Welles to President, Nov. 25 and 30, 1938. All three items from Roosevelt Papers, OF 422-C.

Ickes, *Secret Diary,* II, 510. Moore's opinion regarding repeal by proclamation appeared first in a memorandum dated Mar. 31, 1938, Moore Papers, box 15.

12. The major papers relevant to the dialogue involving the President, the Department of State, and the Attorney General's Office are found in the Roosevelt Papers, PSF Spain (some of these items are copies of those located elsewhere): Secretary of State to Raymond Leslie Buell (press release), Mar. 21, 1938; memorandum by Moore, Mar. 31, 1938; memorandum by Green, Apr. 11, 1938; Ickes to President, Nov. 23, 1938; Welles to President, Nov. 25, 1938; FDR to Attorney General, Nov. 28, 1938; Welles to President, Nov. 30, 1938; Bell memorandum, Dec. 5, 1938; Cummings to President, Dec. 19, 1938; FDR memo to Welles, Dec. 21, 1938. Also relevant is an item from Welles to McIntyre, Jan. 30, 1939, Roosevelt Papers, OF 422.

13. Ickes, *Secret Diary,* II, 528; Pittman to President, Jan. 11, 1939, Roosevelt Papers, PPF 745; Moore to Hull, Feb. 24, 1939, Moore Papers, box 15; and Moore to President, March 8, 1939, Moore Papers, box 15.

14. Stimson to Hull, Jan. 18, 1939, Hull Papers, carton 44; Stimson's letter to *New York Times,* Jan. 23, 1939; Arthur Hays Sulzberger to Stimson, Jan. 17, 1939, and Stimson to Sulzberger, Jan. 21, 1939, Stimson Papers; Stimson, memorandum of tele-

phone conversation with Hull, Jan. 23, 1939, Stimson Papers. One must accept the possibility that Sulzberger's letter reached Stimson before the former Secretary sent his letter to Hull. Also, Dunn had been informed almost a week previous to the first letter that a group of "left wingers" was urging Stimson to write Hull and "hoped to succeed" (Moffat Diaries, Jan. 23, 1939).

15. Letter to *New York Times*, Jan. 23, 1939.

16. Hooker (ed.), *Moffat Papers,* 226–227, entry for Jan. 19, 1939. Present at the meeting were Hull, Moore, Hackworth, Dunn, and Moffat. Bullitt apparently arrived in the middle of the discussion.

17. The fate of the Stimson letter, after it reached Secretary Hull, is documented in the following: Hooker (ed.), *Moffat Papers,* 227–228, entry for Jan. 23, 1939; Moffat Diaries, Jan. 20–23, 1939; draft of suggested reply to Stimson, Moore Papers, box 11; and, Hull to Stimson, Hull Papers, carton 44.

See *New York Times,* Jan. 26 and 31, 1939, for the Conboy and Burlingham-Jessup letters.

18. Bullitt to Secretary, Feb. 6, 1939, DSR, 740.00/568; and Biddle to Secretary, Feb. 17, 1939, DSR, 852.00/9009. Also Bullitt to Secretary, July 26, *FR 1938,* I, 57–59.

Phillips to Secretary, Feb. 2, 1939, DSR, 740.00/564; Pell to Roosevelt, Mar. 15, 1939, Roosevelt Papers, PSF State Department 1939; and, Phillips to Secretary, Mar. 28, 1939, DSR, 852.00/9074.

Bowers to Secretary, Sept. 26, 1938, DSR, 852.00/8409. Moffat, memorandum of conversation with Spanish ambassador, Feb. 10, 1939, DSR, 852.00/8953. De los Ríos proved to be most prophetic: "The Ambassador looked towards a period of blackmail on the part of Franco, during which he would alternate his favors to the dictators and the democracies, trying to make each one pay him for his friendship" (Moffat Diaries, Feb. 10, 1939).

19. Hull, *Memoirs,* I, 616–618; Hull to President, Feb. 23, 1939, DSR, 852.01/476; American consulate (Barcelona) to Secretary, Mar. 16, 1939, DSR, 852.00/9051; Hooker (ed.), *Moffat Papers,* 236–237; and Moore, memorandum for the Secretary, March 30, 1939, Moore Papers, box 19. Also Ickes, *Secret Diary,* II, 608–609; and Moffat Diaries, Feb. 27–Mar. 10, 1939, and Mar. 31, 1939. The formal diplomatic exchanges took place on April 3, 1939.

20. Bowers, *My Mission to Spain,* 419.

11. PRESIDENT, AMBASSADOR, AND SECRETARY

1. Josephus Daniels, copy of notes on conversation with President Roosevelt on Jan. 14, 1939, Roosevelt Papers, PPF 86 (Josephus Daniels).

2. For information received by the President on the comparative armament situations in the major European nations: Louis Johnson to McIntyre, June 23, 1938, Roosevelt Papers, PSF War Depart-

ment (Louis Johnson); Hugh Wilson to President Roosevelt, Aug. 31, 1938, PSF Germany (Wilson); Johnson to President, Oct. 15, 1938, PSF War Department (Louis Johnson); Welles to President, Dec. 23, 1938 (with attached memorandum), PSF Germany; and Josephus Daniels, notes of conversation with the President, Jan. 14, 1939, PPF 86 (Josephus Daniels). Also FDR to Pell, Nov. 12, 1938, Roosevelt Papers, PSF Portugal.

On August 31, 1938, Roosevelt wrote Bowers: "Perhaps a little later on—if the Czech situation does not end disastrously—I can make some kind of move for the purpose of at least aiding in ending the Spanish War" (Roosevelt Papers).

3. The President, according to Ickes, made such a statement at a cabinet meeting on January 27, 1939. Ickes, *Secret Diary*, II, 570 (entry for Jan. 29, 1939).

4. That only a few American ships were sunk by the Germans in World War I, before American entry, is beside the point. Much had been done since that war to demonstrate that the "merchants of death" were responsible for getting the United States into the world conflict. The American public could not have been expected to look favorably, in 1936, upon a policy which permitted munitions-makers to sell their wares and only morally prohibited them from shipping them.

5. Bowers to Hull, Feb. 25, 1938, Hull Papers, carton 42.

6. Bowers to Hull, June 10, 1938, DSR, 852.00/8133.

7. Bowers to Hull, Dec. 7, 1938, DSR, 852.00/8700.

8. Moore, memorandum to Secretary of State, Dec. 20, 1938, and Moore to Welles, Dec. 22, 1938, Moore Papers, box 9, Memoranda on Departmental Matters. Also, Welles to President, Dec. 22, 1938, DSR, 852.00/8746. Welles' letter to Roosevelt followed very closely the words of Moore's note to Welles.

9. Bowers to Welles, Dec. 20, 1938; Welles to Moffat, Jan. 3, 1939; Moffat to Welles, Jan. 28, 1939; and Welles to Bowers, Jan. 2, 1939 (all items, DSR, 852.00/8938). Also Bowers to President, Jan. 7, 1939 and Roosevelt to Bowers, Jan. 26, 1939 (Roosevelt Papers, PPF 730). Also Wilson to Secretary, Jan. 16, 1939 (DSR, 741.65/695) and Jan. 26, 1939 (DSR, 751.00/90); Biddle to Secretary, Jan. 18, 1939 (Hull Papers, carton 44); Bowers to President, Jan. 13, 1939 (Roosevelt Papers, PSF box 45, Spain 1939); and Moffat Diaries, Jan. 28–Feb. 3, 1939.

10. Bowers to President, Aug. 26, 1936; Sept. 23, 1936; Dec. 16, 1936; and Feb. 16, 1937 (all in Roosevelt Papers). In the first of these four letters, Bowers expressed his conviction that the United States must not meddle in Spain's domestic quarrel. He thought America should confine itself strictly to getting Americans out of Spain and to looking after American interests alone.

11. Bowers, *My Mission to Spain*, 410–420; and Moffat Diaries, Feb. 27, 1939. In *My Life: The Memoirs of Claude Bowers* (New York, 1962) he treated the civil war years very briefly, concluding:

"But I do not have the heart for further discussion of the Spanish Civil War, which I have described in another book" (p. 283).

12. Bowers, *My Mission to Spain,* 410–420; Bowers to President, July 21, 1937, and Bowers to Hull and Welles, July 21, 1937, Roosevelt Papers, PSF Box 28 Spain; Moffat Diaries, April 1 and 2, 1939; and correspondence relative to the hearings of the Senate Foreign Relations Committee, the Papers of Senate Foreign Relations Committee, SEN 76-F9(142). Before the House Committee, Bowers received a sympathetic hearing. But this was also to be expected. There were a number of men in Congress who shared Bowers' sympathies for the Loyalists. But there is a vast distinction between "sympathy for" and "action in behalf of." Pro-Loyalist expressions came much more readily after the embargo was no longer an active political issue. In *My Life* Bowers relates that Bloom's invitation was proffered at a reception given him by Senator Guffey and that Messersmith encouraged him to accept it (p. 292).

13. Bowers to Secretary of State: July 20, *FR 1937,* I, 362–364; Sept. 2, 1937, DSR, 852.00/6445; Feb. 25 and June 27, 1938, Hull Papers, carton 42; and Oct. 10, 1938, Hull Papers, carton 43. In September 1937, Bowers wrote to Senator Capper that the United States alone was "conceded by both sides to have followed an honest policy of aloofness." He also said that Czechoslovakia would be the "next victim" if the Fascists succeeded in Spain (quoted in Socolofsky, *Capper,* 180).

14. Bowers to Dodd, June 18, 1937, Dodd Papers, carton 50. Dodd differed from Bowers in being optimistic about the use of economic sanctions. In letter after letter he referred to commercial and financial measures; and this was what he meant, for example, when he wrote to Hull "that decisive action on the part of our country would probably defeat fascism in Spain" (April 26, 1937, Dodd Papers, carton 51). Only in 1938, after returning to private life, did Dodd advise repeal of the embargo.

15. As late as January 1938, Bowers wrote that he would not be surprised if the Loyalists triumphed over the Fascist Internationale (to Dodd, Jan. 12, 1938, Dodd Papers, carton 50).

16. Early in the war, Bowers expressed this same fear of precipitating a European conflict. Bowers to Roosevelt, Aug. 26 and Sept. 23, 1936 (Roosevelt Papers).

17. Hull, *Memoirs,* 481–483. When Hull wrote that a contrary course was "unthinkable," he was arguing that, since twenty-seven European nations "had solemnly agreed not to intervene in Spain by sending arms or men to one side or the other," the United States could do nothing but adopt a like policy. One might agree with Hull that in 1936 he chose the wisest course, but that does not mean Hornbeck presented an "unthinkable" alternative in his dissenting memorandum in August 1936.

In what was an obvious contradiction of his later *Memoirs* and of his remarks during the civil war, Hull reportedly said in October 1940: "By 1938 there was no longer any doubt that the existence of the arms embargo provision was definitely having the effect of making widespread war more likely." Quoted in Bendiner, *Riddle of the State Department*, 58.

18. Hull, *Memoirs*, 483–484 and 514–517.

19. As late as October 1938, about two-thirds of those polled by the American Institute of Public Opinion "put more faith" in stricter neutrality laws than in greater presidential discretion for the purpose of keeping the United States out of war (Cantril and Strunk, *Public Opinion, 1935–1946*, 966).

20. Stimson to Hornbeck, Mar. 7, 1939, Stimson Papers; and Moffat Diaries, Nov. 5 and 6, 1938. Bowers and his staff also experienced fatigue, but their responsibility was to carry out the Spanish policy—a small problem compared to the responsibilities of the topsiders in the Department.

INDEX

DATE DUE